Measuring Prison Performance

VIOLENCE PREVENTION AND POLICY SERIES

This AltaMira series publishes new books in the multidisciplinary study of violence. Books are designed to support scientifically based violence prevention programs and widely applicable violence prevention policy. Key topics are juvenile and/or adult community re-entry programs, community-based addiction and violence programs, prison violence reduction programs with application in community settings, and school culture and climate studies with recommendations for organizational approaches to school-violence reduction. Studies may combine quantitative and qualitative methods, may be multidisciplinary, or may feature European research if it has a multinational application. The series publishes highly accessible books that offer violence prevention policy as the outcome of scientifically based research, designed for college undergraduates and graduates, community agency leaders, school and community decision makers, and senior government policy makers.

SERIES EDITOR:

Mark S. Fleisher, Director, The Dr. Semi J. and Ruth W. Begun Center for Violence Research Prevention and Education, Case Western Reserve University, 10900 Euclid Avenue, Cleveland, OH 44106-7164 USA, 216-368-2329 or msf10@po.cwru.edu

EDITORIAL BOARD MEMBERS

BOOKS IN THE SERIES:

1. *Gang Cop: The Words and Ways of Officer Paco Domingo* by Malcolm Klein (2004)
2. *Measuring Prison Performance: Government Privatization and Accountability* by Gerald G. Gaes, Scott D. Camp, Julianne B. Nelson, William G. Saylor (2004)

Measuring Prison Performance
Government Privatization and Accountability

Gerald G. Gaes
Scott D. Camp
Julianne B. Nelson
William G. Saylor

ALTAMIRA
PRESS

A Division of Rowman & Littlefield Publishers, Inc.
Walnut Creek • Lanham • New York • Oxford

ALTAMIRA PRESS
A Division of Rowman & Littlefield Publishers, Inc.
1630 North Main Street, #367
Walnut Creek, California 94596
www.altamirapress.com

Rowman & Littlefield Publishers, Inc.
A Member of the Rowman & Littlefield Publishing Group
4501 Forbes Boulevard, Suite 200
Lanham, MD 20706

PO Box 317
Oxford
OX2 9RU, United Kingdom

British Library Cataloguing in Publication Information Available

Library of Congress Cataloging-in-Publication Data

Measuring prison performance : government privatization and accountability /
Gerald G. Gaes, . . . [et al.].
    p. cm.—(Violence prevention and policy series ; 2)
  Includes bibliographical references and index.
    ISBN 0-7591-0586-3 (hardcover : alk. paper)—ISBN 0-7591-0587-1 (pbk. : alk.
paper)
  1. Prisons—United States. 2. Privatization—United States. 3.
Corrections—Contracting out—United States. I. Gaes, Gerald G., 1947– II.
Series.

HV9469.M43 2004
365'.973'068—dc22

                                                        2004005396

Printed in the United States of America

∞™ The paper used in this publication meets the minimum requirements of American
National Standard for Information Sciences—Permanence of Paper for Printed Library
Materials, ANSI/NISO Z39.48-1992.

CONTENTS

CONTENTS

ACKNOWLEDGMENTS

W e extend our thanks and appreciation to Jesse Krienert, Michael Gilbert, Bert Useem, Tom Kane, Jesse Shapiro, and Shawn Bushway who have critiqued previous versions of this book. A special thank you goes to Jean Gaes who spent countless hours reading and providing feedback that greatly improved this manuscript. The opinions expressed in this book are solely those of the authors and do not represent the policies of the National Institute of Justice, Federal Bureau of Prisons, or the U.S. Department of Justice.

INTRODUCTION

The Motivation for the Book and a Statement of the Issues

How many of us care about what happens inside a prison? If we are indifferent about prison quality, we are certainly concerned about the released offender when he returns to our community, our neighborhood, our street. If one believes the two ideas are connected—what happens inside affects how the ex-offender behaves on the outside—then almost everyone should care about prison performance and government oversight.

Add to this theme the idea that there has been an evolution (some say a revolution) in the way governments and economies interact. Daniel Yergin and Joseph Stanislaw provide a recent historical account of this interaction in their book *The Commanding Heights*. The boundaries and relationships between governments and economies have undergone a radical transformation worldwide. The evolution from government-managed economies and government ownership and production to private interests has gained momentum in the last thirty years and has involved such disparate economies as those of China, the former Soviet Union, Great Britain, and the United States. Yergin and Stanislaw describe this historical movement almost as if it were trench warfare. "Where the frontier between state and market is to be drawn has never been a matter that could be settled, once and for all. . . . Instead, it has been the subject, over the course of this century, of massive intellectual and political battles as well as constant skirmishes" (Yergin and Stanislaw, 1998: 11). Prison privatization is one of those battles. These are the two themes captured in this book—government accountability and prison privatization. You cannot discuss one intelligently unless you discuss the other.

As part of this recent history in the United States, in March 1988 a presidential commission published *Privatization: Toward More Effective Government* (1988). The commission's report to President Ronald Reagan referred to the global momentum toward privatized services. It also called for the widespread use of privatization by state and local governments in the United States and articulated a conviction that the government should strike a new commitment to rely "on the talents and ingenuity of private citizens to develop better ways to accomplish what is now the government's business" (President's Commission on Privatization, 1988: 6). Chapter 6 of the commission's report made recommendations regarding federal, state, and local prisons. The commission endorsed the privatization of prison administration; it called for the privatization of entire prisons, not just some functions; it recommended that the Bureau of Prisons do an analysis based on Office of Management and Budget guidelines to uncover the "true" costs of prison administration; it suggested that the Bureau of Prisons set up a demonstration and evaluation project by privatizing one of its facilities comparing the performance of the privately managed institution to its public counterpart; and the commission directed the Department of Justice to give priority to private sector involvement in corrections. At this point in the history of prison privatization there was a great deal of growth in the industry and enthusiastic optimism—at least among the private industry advocates and some public officials—that prison privatization would eventually gain a large share of the prison market in the United States. Was this enthusiasm and optimism premature?

People with different perspectives will read the recent trend in slower growth of American prison privatization in different ways. Scholars who take this matter seriously are still asking the most fundamental questions. In his summary of the state of knowledge about private prisons, Richard Harding (2001) asserts that "The ultimate question is whether private prisons can and do provide good, or even superior, quality correctional services" (p. 324). Harding's conclusion presupposes that there are definitive ways to compare prison quality. In our judgment, the literature on prison performance and the research comparing the quality of private and public management is essentially flawed because there has been no coherent approach to the problem. In this book, we try to develop the conceptual and empirical underpinnings of prison performance measurement. While this effort has always been important in penology, we believe it is even more decisive in the current correctional climate that pits private enterprise against government management. In this arena, there has been more rhetoric than reality,[1] more speculation than specifics, and more postulation than proof.

As background, we consider the fundamental purposes of prison. However, this is not a book about what prisons should do, but rather one about how to evaluate prison performance once the goals have been established. Much of the current social science literature on prison performance has been a side effect of the interest in comparing the quality of publicly and privately operated prisons. Although our primary concern in this book is to address the fundamentals of prison performance, many of our examples come from the literature that compares private and public prisons. A second reason for bringing the subject of privatization into our analysis of prison performance is that the literature on privately and publicly operated prisons introduces two themes that had not been given much prior consideration: contract compliance and prison costs. Before prison privatization, prison costs were given much less importance in the analysis of performance. The relevance of cost has been elevated by the claim that private companies can do the same tasks as well, or better, and at a cheaper cost. We devote two chapters to prison costs. In another chapter, we discuss whether contracts change the nature of prison performance.

While we have been critical of the literature on prison performance in the context of the public-private debate (Gaes, Camp, and Saylor, 1998), there has been at least one serious attempt to develop a coherent theoretical and empirical approach to prison performance measurement. The seminal piece was a paper by Charles Logan entitled "Well Kept: Comparing Quality of Confinement in Private and Public Prisons" (Logan, 1992). We review Logan's work in great detail in chapter 1 of this book. In chapter 1, we also discuss the purpose of prison in our society. A clear definition of purpose is important because prison performance must be measured in reference to the mission and goals of the prison system under study. Logan recognized the bridge between mission and performance. Although we begin on the same path as he did, we diverge from the route he took when he presumed to articulate what a prison system's mission *ought to be.* Rather, we begin with what a prison system's mission *is,* as it is defined by the different jurisdictions.

The purpose of prison, which we review in chapter 1, is usually articulated within a jurisdiction by the statement of the mission and goals of that prison system. Those goals and missions may not always be stated clearly. However, we argue that without declared goals, we cannot hold a jurisdiction accountable, and performance measurement is meaningless. Following our discussion of the purpose of prison, we reflect on whether recidivism should be considered the primary prison performance measure. Even though this is only one possible indicator among many others of prison performance, criminal desistance is fundamental to many arguments about the purpose of prison. It is also the yardstick by which analysts measure prison program interventions. By analogy, if we conceptualize the prison experience as a "dosage" of punishment or a dosage of rehabilitation (or both), then we could imagine that some prisons (jurisdictions) are better than others in providing these interventions. Conceptualizing the goals of prison this way shows how the purpose of prison determines the measurement of prison performance. In the section on recidivism, we also consider the methodological and theoretical dilemmas involved in the analysis of recidivism. We believe some of these issues pose formidable problems for researchers to solve. Despite these barriers, we argue that it is a worthwhile endeavor to push recidivism as a measure of institutional performance as far as we can. It is also important to understand the limitations of this measure, and the extent to which we should hold prison administrators responsible for post-release outcomes.

After we review the conceptual and theoretical basis for evaluating prison performance, we focus on the specific methods and indicators, other than recidivism, that analysts have used in their pursuit of prison performance measurement. We believe there is no single best methodology to measure and compare prisons; however, we systematically review the following approaches: prison audits (chapter 2); qualitative approaches to understanding the context, including two examples drawn from the privatization literature (chapter 3); behavioral prison performance indicators (chapter 4); survey instruments that measure the attitudes of inmates and staff (chapter 5); and cost measures (chapter 6). In chapter 7, we discuss the relationship between cost and performance and the role of prison labor in this equation.

There are other important concepts illuminated in chapters 2 through 7. In chapter 2, we discuss how prison audits are the single most important process currently used by prison administrators to hold their prison wardens accountable. We assess one such tool, the prison security audit, in great detail, because we want to demonstrate how such a well-defined procedure can easily be translated into performance data. In this chapter, we show how an audit program can serve two masters—it can be used to give feedback to prison staff on potential weaknesses they must address, and it can be used to generate a database of information that will give managers further insight into most any prison function.

In chapter 3, we present two examples in the prison privatization literature of thoroughly documented instances of prison privatization. We use these examples to show how researchers and prison administrators can learn a great deal about the context of prison performance and privatization from these well-conducted studies. In chapter 4, when we discuss behavioral performance measures, we also introduce the method of multilevel analysis. This is an approach that is used to analyze individual and institutional responses at the same time. It also solves many of the most vexing problems that arise when analysts try to use data summarized across individuals to interpret institutional performance. We give examples of such analyses drawn from some of the work we have conducted, as well as references to assessments of the performance of hospitals and schools. In this chapter, we demonstrate the perils of using summary measures of individual inmates in measuring performance. After this discussion of clustered data, the ecological and atomistic fallacies, and Simpson's Paradox, we show how multilevel models can be used to avoid most of these problems.

In chapter 6, we discuss the principles of a sound cost analysis and some economic theory that may lead us to different expectations than are typically found in the economic literature about whether private prisons will be cheaper than their public counterparts. We provide a great deal of detail about the comparative assessment of costs between private and public competitors. In the current environment, this is a controversial topic, and it is but one of the skirmishes in the battle over privatization. In chapter 7, we continue the discussion of costs by showing how to relate cost and quality. In this chapter, we also refer to the organizational theory called the McDonaldization argument for efficiency. If the private sector is to cut costs, it will probably come from reductions in the expenditures for prison labor. To do this, we suggest that advocates of prison privatization have implied that the routine of prison guards can be broken down and simplified so that prison labor becomes more fungible—the economic term for easily replaceable.

In chapter 8, we discuss comparisons across systems or jurisdictions. Jurisdictional comparisons are difficult because of the unique contexts in which prisons are managed. Nevertheless, it is precisely these contextual differences that make these analyses interesting and productive. After reviewing these methods, in chapter 9, we revisit the issue of measuring prison performance with recidivism and frame the issue in a larger context based upon the life course of criminality literature. In chapter 10, we provide a template for the measurement of prison performance capitalizing on the prior chapters. As an example, we show how we would measure the security and custody functions of a prison. In this same chapter, we also show how the results of performance measurement analysis can be presented in a user-friendly format for administrators. It is because we have spent a great deal of time trying to assess the relative performance of private and public prisons, as well as the performance of individual prisons within a system, that we believe it is time to take a fresh look at the problem and suggest alternative theoretical and empirical solutions. In chapter 10, we also briefly discuss contract compliance and its implication for measuring prison performance for privately operated prisons. We discuss this subject to placate those who believe it should be part of the prison performance discussion. However, we believe it is a distraction from the real issues, and we explain our reasoning for that conclusion.

Although this book is devoted to an exposition of prison performance, it is rather easy to show how the framework, both theory and method, can be applied to other criminal justice components: policing, prosecution, adjudication, and post-release supervision. Public policy analysts will also see how this general framework could be applied to evaluating the privatization of almost any publicly administered service. To show how this approach fits into the broader public policy debate, we devote chapter 11 to a review of the research on government performance and the privatization of government services covered in the public administration domain. While we do not consider ourselves to be thoroughly familiar with this discipline, as we review the literature, the reader should quickly discover, as we did, how the paradigm we are proposing applies to the possible measurement of any government service. In a sense, we have developed a generic paradigm by starting with a specific service, prisons, and implicitly showing how this approach applies to the broader public policy debate about the extent to which a government service can and should be partially or completely privatized. Each of the steps we propose in the succeeding chapters of this book can be applied, to a greater or lesser extent, to such public services as trash collection, administration of welfare, policing, and the operation of public parks, to name a few. Even if an argument can be made that a function is inherently governmental (such as, perhaps, adjudication and prosecution), the steps we propose in this book at least allow policy analysts to identify the performance parameters and the unalloyed costs of that function. In chapter 11, we also discuss some of the unintended consequences of prison performance. We capitalize on a paper we found in the public administration literature by Peter Smith (1995) that outlines eight different dimensions of unintended consequences.

In chapter 12, we summarize the essential themes of this book and provide future direction for the next generation of prison performance research. However, in every publicly administered service, we must start with the most basic question. How do we conceptualize the purpose of that service?

CONCEPTUALIZING PRISON PERFORMANCE

An understanding of prison performance should begin by deriving goals and objectives from the mission of the prison system. The mission expresses the purpose of incarceration for a particular jurisdiction. Such missions not only guide the performance measurement strategy, but they also provide a justification of the system, promoting an understanding of the connection of the prison to the larger goals of criminal justice practices. This is not unique to prisons. Books on performance measurement typically refer to an agency and its mission, goals, and objectives. For example, the Department of Energy's manual on this topic states, "Performance measures are always tied to a goal or an objective (the target)" (Department of Energy, 1995: 1). Harry Hatry, one of the innovators of the performance measurement process as a way to hold governments accountable, makes this same point in much of his work (c.f. Hatry, 1999).

To set the stage, we first review different scholars' writings on the purpose of prisons and other criminal justice institutions. This discussion of purpose demonstrates that prison performance is entirely dependent on one's expectations about what prisons are supposed to do. The discussion culminates with a detailed description of Charles Logan's confinement model. Arguing from the perspective of just desserts, Logan has asserted that we ought to limit the goals (purpose) of prisons. His approach leads to a specific model of performance measurement. We consider this argument in detail, because it is instructive to show how assumptions about purpose lead you into, and away from, certain performance dimensions. In the following section of this chapter, we further define what we mean by mission and goals and show how these are represented by the mission statements of state, federal, and Canadian adult correctional systems.[1] We categorize these missions along different dimensions, such as public safety

1

and rehabilitation, showing that the safety of inmates, staff, and the public is the most frequently mentioned goal of these correctional systems. To flesh out the strategies required of an agency to satisfy its mission, jurisdictions must translate them into objectives. These, in turn, lead to quantifiable dimensions of prison performance. To complement this discussion, the research by James, Bottomley, Liebling, and Clare (1997) is presented to demonstrate how a study of performance measurement is dependent on this framework.

Most of the remaining discussion in this chapter focuses on recidivism as a measure of prison performance. While this is only one measure among many others, the importance of this dimension elevates it to a position of prominence. This is also warranted by the controversies surrounding its measurement, by the difficulty in attributing causation, and by what we believe to be a lack of clear thinking about the meaning of recidivism. Measuring the recidivism level of prisons adds a layer of complexity to a problem that is already difficult to understand and analyze even when the research is relegated to the behavior of individually released offenders. In this part of the chapter, we also review recent attempts to compare public and private prison recidivism rates, a discussion intended to demonstrate the inherent difficulties in conducting these studies. We conclude this chapter by referencing other dimensions of prison performance that do not have the same theoretical and empirical intricacies.

The Purpose of Prison

John DiIulio's (1993) introductory paper to a volume sponsored by the Bureau of Justice Statistics (1993) illustrates the many purposes of criminal justice. DiIulio proposes that the criminal justice system is intended to punish, rehabilitate, deter, incapacitate, and reintegrate. While these goals reinforce the social order, DiIulio asserts that the community wants these goals achieved "without violating the public conscience (humane treatment), jeopardizing the public law (constitutional rights), emptying the public purse (cost containment), or weakening the tradition of State and local public administration (federalism)" (DiIulio, 1993: 6). DiIulio recognizes that the whimsy of public sentiment can shift the locus of attention from one objective to another. From our perspective, different constituencies advocate the importance of some goals to the exclusion of others. This makes it very difficult for prison administrators and public policy makers who have to balance the objectives of all constituencies simultaneously. Restorative justice has also been advanced as a goal or purpose of corrections. Restorative justice focuses on the harm to crime victims and on the offender's need to repair the harm to the victim and to the community.

DiIulio's own prescription for establishing a new paradigm of criminal justice measurement is to elevate four "civic ideals" (DiIulio, 1993: 10). These ideals are: doing justice, promoting secure communities, restoring crime victims, and promoting noncriminal options. These ideals roughly correspond to the notions that defendants are to be treated fairly; that the criminal justice system must ensure the safety of the citizenry; that victims of crime ought to be restored as closely as possible to the state they were in prior to their victimization; and that offenders ought to be given the opportunity to participate in meaningful activities. Some of these civic ideals obviously overlap with the previously mentioned goals of criminal justice. Although DiIulio was proposing a schematic for a new paradigm encompassing the entire criminal justice system, these goals and ideals equally apply to our narrower interest in this book—defining the goals of any prison system.

In the last paper in that same Bureau of Justice Statistics (BJS) volume, James Q. Wilson makes an interesting argument about police performance measures. Wilson reasons that most attempts to measure police performance have concentrated on measures of public safety or proxies of public order that depend on crime indices. Wilson argues that criminality is often unrelated or marginally related to what police actually do. It is Wilson's contention that the public should not blame the police when crime goes up. Nor should it give them credit when crime goes down. Furthermore, it is difficult to define public order much beyond the information crime statistics give us. Wilson's suggestion is to first consider what citizens want that might be related to police behavior. He posits that "People want to live in safe orderly neighborhoods" (Wilson, 1993: 161). By definition, this means that people want "streets free of drug dealers, rowdy juveniles, threatening derelicts, soliciting prostitutes, and predatory criminals; buildings without graffiti or other signs of decay; no drive-by shootings, and so forth" (Wilson, 1993: 161). Wilson understands that some neighborhoods are "self-policing"; the citizens themselves insure public order. Other neighborhoods are almost beyond help; decay and disorder prevail. Wilson advocates a two-tiered system of measurement. First, establish the level of orderliness of the neighborhood, then measure how well police do in juxtaposition to that inherent level of orderliness. Neighborhood measures may include strategies like random observations of the streets, noting how many panhandlers, suspected drug dealers, and sleeping vagrants are present. One can also gauge orderliness using telephone surveys of residents. As Wilson notes, these measures of order may be going in an opposite direction from measures of crime reported to the police or victimization reports. Police performance measured this way, according to Wilson, assesses the preconditions of public order without "attacking ultimate outcomes" (Wilson, 1993: 165). Because crime has multiple causes, many of which are beyond the control of police, the measurement process proposed by Wilson concentrates on those problems the police can ameliorate.

One of the reasons Wilson's argument is so interesting in the context of this book is that it resonates with Logan's assessment of prison performance. Both theoreticians draw a distinction between those aspects of the social order that criminal justice practitioners can have an effect upon, and those that they cannot. This is also Charles Logan's reasoning for rejecting recidivism as a goal of prison performance. It is our contention that ultimate performance indicators—crime indices, recidivism—ought to be evaluated in conjunction with those measures on which criminal justice agencies have a more direct impact. Even if police have a limited effect on crime, are we willing to concede that police have *no* impact on crime? Despite the many barriers ex-offenders must overcome when they return to the community, are we willing to concede that prison programs or the prison environment have no effect on the post-release success of inmates? These questions anticipate an argument we make about the importance of recidivism as a performance outcome measure for prisons. Even though we recognize the merit of the Wilson/Logan argument, that crime and recidivism may have many causes, we are not willing to abandon those outcomes once we have developed a well-constructed theoretical framework and an appropriate measurement model. In the chapter on a life course perspective of recidivism, we show how an analyst can develop an expected rate of crime for a community or an expected rate of misconduct for a prison based on characteristics of the people and inmates in those communities and prisons. Then we can analyze how other factors, some of which are under the control of criminal justice agents, increase or decrease those expected rates. This approach circumvents the Wilson/Logan argument for ignoring crime rates as an indicator of either police or prison performance. We examine Logan's arguments closely below. He was one of the first policy analysts to rigorously examine what a prison *ought* to do as a prerequisite to meaningful performance measurement.

Charles Logan's Confinement Model

Charles Logan's analysis of prison performance measurement begins with the most fundamental of all questions: "What is criminal justice?" (Logan, 1993: 20). His answer launches him in a direction that minimizes the instrumental goals of imprisonment and emphasizes the desserts model. Logan states that:

> Justice is the quality of treating individuals according to their rights and in ways that they deserve to be treated by virtue of relevant conduct. Criminal justice is rights-respecting treatment that is deserved by virtue of criminal conduct. (Logan, 1993: 20)
>
> Justice by this definition is backward-looking. It requires that we treat people according to what they have done, not what they (or others!) might do in the future as a result of how we treat them now. Justice requires that all persons, including offenders be treated as autonomous and responsible actors and as ends in themselves, not as means to social ends. (Logan, 1993: 21)

To understand why Logan rejects the utilitarian goals of imprisonment—rehabilitation, incapacitation, deterrence, reintegration—in favor of the desserts model emphasizing punishment and its symbolic effect on the individual and the community, consider his appraisal of the internal and external pressures on the prison system.

> We ask an awful lot of prisons. We ask them to correct the incorrigible, rehabilitate the wretched, deter the determined, restrain the dangerous, and punish the wicked. We ask them to take over where other institutions of society have failed and to reinforce norms that have been violated and rejected. We ask them to pursue so many different and often incompatible goals that they seem virtually doomed to fail. Moreover,

when we lay upon prisons the utilitarian goals of rehabilitation, deterrence, and incapacitation, we ask them to achieve results primarily outside of prison, rather than inside. By focusing on external measures, we
set prisons up to be judged on matters well beyond their direct sphere of
influence. (Logan, 1993: 23)

The Logan argument to limit the measurement goals of imprisonment
is the same as the Wilson argument to limit the measurement goals of the
police, that is, we ought *not* to hold agencies responsible for ultimate outcomes over which they have limited influence. We reject this argument as
being too extreme. We concede that there are a myriad of causes for criminality (recidivism); however, there are many jurisdictions that articulate its
mission based upon the instrumental purposes of prison. For that reason,
we should hold criminal justice agencies responsible for their contribution
to providing incentives and skills to inmates who will then have a better
opportunity to make law-abiding decisions upon release from prison. We
certainly recognize the importance of other determinants of offending that
are typically beyond the control of criminal justice agencies: early childhood influences, the macro social and economic environment, the conditions and norms in neighborhoods. These external factors do not diminish
the responsibility of our criminal justice agencies to bring about socially desirable changes in individuals. As we have already stated, this is not a book
on *what prisons ought to do.* This is a book on conceptualizing prison performance once a jurisdiction *decides what it ought to do.* Nonetheless, it is
incumbent on the analyst who studies specific deterrence to demonstrate
the extent to which criminal desistance depends on skills acquired in
prison, as opposed to the level of punishment, or community influences. In
a sense, Logan's argument begs the question of whether prison can impact
post-release outcomes. If we assume it cannot, and make no effort to test
the assumption, then we will never discover whether the premise is true.

While we reject the Logan/Wilson thesis, we acknowledge that we
must be circumspect in measuring these ultimate criminal justice outcomes.
Admittedly, we need a much more refined understanding of the process that
leads to recidivism. In chapter 9, we capitalize on recent developments in life
course research to inform our understanding of criminal desistance. The desistance perspective sensitizes us to the cumulative experiences of the individual and the relationship between prior criminality, behavior in prison,

and the course of conduct after release from prison. In this way, it can inform the debate on the extent to which the criminal justice system can have an impact on the criminal activity of inmates after their release from prison.

It is also desirable to have more direct measures of intermediate changes to human behavior that precede desistance, and that may be influenced by criminal justice interventions. We need more refined measures of educational skills, changes in cognitive functioning, and changes in attitudes about substance abuse that are acquired in prison. All of these represent the development of intellectual and social capital of the inmates. In our analysis of recidivism below, we recognize that forces beyond the control of criminal justice agencies do impinge upon the offender. However, rather than throw up our hands in surrender, we argue that social scientists should push ultimate outcomes as far as they can be pushed. This analysis calls for a model that represents intermediate outcomes, those that Logan and Wilson believe are under the control of criminal justice agencies, in relation to post-release outcomes. We develop this model throughout this book and present a template on exactly how to specify such a model in chapter 10. Logan's confinement model is an excellent typology of some of the most important dimensions of intermediate prison outcomes. However, we believe it is primarily a first approach to the classification and construction of prison performance objectives, and not a fully articulated theoretical model.

The confinement model calls for an assessment of the following dimensions: security, safety, order, care, activity, justice, conditions, and management. In Logan's clever terminology, this taxonomy corresponds to: "keep them in, keep them safe, keep them in line, keep them healthy, and keep them busy—and do it with fairness, without undue suffering, and as efficiently as possible" (Logan, 1993: 20). Subsumed beneath these eight dimensions, Logan lists performance criteria. Underneath the performance criteria are the specific measures or indicators. For example, under the security dimension are listed the following criteria: security procedures, drug use, significant incidents, community exposure, freedom of movement, staffing adequacy. Under the criterion security procedures, Logan lists: perceived frequency of shakedowns in the living area; perceived frequency of body searches; proportion of staff who have observed either specific security problems (involving lax security, poor assignment of staff, inmate security violations, staff ignoring inmate misconduct, staff ignoring disturbances), or other problems; information on the actual number of shakedowns; information on inmate drug testing; drug-related inmate mis-conduct; significant incidents (assaults, disturbances, escapes); information on inmate furloughs to the community; perceived freedom of inmate movement; and ratio of inmates to security staff. Thus, Logan presents a system that articulates a just desserts model of criminal justice into a set of specific indicators. Since each dimension has many criteria and each crite-rion has many indicators, the total list of indicators can be substantial. In Logan's appendix he lists several hundred.

Logan combined and scored these indicators to produce a rating that he could use to compare prisons in his study of the privatization of a state women's facility in New Mexico (Logan, 1991, 1992). In Logan's 1993 pa-per that we are citing extensively in this section, he claims that one should not "prejudge the question of just what standards should differentiate good, fair or poor performance. Such standards probably cannot be articulated in abstract or absolute terms. Rather, prison performance should generally be viewed as a relative or comparative matter, and preferably within contexts that hold constant or adjust for such factors as the population type, secu-rity level, or other characteristics of the prisons being compared" (Logan, 1993: 39). While we have been critical of Logan's application of his system of prison performance measurement when he applied it to the New Mex-ico privatization analysis (Gaes et al., 1998), we have also given him credit for the most systematic approach that anyone has yet applied. We agree with Logan that context is crucial. We think Logan essentially disregarded context in his analysis of privatization in New Mexico. We also disagree with Logan that we should not "prejudge" standards that determine a good prison from a bad one. Standards follow from the mission declared by the prison system.[2] Before we elaborate what we mean by this, we define some terms so that we can be consistent in our representation of the theoretical and methodological model we are proposing.

The Missions and Goals of Adult Correctional Agencies in the United States and Canada

By a prison system's "mission," we mean the specific language that articu-lates the purpose of imprisonment within a jurisdiction. A good mission statement sets out a series of goals to be achieved by the jurisdiction. Some jurisdictions have clear, precise mission statements. Some are vague. If a system subscribes to a multifaceted set of purposes, then we should hold that system accountable for all of them. Who sets the jurisdictional mission is a matter for legislators, jurisdictional executives (governors, mayors, and sheriffs), prison administrators, philosophers, pundits, and the community. In table 1.1, we list the goals defined in mission, vision, and core values statements found at the World Wide Web sites of correctional systems listed in the American Correctional Association's reference book (American Correctional Association, 1999).

Some have expressed the point of view that to hold a jurisdiction to the goals specified in their mission statements may not be fair, since these goals were not explicitly meant to be the basis for performance standards. Another, more cynical group of critics has suggested that a mission should be understood by the concept of "revealed choices." If an agency emphasizes rehabilitation in its mission, and spends little or no money on these activities, its true mission is revealed by budget priorities. Both of these insights further emphasize that if mission statements are to be taken seriously and used as a basis for articulating objectives and performance standards, agencies should carefully conceptualize them and develop strategies and policies to meet the goals and expectations of those statements. The jurisdictions we are familiar with spend a great deal of time and energy using their most senior administrators to develop their missions, goals, and objectives. They revisit these decisions constantly, trying to find ways to maintain these objectives in an era of fiscal constraint.

After examining these missions, visions, and core values, it was apparent that there were certain themes emphasized by most of the adult correctional systems. The specific jurisdictional themes are found in table 1.1. Here we list each main theme and the percentage of jurisdictions that included that theme in their mission, vision, or core value statements: guaranteeing the safety of the public, staff, and inmates (96.2 percent); providing the opportunity for inmate self-improvement, treatment, and rehabilitation (65.4 percent); reducing recidivism or assisting the offender's reintegration into society (53.9 percent); respecting the dignity of inmates and treating them humanely (48.1 percent); operating cost-efficient and well-managed institutions (30.8 percent); insuring victims' rights by promoting the goals of restorative justice (26.9 percent); and offering meaningful work either as an end unto itself or as a goal of rehabilitation (21.2 percent).

Table 1.1. Goals Represented in Department of Corrections Mission Statements

Jurisdiction	Reduce Recidivism/ Assist Reintegration	Humane Confinement/ Dignity of Inmates	Rehabilitation/ Treatment/ Self-Improvement	Public Safety Including Staff & Inmate Safety	Meaningful Work	Victims' Rights/ Restorative Justice	Cost Effective/ Efficient/ Well Managed	Miscellaneous
Federal Bureau of Prisons	✓	✓	✓	✓	✓		✓	
Correctional Service of Canada	✓	✓	✓	✓				Respecting the rule of law
Alaska	✓	✓	✓	✓			✓	
Alabama			✓	✓	✓	✓		
Arizona		✓	✓	✓	✓		✓	
Arkansas	✓	✓	✓	✓	✓		✓	Opportunities for spiritual and physical growth
California	✓		✓	✓	✓			Public education on the role of correctional programming Cooperative efforts with other criminal justice agencies and other agencies
Colorado	✓	✓	✓	✓	✓		✓	
Connecticut		✓		✓				Climate that promotes professionalism, respect, dignity, and excellence

State	Hold prisoners accountable for their behavior upon release	Promotion in recognizing the value of human resources as represented by volunteers, offenders, their families, and community members	Health and well-being of committed are sustained	Comply with established mandates in preparing inmates for reentry into the community	Work in partnership with communities to supervise offenders at the appropriate level to manage risk	Be active in the community's efforts to prevent crime
Delaware	✓		✓			
Florida	✓		✓	✓		
Georgia	✓	✓	✓			
Hawaii	✓	✓	✓			
Idaho	✓		✓	✓		
Illinois						
Indiana	✓		✓			
Iowa	✓		✓			

(continued)

Table 1.1. Goals Represented in Department of Corrections Mission Statements (continued)

Jurisdiction	Reduce Recidivism/ Assist Reintegration	Humane Confinement/ Dignity of Inmates	Rehabilitation/ Treatment/ Self-Improvement	Public Safety Including Staff & Inmate Safety	Meaningful Work	Victims' Rights/ Restorative Justice	Cost Effective/ Efficient/ Well Managed	Miscellaneous
Kansas			✓	✓				
Kentucky		✓	✓	✓				
Louisiana	✓			✓				
Maine	✓					✓		
Maryland	✓	✓	✓	✓		✓		
Massachusetts			✓	✓	✓		✓	Appropriate classification of inmates Sound correctional policies and procedures Proactively informing and educating the public consistent with established correctional policies Professional and rewarding work environment for staff
Michigan		✓	✓	✓	✓	✓	✓	Just punishment
Minnesota				✓	✓			Provide effective correctional practice
Mississippi	✓		✓	✓	✓		✓	Value all employees and commit to their professional development and well-being

	Ongoing assessment	Custody classification	Continuum of supervision strategies	Promote public trust	Programs that emphasize offender accountability	Promote staff development and personal growth in a safe environment	Appropriate level of custody. Inmates provides care, discipline, training, and treatment for reintegration	Provide programs and services for offenders	Offer staff a variety of opportunities for career enrichment and advancement
Missouri *	✓		✓					✓	
Montana	✓			✓	✓				
Nebraska	✓		✓		✓				✓
Nevada	✓		✓		✓				✓
New Hampshire	✓				✓	✓			
New Jersey	✓		✓				✓		
New Mexico	✓							✓	
New York State			✓					✓	✓

(continued)

Table 1.1. Goals Represented in Department of Corrections Mission Statements (continued)

Jurisdiction	Reduce Recidivism/ Assist Reintegration	Humane Confinement/ Dignity of Inmates	Rehabilitation/ Treatment/ Self-Improvement	Public Safety Including Staff & Inmate Safety	Meaningful Work	Victims' Rights/ Restorative Justice	Cost Effective/ Efficient/ Well Managed	Miscellaneous
North Carolina	✓		✓	✓				Growth and development of staff; Community involvement
North Dakota				✓		✓		
Ohio	✓	✓	✓	✓		✓		
Oklahoma	✓	✓	✓	✓			✓	Responsibilities toward employees: secure, healthy environment; equitable pay, grievance procedures; no discrimination; professional growth. Responsibility toward inmates: climate of fairness, safety, helpfulness, and courtesy
Oregon Docs	✓			✓				Hold offenders accountable for their actions
Pennsylvania	✓		✓	✓		✓		
Rhode Island	✓	✓	✓	✓				
South Carolina				✓				
South Dakota				✓				

State		Become a nationally recognized leader for the economic and social contribution provided to the State of Tennessee and its taxpayers
Tennessee		✓
Texas	✓	✓
Utah	✓	✓
Virginia		✓ ✓
Vermont	✓	✓
Washington State	✓	✓
	Hold offenders accountable	
	Administer effective correctional programs	
	Provide leadership for the future	
Wisconsin	✓	✓
	Appropriate classification	
	Staff function honestly and professionally	
	Treating a diverse workforce as valued partners by fostering staff development and effectiveness.	

(continued)

Table 1.1. Goals Represented in Department of Corrections Mission Statements (continued)

Jurisdiction	Reduce Recidivism/ Assist Reintegration	Humane Confinement/ Dignity of Inmates	Rehabilitation/ Treatment/ Self-Improvement	Public Safety Including Staff & Inmate Safety	Meaningful Work	Victims' Rights/ Restorative Justice	Cost Effective/ Efficient/ Well Managed	Miscellaneous
West Virginia		✓		✓				Holding offenders accountable for their actions through sanctions, restitution, and restoration
Wyoming	✓	✓	✓	✓				Developing individualized correctional strategies based on the uniqueness of each offender
								Educating the public on what we do and how we do it
Total Counts	28 (53.9%)	25 (48.1%)	34 (65.4%)	50 (96.2%)	11 (21.2%)	14 (26.9%)	16 (30.8%)	43 possible entries in each column

* This information comes from the Department Overview at www.corrections.state.mo.us/overview.htm

By far, the greatest emphasis is placed on public safety. We should not expect that simply because a theme was not explicitly stated in these mission statements, a correctional agency does not internally emphasize that theme. Nonetheless, it is interesting to note the relative importance of safety above all other themes. This should not be surprising to anyone who has studied corrections, or who has worked in a prison. The primary responsibility of prisons is to public, inmate, and staff safety. However, it is also noteworthy that rehabilitation and/or reintegration roles are also emphasized by most jurisdictions. Typically, these latter goals are cautiously stated. Consider the following examples:

> It is the mission of Federal Bureau of Prisons to protect society by confining offenders in the controlled environments of prisons and community-based facilities that are safe, humane, cost-efficient, and appropriately secure, and that provide work and other self-improvement opportunities to assist offenders in becoming law-abiding citizens.
>
> The Correctional Service of Canada (CSC), as part of the criminal justice system and respecting the rule of law, contributes to the protection of society by actively encouraging and assisting offenders to become law-abiding citizens, while exercising reasonable, safe, secure, and humane control.
>
> In partnership with the citizens of Alaska, protect the public from repeat offender crime by using the best correctional practices available to provide a continuum of appropriate, humane, safe, and cost effective confinement, supervision, and rehabilitation services. The Department will carry out its responsibility while respecting the rights of victims and recognizing the dignity inherent in all human beings.
>
> The Alabama Department of Corrections, charged with the confinement and management of convicted felony offenders, is committed to public safety and to self-improvement activities for inmates, including meaningful work and treatment opportunities.
>
> The mission of the Colorado Department of Corrections is to protect the public through effective management of offenders in controlled environments which are efficient, safe, humane, and appropriately secure, while also providing meaningful work and self-improvement opportunities to assist offenders with community integration. (American Correctional Association, 1999)

Rehabilitation and reintegration are incorporated into these mission statements using verbs such as *provide, assist,* and *encourage.* This is probably an indirect acknowledgment that rehabilitation is a difficult enterprise, requiring the efforts of both the inmates and staff, and with the realization that once released, former offenders must navigate a difficult road to prevent criminal relapse. When we review recidivism as a measure of prison performance, we provide a road map of the difficult terrain inherent in disentangling the effects of prison rehabilitation from the myriad influences emanating from the post-release environment.

It should also be obvious that almost every correctional philosophy is mentioned in most mission statements. Incapacitation is represented by "public safety," rehabilitation by "treatment" and "self improvement," reintegration by explicit reference or by referring to "law abiding citizens," restorative justice by "victim's rights" or explicit reference. Even just desserts can be found in a few mission statements that refer to "holding prisoners accountable for their behavior," or "respecting the rule of law."

Objectives and Performance Indicators

Once a mission is defined, we can break it down into specific components. If one of the goals of the mission is to reintegrate an offender into the community, then the objectives that follow from that prescription might be: increasing the offender's level of education; providing an inmate with specific marketable skills; preparing an inmate for release by insuring that he or she has requisite documents such as proof of a GED, a social security number, and so on; providing the inmate with community transitional help in the form of supervision or programs; or, insuring that the inmate has sufficient funds to provide an economic safety net while he or she is trying to reintegrate back into society.

Underneath each objective may be subobjectives; however, ultimately, as social scientists, we need something to measure. These measures are the indicators of prison performance. Petersilia (1993) in describing performance measures for community corrections, laid out a similar logic. She specified the four pillars of mission, goals, methods, and indicators. Although Logan used different terminology than we are using here, he has brought us a long way. He articulated the relationship between mission, objectives, and performance indicators. Nevertheless, there is a considerable distance yet to go. In this book, we try to build upon Logan and others to develop a model for prison performance and to demonstrate the different measurement methods that one can use to evaluate prison performance.

From Mission to Performance Measurement: A Case Study of the Wolds Remand Prison

The James, Bottomley, Liebling, and Clare (1997) study of the Wolds Remand Prison (similar to a U.S. jail) in England provides a clear example of how a mission can and should determine the performance criteria for a prison or jail.[3] Wolds was one of the first jails to be privately operated in England. The contract for operation was awarded to the company Group 4. The Group 4 tender and the subsequent contract outlined the mission, goals, and even some specific objectives to be achieved by the company. These goals were also promoted and endorsed by the Home Office.[4] In fact, the Home Office tender documents stipulated that by contracting out a remand prison, the government had a unique opportunity to establish a new, more humane approach to inmate treatment in remand prisons. According to James et al. (1997), in contrast to the regimented, authoritarian, minimalist government of the typical remand prison, the Wolds regime[5] was to be based upon a philosophy that the remand prisoners were presumed innocent. Only those restrictions that were absolutely necessary to insure order and public safety would be imposed. The contract was supposed to insure that Group 4 would maintain high standards even under pressure to crowd Wolds. For example, the contract specified that prisoners would "receive 15 hours out-of-cell every day, 6 hours of education and gym per week, daily visits lasting a minimum of one hour, access to card phones on the living units, etc." (James et al., 1997: 67). Apparently, public remand prisons afforded very little out-of-cell opportunities and few program amenities.

The main point of the Wolds story is that both the Home Office and the contractor had clear expectations about the purpose and mission of the remand prison and even some of the specific objectives. This served as a framework for the James et al. evaluation of Wolds. In our chapter on qualitative assessment of prison performance, we describe how James and his colleagues contrasted the performance of Wolds and public sector prisons.

In subsequent chapters, we consider different ways we can define and measure performance indicia that are used to calibrate objectives within prison. Once again, these objectives ultimately stem from the goals of the particular jurisdiction. The model we are proposing is generic enough that it could correspond to any particular jurisdiction regardless of how it may limit or expand its mission statement. In the next part of this chapter, we take up the issue of recidivism as a measure of prison performance. In subsequent chapters we discuss other performance measures.

Recidivism

Michael Maltz's book, *Recidivism* (Maltz, 1984) is still the most comprehensive treatment of the topic. Other researchers such as Schmidt and Witte (1988) have provided technical treatments of survival models to measure recidivism; however, Maltz not only discussed the technical merits of such models, he also conceptualized the definitional and measurement issues inherent in assessing recidivism. We refer to his book throughout the remainder of this chapter.

Maltz shows how recidivism can be construed as a measure of special deterrence, incapacitation, and indirectly of rehabilitation. For recidivism to be a measure of rehabilitation, the analyst must also conceptualize, assess, and demonstrate the relationship between an offender's deficiencies and criminality. In the context of treatment, the analyst must demonstrate the relationship between treating such deficits and post-release recidivism. From this point of view, recidivism is the final measurement in a series of measurements intended to explain a rather complicated process. Maltz's explication focuses on the process of recidivism for an individual. A host of other problems arise when one tries to use an aggregate measure of recidivism to measure institution performance.

Some researchers have argued that recidivism ought to be the single most important criterion in measuring the performance of an individual prison or a prison system (see especially Harding, 2001). A study by Lanza-Kaduce and Parker (1998) and Lanza-Kaduce, Parker, and Thomas (1999) presented data on recidivism rates of offenders released from publicly and privately operated prisons in Florida. The study was an earnest attempt to measure the comparative differences in recidivism rates of public and private prisons. We review these papers closely, as well as a later paper updating information on the same release population. We also critique a more recent study conducted in Florida, which corrected for some of the methodological shortcomings of the prior research. Not only is it important to understand these shortcomings, but it is also essential that we consider theoretical explanations and causal mechanisms that should lead us to expect why one sector, public or private, should be more effective than the other in reducing recidivism. Would we expect a difference because one sector is more punitive? Or is it because one sector has better treatment programs? Or is it because one performs better in preparing an offender for the reintegration process? If we treat recidivism as a global measure of institutional or jurisdictional success, what do we really learn? As Maltz argues, when we conceptualize corrections as a process that leads to reduced criminality, we want to be able to decompose that reduction in criminality into specific program or regime effects. Since criminal desistance is such a complicated process, we want to be able to disentangle from one another the impacts of such programs as education, cognitive skills training, vocational training, addictions amelioration, and perhaps the impact of punishment. This is an ambitious goal, but, nevertheless, one that must be achieved if we are to make any sense of recidivism results.

Maltz (1984) also describes specific problems with using recidivism as a social indicator. First, if there are changes in arrest or revocation policy over time, these can affect the level of recidivism independent of the rate of underlying crime. Second, by focusing exclusively on a measure of failure other important social indicators are precluded from analysis. For example, much can be learned by studying post-release employment. Third, Maltz points out that there can be imprecision in the measurement process as well as potential artifacts that result from using pre- and post-custody rates of offending. One issue is that offenders who have been given a period of custody may be in a higher state of criminal activity than those who have not been given a period of custody. Their rate after prison returns to the average rate of high and low activity offenders and, as an artifact, looks lower than the pre-custody level. Another issue is that pre- and post-custody comparisons of officially recorded arrests may suffer from regression to the mean artifacts. Maltz does an exceptional job in explaining a very nonintuitive problem (Maltz, 1984: 34–40). Although these can be formidable challenges, as Maltz notes, "problems of this nature are common to the measurement of virtually all social phenomena" (Maltz, 1984: 25). While Maltz's critique applies to the calculation of individual level measures, there are other complications in using recidivism as a measure of institutional performance. We briefly describe these problems under the rubrics of prisoner movement, prisoner backgrounds, release neighborhoods, and decomposing criminality from jurisdiction supervision levels.

Prisoner Movement

One of the features of most prison systems is that inmates often transfer from one prison to another during the course of their prison stay. But how do we determine the role of the prison when inmates are moving from one to the other? Do we allocate a success or failure to the prison the inmate was released from, to the prison the inmate spent the most time in, or to all of the prisons in which the inmate spent time? Do we allocate the successes and failures based on the prisons where the inmate received the most programming, the best programming, or the institution in which the inmate had his change of heart? We do not wish to exaggerate the idea that inmates suddenly discover prosocial attitudes or that their orientation to crime changes instantaneously. It is more likely that the change is gradual, or proceeds erratically, sometimes moving forward, sometimes backward. Given the current technology of inmate skills measurement, a researcher may be hard pressed to demonstrate the process by which inmates' attitudes and skills are changing. This makes it very difficult to say precisely in which institution(s) an inmate acquires the social capital or changes attitudes to launch him or her toward a noncriminal lifestyle.

Prisoner Backgrounds

There is a great deal of data to demonstrate that post-release outcomes are very much dependent on a host of background characteristics of inmates. Prior criminal history, age, sex, education level, and gang participation are some of the major post-release predictors (Gendreau, Little, and Goggin, 1996). Any comparison among institutions would have to account for the compositional differences among inmates. There are many reasons why these average criminal risk levels can vary among prisons. As Maltz points out, there may be jurisdictional differences in the level of the use of probation. Districts or jurisdictions that use a lower level of probation as a sanction, assuming the criminal event is the same, will result in lower average criminal risk pools of offenders sentenced to a term of prison. Jurisdictions also assign prisoners in a nonrandom fashion to prisons. Correctional systems use prisons that have varying levels of security, usually assigning these levels as minimum, medium, and high. Offenders with higher criminal propensities, especially violent propensities, are assigned to the higher risk institutions. Even within an institution security level there may be variability from district to district. This is especially true when a second rule is used to assign prisoners to institutions by placing them as close as possible to their residence and their family. Thus, even within an institution security level, some prisons will house prisoners with higher average criminal risk than others because of the propinquity to a particular city.

Release Neighborhoods

A great deal of evidence has now accumulated that demonstrates the impact of the community and neighborhood on criminality (Raudenbush and Sampson, 1999a, 1999b). There is also much new information coming from research on crime mapping and other geo-coding techniques that demonstrates that in the United States, many ex-offenders are returning to some of the most disadvantaged and crime-prone neighborhoods (Cadora and Swartz, 1999), or to neighborhoods with a high number of parolees and ex-offenders (Lynch and Sabol, 2001). If we are to conduct recidivism studies that try to evaluate institutions and jurisdictions, then we must take into account the impact of these neighborhood effects on individual and ultimately aggregated criminality. This obviously introduces yet another layer of complexity and noise into our understanding of institutional measurement.

Differentiating Criminality from Criminal Justice Levels of Supervision

Petersilia (1993) has noted that if the correctional goal is to emphasize public safety, then increasing recidivism rates could be interpreted as a positive instance of performance. If the goal is rehabilitation, then an increasing recidivism rate may be interpreted as failure. While criminal justice events may be interpreted in various ways, we also see a problem given the level of discretion in the system. As Maltz (1984) recognized, post-release supervision policy and requirements are implicated in the measurement of recidivism. Within a jurisdiction, law and policy governing supervision are probably relatively uniform. However, there are many focal points in the supervision process where judgments and the role of discretion can cause differences in the revocation process. Thus, even within a state, there may be district variations in the choices made by the court, parole, or other supervision agents that monitor the offender. These are the agents that interpret law and policy that may lead to a revocation. If one compares prison releasees in one district to prison releasees in another, the role of judgment and discretion by these agents should be acknowledged and some consideration should be given to measuring decision-making differences in these jurisdictions.

Let's assume we can separately measure the level of surveillance from the level of criminality. Suppose that we use measures of level of supervision such as the number of police in a jurisdiction, the number of parole or probation officers supervising released offenders, and the amount of money spent on criminal justice. Then we may be able to isolate the degree to which recidivism rates depend on surveillance rather than the level of crime. This way one can draw conclusions about both public safety goals and the impact of rehabilitation. This is similar to the analysis of neighborhood effects; however, when we study neighborhoods, we are typically concerned with informal social control mechanisms. When we evaluate supervision levels in districts, we are concerned with formal social control mechanisms and the discretion involved in the interpretation of policy and law.

While there are a variety of indicators to measure the level of surveillance, it may be more difficult to measure discretion. Nevertheless, it may be possible to develop indicators. For example, the average number of positive urinalyses that occur prior to revocation is an indirect measure of the level of supervision, as well as the number of opportunities to exercise discretion in a jurisdiction.[6]

Comparing the Public and Private Sector Institutional Recidivism Rates

There have been several attempts to compare the recidivism rates between publicly and privately operated prisons in Florida. A close reading of these studies shows how many of the factors we have presented as being crucial to the understanding of prison recidivism rates have been almost entirely ignored in these studies. There have been papers by Lanza-Kaduce and Parker (1998) and Lanza-Kaduce, Parker, and Thomas (1999); however, they are essentially different versions of the same study. To get an "apples-to-apples" comparison of recidivism rates, these authors matched inmates who were released from two privately operated facilities with inmates released from publicly operated institutions. The matching variables were gender, classification level (minimum, medium), offense, race, prior record based on number of prior incarcerations, and age category. Lanza-Kaduce et al. (1999) found lower average recidivism rates among the inmates released from private facilities than the inmates released from public facilities. However, a survival analysis did not indicate any difference over the entire twelve-month follow-up period. This latter technique allows an analyst to compare the amount of time from release to arrest for the different groups. Given this mixed set of results, it is not clear why Lanza-Kaduce et al. were so emphatic in their inference that "Only one conclusion can be drawn from the results: Private prison releasees were more successful than were their public prison matches" (Lanza-Kaduce et al., 1999: 42).

A critical assessment of this study was written by the Florida Department of Corrections, Bureau of Research and Data Analysis (1998), noting significant problems. As the Bureau of Research and Data Analysis (BRDA) report showed, publicly released inmates served a longer time period, had longer sentences, and were more likely to have a term of supervision. These were not variables used in the matching. Although Lanza-Kaduce et al. used the custody level, minimum and medium, to match offenders, the BRDA found that the underlying continuous score measuring custody level was more often higher for the publicly managed offender in the matched pair than for the privately managed offender. Finally, by examining the data more closely, the BRDA found that the way in which Lanza-Kaduce et al. categorized prior incarcerations underrepresented the seriousness of a prior offense. While Lanza-Kaduce et al. chose two or more prior incarcerations as a cutoff, the BRDA found that public offenders in the matched pairs were more likely to have more prior incarcerations overall. All of these variables point to a failure in matching and an increased likelihood that public sector releasees were from a higher risk pool and would be more likely to recidivate. As the BRDA researchers pointed out, supervision can increase the likelihood of surveillance and a recidivistic event, in and of itself. Based on the differences found by BRDA, one might expect that in addition to a higher propensity to commit crime when they were released, the publicly released offenders may have also had higher levels of supervision.

There were other problems as well. The Lanza-Kaduce et al. article states that "[i]f inmates were transferred between public and private institutions during the year, the last institution at the time of release was used to determine whether the release was from a private or a public facility" (Lanza-Kaduce et al., 1999: 32). They did not provide data on the percentage of releasees from these institutions who had transferred from either another publicly or privately managed prison. The BRDA did some follow-up assessment of the same data and found that 35 percent of the 198 matched inmates released from the private facility had spent time in a public facility. Of these sixty-nine mixed cases, fifty-two offenders spent more time in a public facility during the course of their imprisonment. This is symptomatic of the problems we discuss above. This is a dilemma that must be solved, especially in jurisdictions where there will be many transfers between private and public facilities. Lanza-Kaduce et al. chose to allocate these transfers to the facility from which the inmate was released. However, in this case, a plausible argument could be made that these inmates should have been allocated to a public facility. Only one offender identified as a public prison releasee had spent time in a private facility.

While many of these criticisms might be circumvented by a reanalysis of the data, there was one flaw noted by the BRDA researchers that could mean the recidivism results were an artifact of the measurement process. Apparently, privately released offenders were discharged between seventeen and fourteen months prior to the recording of the recidivism events. Matched publicly released offenders were discharged between twenty-two and fourteen months prior to the recording of the event. Since the researchers used a twelve-month follow-up "risk period," all releasees would have had the same time at risk. However, public releasees had a longer period, for some an additional five months, during which the event could be adjudicated, and thus had a greater likelihood of being recorded in the Florida Department of Corrections information system. This was the system the researchers used to code the recidivism events. The BRDA researchers examined the records system two months after the original research team had recorded their data. They provided an example of a privately released offender whose arrest actually occurred during the twelve-month risk period, but the event was not recorded at the time of the original data coding because the inmate had not yet been adjudicated.

A follow-up paper by Lanza-Kaduce and Maggard (2001) used the same release cohort of 198 inmates and collected recidivism data over a longer time period, forty-eight rather than twelve months. Releasees from privately operated prisons had lower forty-eight-month recidivism rates than the releasees from publicly operated facilities. Although Lanza-Kaduce and Maggard argue that a longer time period debunks some of the prior criticisms of their twelve-month follow-up, the BRDA criticisms still hold with respect to matching and even differences in possible length of the follow-up risk period.

The BRDA researchers essentially point out weaknesses with the Lanza-Kaduce et al. studies based on prisoner movement, prisoner backgrounds, and to some extent jurisdictional supervision levels. There is no mention of release neighborhoods, and we have no reason to assume one way or another that inmates were released to neighborhoods of equal risk. Since inmates did seem to be exposed to higher levels of supervision risk if they were released from a public facility, the authors of this study should have made some effort to control for not only time at risk, but the level of supervision risk as well.

A more recent study by Farabee and Knight (2002) corrected for some of these deficiencies. Farabee and Knight used the pool of all offenders re-leased from the Florida public and private prisons between January 1, 1997, and December 31, 2000, who did not have a detainer, were classi-fied as minimum, medium, or close custody, and had spent at least six months in the releasing facility. Matching was done on commitment of-fense, custody level at the time of release, race, ethnicity, age at release, ed-ucation level, prior recidivism, time served, and months since release. The final sample included 2,341 offenders released from private facilities and 4,912 released from public institutions.

Farabee and Knight found that during their prison stay inmates in privately operated prisons were more likely to participate in and complete institution programs than their public counterparts. Adult women and youthful offenders released from private prisons had fewer major discipli-nary reports than their public sector counterparts. This latter finding was not true for adult males. When recidivism was measured as a reoffense, there were no differences between private or public male or juvenile re-leasees. Women released from private facilities had lower reoffense rates than their public counterparts. The same relationships were found when recidivism was measured as reincarceration.

While Farabee and Knight seem to have increased matching precision over the methods used by Lanza-Kaduce and colleagues, it is still not clear how Farabee and Knight handled the inevitable problem of institution transfer. They only mention that an inmate had to be at a releasing institution for six months but do not consider where else the offender might have been in his or her "career" in the Florida prison system. Furthermore, the matching algorithm they used randomly chose matched pairs based on the criteria listed above. One problem not addressed by this kind of matching approach is that it does not handle potential selection bias artifacts. If there is some process that determines who is assigned to an institution that may be correlated with institutional or post-release behavior, the analyst is supposed to use a method designed to tackle selection artifacts. One such technique that could have easily been used is Rubin and Rosenbaum's propensity score method (Rosenbaum and Rubin, 1984). This technique allows an analyst to measure the probability (propensity) that an offender would have been selected into a private rather than a public institution. We suspect that assignment to private prisons may involve some "creaming" of the better behaved prisoners and an adjustment should be made to account for this selection artifact.

Although Farabee and Knight used two measures of recidivism, conviction or reincarceration (following either an offense or technical violation), the former is flawed. According to the authors, "reoffense" did not take into account someone who had technically violated their supervision but had no conviction. In the language of survival analysis, someone who technically violates his or her supervision and is returned to an institution is "censored." The censored individual is removed from the pool of those that could be reconvicted. Those offenders that technically violated their supervision, however, may have been the most risky of the released population and the most likely to be convicted for a new offense if they have not been returned to prison. This kind of "informative" censoring can lead to misinterpretations of the data.

The authors also reported that they used major disciplinary reports as an outcome. The lower disciplinary rates among youth and women at the privately operated prisons might reflect the selection bias we mention above, if less problematic inmates were assigned to private prisons. It could also mean that the private institutions manage their prisons better, or it could mean that private prisons are less likely to record and report institutional misconduct than their public sector counterparts. Regardless of the explanation, Farabee and Knight could have analyzed the outcome data with survival methods controlling for all of the matching variables as well as misconduct. To eliminate the possible selection artifacts they could also have subclassified offenders on a propensity score. Nor does the Farabee and Knight analysis take into account the release context of offenders.

Future studies of institutional recidivism levels will have to address not only the problems we note above, but also the issues associated with making inferences at the institutional level by using data that characterize both the individual offenders and the compositional characteristics of the institution. Multilevel models are required to draw inferences about the institution, while controlling for compositional differences in the offender population. We address this problem below when we discuss multilevel models within an organizational context.

Measures of Prison Performance Other than Recidivism

Although we revealed our hand when we began our discussion with recidivism as a prison performance measure, there are many other performance measures that can be used that do not carry the same methodological and theoretical "baggage" as recidivism. Institutional measures of performance, consistent with the many purposes of prison, can be used to monitor the different prison functions. We take up many examples of these measures in subsequent chapters. Unlike recidivism, many of these have the advantage of being "real time" contemporary indicia of events as they are occurring within the institution, day to day and month to month. One of the arguments against the practicality of using recidivism is that it is measured months or years after the interventions that are intended to affect the outcome. It is difficult to hold current employees accountable for retrospective interventions for which they may have had little or no involvement.

Contemporaneous measures such as escapes, contraband, random drug hit rates, and GED completion rates are not only easily monitored with fewer measurement problems, they also allow managers to make improvements or contemplate changes soon after the data have been collected. Changes in these indicators may signal a systemic problem, such as the necessity for more training or more resources. Or they could signal a problem in individual behavior.

Unless employees are negligent, it is better from a management perspective to interpret changes in indicators as a system-level problem to be addressed by further inquiry and structural improvements. If employees believe performance measurement is simply a way to generate a list of staff failures, the system may be subverted by those employees it is intended to monitor. However, if staff believe that performance monitoring is indeed a way of promoting continuous process improvement, then they will be more likely to buy into the system and not subvert the measurement process itself. We have much more to say about unintended consequences of performance measurement in chapter 11. In the next several chapters, we show how different measurement processes can be used to generate real-time performance measurement. We return to recidivism toward the end of the book and frame the issue in the broader criminological area of life course literature.

CHAPTER TWO
PRISON AUDITS

Prison audits, more than any other technique, are the primary method administrators use to monitor and evaluate their institutions. Teams from accrediting agencies, external monitors, and employees who are experts in a particular area visit a facility and evaluate some programmatic function such as food service, security, health services, or occupational safety. The audit establishes whether a particular function is in compliance with policy, regulations, law, and standards established by the agency, the courts, the government, or an accrediting institution.

Prison audits are a rich resource of material that can be used to collect data on processes and outcomes. The distinction between process and outcome is important for many reasons. Process data are those that can be used to inform our understanding of procedures and practices that are intended to affect outcomes or consequences. For example, health screening is a process that involves interviewing patients, conducting diagnostic tests, and using clinical judgment to ensure good health outcomes for inmates and staff alike. Process indicators can include such measures as compliance with screening standards, whether or not an agency uses modern clinically acceptable screening procedures, and the number of medical staff available to treat the inmate population. Outcomes would be measures of inmate health such as the incidence of infectious diseases. It is rather straightforward to develop process and outcome indicators for almost any prison function, including health, inmate programs, and inmate security. In most jurisdictions, all of these functions are monitored with audit procedures that lend themselves to the development of process indicators. As we demonstrate in subsequent chapters, we can use process and outcome indicators in statistical models that allow us to draw conclusions about the impact of procedures and practices on important outcomes. This is implicitly what the prison audit is about. Those who govern prisons assume that if an audit establishes that policy and procedures are being followed, then the institution will continue to run without incident. While most policy is based on the collective wisdom of professionals, the field of corrections has benefited before from rigorous scientific investigation of the impact of policy or procedures on outcomes. As we show in subsequent chapters, we can gain a rich understanding of the relationship between processes and outcomes when we apply an explicit model. In this chapter, we demonstrate how an extremely valuable prison security audit can be modified, ever so slightly, to provide not only institutional guidance on security issues, but also a database that could be used to monitor the security strengths and weaknesses of the entire prison system.

We are unaware of a single instance in the published social science literature in which a researcher has incorporated prison audits into the evaluation of prison performance. If there are such studies, they are not a significant aspect of the social science of prison performance. This is unfortunate, since prison audits are the primary instrument used by public officials to monitor both public and private prison performance. As an example of how one state systematically uses prison audits, we consider the Department of Corrections for Arizona.

The state of Arizona is required by enabling legislation to evaluate private prisons against the performance of public prisons.

Arizona uses audits to compare prisons in functional areas such as security, inmate management, safety, sanitation, administration, food service, personnel practices, staff training, inmate health systems, inmate discipline, business practices, public access to information, inspections and investigations, and other matters determined by the director. A report by the Arizona Department of Corrections (Stewart, 2000) depicted the results of audits conducted by staff of the General Inspections Program. Based on this report, the private prisons performed at or above the average level of public prisons 62.3 percent of the time. The report also claims that the state saved $5.5 million in fiscal years 1998 and 1999. Because this assessment does not explicitly account for potential differences in the populations served and differences in characteristics of the prisons themselves, we make no judgment about the veracity of these differences. However, the Arizona approach seems to be based on a comprehensive internal assessment of objectives to be achieved within each of the functional areas they inspect. This is a major step in what we conceive of as an optimal performance measurement system for corrections. In following chapters, we describe other components necessary to make a fair comparison among prisons that are lacking in the Arizona analysis. Nevertheless, Arizona is one state that has made a concerted effort to incorporate audit information into an objective analysis of prison performance.

In some of the other private prison literature, government agencies have used compliance with American Correctional Association standards (Tennessee Select Oversight Committee on Corrections, 1995) or state audit instruments to compare publicly and privately operated prisons. While it may appear to the social scientist's naive eye that audits are too subjective to be used in a scientific assessment, we demonstrate that the best audit instruments contain domain-specific objective information that could easily be translated into "hard" data. Furthermore, because these instruments have been developed to evaluate specific functional domains such as prison security or health services, an analysis of audit data would tell us precisely where prisons are succeeding or failing, and how prisons compare. The reason that audits have not been used in the social science literature is that most of these instruments have not been articulated as a measuring device, and the audit results have not been recorded as data.

A Model Audit for Prison Security

The best audits are those that establish not only whether there is good policy and procedure in place, but whether those rules are consistently followed by staff. To demonstrate how an audit can provide valuable information on institution performance, we chose as an example the *Security Audit Program: A "How To" Guide and Model Instrument for Adaptation to Local Standards, Policies, and Procedures* (Atherton, Czerniak, Franklin, and Palmateer, 1999). This audit was developed under the auspices of the National Institute of Corrections (NIC). The audit's primary contributors and writers represent the document as "the combined thinking and observations of numerous corrections professionals representing many agencies from all parts of the U.S." (Atherton et al., 1999: acknowledgments). We deliberately chose the security audit, because it measures one of the least controversial and most essential purposes of prison: the safety of inmates, staff, and the public.

The first author of this book witnessed how this audit is applied in practice. He accompanied one of the audit authors, Joan Palmateer, during three different site visits. Some prison administrators have argued that the best administrators manage by "walking around." A good auditor walks, listens, observes, questions, measures, inspects, reads, and records. Depending on the size of the prison, an audit in one specific functional area can take three to five days, eight to ten hours a day. As Ms. Palmateer says, "Get your hands dirty and wear comfortable shoes."

To give the reader an indication of the comprehensiveness of the NIC security audit, we list the twenty-five audit areas in table 2.1. While some of these areas may not seem appropriate to those new to prison security issues, all of them have security implications. For example, consider food service. It is not difficult to think of potential weapons available in a kitchen—knives, spatulas (which can easily be sharpened into knives), and other cooking devices. Only the security specialist would think of yeast and cayenne pepper as a security issue. Yeast can be used to make "home brew." Cayenne pepper can be used to deter drug-sniffing dogs, or to make a spray to be used against other inmates or prison staff.

Table 2.1.   National Institute of Corrections Security Audit Areas

armory/arsenal
communications
contraband and contraband management
inmate counts
control centers(s)
controlled movement
fire safety
food service
use of force
hazardous materials management
inmate mail
inmate visiting
inmate property
inmate work assignments
inmate transportation
key control
medical services
perimeter security
physical plant
post orders
admission and discharge
searches
security inspections
segregation (special management)
tool control

In its current manifestation, the security audit is a report tailored to address specific institutional concerns. As each of the areas is reviewed, the auditor records notes about what he or she is finding. For example, under perimeter security, there are a number of audit guidelines, each specifying a different requirement. The auditor makes a comment when he or she observes a violation or can make a suggestion or recommendation. Joan Palmateer's review of a facility in Oklahoma had the following kinds of comments concerning perimeter security:

> Repeater tower directly adjacent to the administration building creates access to administration rooftop, if inmate(s) compromise the one interior fence.
>
> Razor ribbon on exterior fence is not "collapsible/enveloping" type. There are hog rings set at frequent spacing on razor coils around the entire perimeter fence. This increases the strength of razor rolls allowing an individual to actually use the razor ribbon to climb the fence minimizing injury. It was viewed as a true deterrent when it was designed, but actually creates potential aid to affect an escape.
>
> The bottom of interior vehicle gates have loose ties and fencing around the bottom support pole. This area could be easily compromised by inmates attempting to escape.
>
> Mobile patrol officer was asked when he would be authorized to shoot/use lethal force if inmate(s) were breaching the fenced perimeter. His response was to shoot when inmate(s) are in between the two fences. The Chief, who was accompanying us, indicated that was not correct. Shots can be fired when inmate(s) breach the first interior fence. The mobile patrol officer was also asked what he would do if there were an aircraft intrusion. He responded that if inmate(s) got in a helicopter and it took off, he would fire upon the aircraft. The Chief indicated this was also incorrect; however, there is no training to address this issue. The post order for mobile does not address either the breach of the perimeter by an inmate or an aircraft intrusion.
>
> All cross fencing intersecting with interior perimeter fence have brackets which create a self-climb ladder. "No climb" or vertical razor ribbon could enhance the perimeter security.

A New Approach to Using Prison Audit Data

These previous comments and recommendations are invaluable to the audited institution. However, the audit instrument could be modified slightly to enhance its utility systemwide. When an auditor tours the institution, he or she records comments in response to specific guidelines. For example, guideline 18.02.12 reads: "A crash barrier is installed at every breach in the perimeter fence created for the purpose of vehicular access to the institution." Guideline 18.04.09 reads "Security procedures prevent inmate access to buildings located on the perimeter that are points of facility entrance and egress." These security guidelines could easily be coded to indicate whether or not a facility was in compliance with a particular guideline. Some of the guidelines could be transformed into continuous measurement scales of institution policy compliance. For example, the security guidelines on hazardous materials recommend a "perpetual inventory." A perpetual inventory of caustic materials is the amount of the material by weight recorded every time the material is used. When an auditor checks on compliance with this standard, he or she weighs the material to see how close the recorded perpetual audit amount is to the actual current weight. The result of this calculation, from a scientific point of view, is a continuous measure of the extent to which an institution adheres to a perpetual inventory. These kinds of continuous data, and the nominal data that are produced when one records the compliance, or lack of it, with other security guidelines, could be compiled on each specific guideline for every institution on which the security audit is conducted. Furthermore, given the current software technology, many of the recommendations or comments that appear in these reports could be worked into lists. If the audit were automated and was designed for a laptop computer or even a personal data assistant (PDA), auditors could simply choose from "pick lists." This would speed up the audit. It would also provide a great deal more systematic data collection for security specialists that would allow them to study the security issues throughout the system. After these procedures were honed, the security data could then be analyzed in conjunction with other objective data, such as assaults, or escapes, creating a scientific assessment of security issues.

We believe that the primary reason why this measurement approach has not been embraced by jurisdictions is because auditors are trained to be responsive to a specific institution. Administrators reacting to the critique also view the problems as localized issues. The transformation of the security audit into a data collection tool would not change its utility to the individual institution. Reports could still be tailored to local issues. In addition, by slightly modifying the security audit, the instrument would become a tool to study systemwide, even nationwide, security issues. A lot of effort has already gone into the security audit procedures developed under the auspices of the National Institute of Corrections. With a little more work, the audit could become a standard for developing a national database of security information. These audit instruments already exist for other domains of institution performance such as health services, case management, sentence computations, and inmate programs. Each of these could be adapted into a scientific measurement instrument. Having these measurements on every institution in a system would allow comprehensive analysis of institution performance that has eluded corrections to this point. While audits seem to be lagging in their development into objective performance measures, the American Correctional Association (ACA) has embarked on developing objective standards.

The American Correctional Association's Performance-Based Standards

The American Correctional Association has published performance-based standards for adult community residential services (American Correctional Association, 2000) and for correctional health care in adult institutions (American Correctional Association, 2002). The ACA Standards Committee has decided to develop performance-based criteria for all of its standards manuals.

The performance-based manuals distinguish between outcome measures, expected practice, protocols, and process indicators. The outcome measures are organized by the different sections or components of the standards manual. The health care standards manual includes the following sections: continuum of health care services, staff training, offender treatment, performance improvement, offender hygiene, safety and sanitation, and administration. As an example, the rate of positive tuberculin skin tests is an outcome measure of the continuum of health care services. There are fifty-nine outcome measures spread across the different components. An expected practice is an activity that achieves a specific goal. For example, one of the mandatory expected practices (formerly called a mandatory standard) is that an offender, upon arrival at a facility, is informed about access to health systems and the grievance procedure. A protocol, according to this nomenclature, is a policy, an inmate handbook, and/or a statement of the grievance procedure that describes implementation of the expected practice. A process indicator is a measure that establishes whether the practice is being carried out.

As an example, a process indicator could include documentation that offenders are informed about health care access. Alternatively, auditors could interview offenders asking them whether they received information on health care access. At this point, the process of accreditation is similar to what it has always been. Institutions must pass all mandatory expected practices and a certain percentage of nonmandatory expected practices. ACA has not set any criteria establishing a minimal level of success with respect to the outcome performance measures. Nor have they established a threshold for any particular process indicator. Thus, ACA is currently silent on an acceptable level of infectious disease. From a performance perspective, it may make more sense to assess incidence in addition to the prevalence of infectious disease as ACA currently does. This would parallel some of the other incident information that is collected, such as the rate of suicides. The prevalence of infectious disease indicates the potential for transmission. Ideally, a prison system should monitor the level of infectious disease when an inmate first arrives and record that diagnostic so that a prevalence rate can be computed for an admission cohort. A prison cannot be held accountable for the number of infected inmates who are admitted to their system. However, they can be held accountable for new cases, or for the incidence of infectious disease. The prevalence of disease in an admission cohort alerts the health administrators to how many resources they may need to treat the inmate population, and to emphasize procedures that minimize the risk to staff and inmate exposure.

If jurisdictions are able to collect this performance data and submit the data to ACA, this will generate a very rich source of outcome and process measures that could be analyzed in a manner we suggest in chapter 4 of this book. The more objective and independent the audits, the more outside constituencies will have faith in the results. However, prison administrations typically want an honest accounting of the level of functioning of their prisons. Independent and critical audits insure accountability and proper management. They can also be used to promote knowledge transfer and good performance. The ACA strategy is very important to the development of prison performance measurement. The relationship between process and outcome indicators may pave the way for an eventual national system of prison performance.

CHAPTER THREE
UNDERSTANDING THE MEASUREMENT
CONTEXT—QUALITATIVE ASSESSMENT

I n chapter 2, we discuss the techniques prison administrators are most likely to use to monitor and evaluate institution performance. In this chapter, we discuss the merits of the least likely method to be used by prison administrators—systematic qualitative assessment. First, we should clarify what we mean by *qualitative assessment*. Qualitative assessments are descriptions of the context in which performance is measured. Qualitative measures add meaning and dimensionality to our understanding of quantitative performance indicators. To develop a qualitative assessment, the researcher can observe staff, conduct focus groups, or engage in informal discussions. The observations and information add a contour and understanding of the quantitative data that is collected. As an example of such measures, we briefly highlight some of the main findings of the study by James, Bottomley, Liebling, and Clare (1997) who evaluated private remand prisons in England. We also summarize a study by C. Elaine Cummins depicting the growth of prison privatization in Texas. Although both of these were academic expositions, the work by James and others was done for the British government. Both are excellent examples of the added understanding that can be achieved when the entire context of a policy change is considered in a comprehensive report. While these kinds of assessments take a great deal of time and are rather expensive, they may be warranted in special situations where a prison administrator requires a thorough understanding of the context of the operations of their prisons. Such studies are often undertaken by prison administrators as after-action reports to dramatic prison events such as riots, an unusual number of homicides, or mass escapes.

While we describe these studies as qualitative or ethnographic, they also incorporate data into their exposition. They are ethnographic in the sense that the authors observe behavior by spending time among inmates, staff, administrators, legislators, and other key participants. It is, however, the added dimensions, provided through analyses of staff and inmate interviews, explanations of enabling or guiding legislation, discussions of relevant policy, portrayals of historical context, and illustrations of legal, social, and economic factors, that make these types of studies so valuable.

The Study of the Wolds Remand Prison, Her Majesty's Prison Service—Revisited

This work is described in the first chapter and clearly demonstrates that to conduct an evaluation of a prison the researcher must have an understanding of the mission, goals, and objectives of the prison system. Wolds was one of the first privately operated correctional institutions in England. The government objective was to change the entire culture of remand prisons from the publicly managed orientation that was authoritarian, regimented, and minimalist to one that encompassed a philosophy that incorporated a presumption of innocence toward pretrial inmates and a concomitant approach to their treatment. One of the objectives coming out of the new mission of Wolds was to import the U.S. prison management strategy of direct supervision[1] into the English system. Direct supervision was introduced into Wolds as a management innovation. James and his co-authors describe the particular problems that resulted from direct supervision because of staffing shortages and the inability of staff to sanction prisoners. One solution to the problem was to introduce a unit to house the most recalcitrant prisoners. This had the intended effect of isolating the most troublesome prisoners; however, because the "problem" unit had to have higher staffing levels, fewer people were available to staff the remaining posts in the institution. Indeed, James et al. describe how chronic labor shortages were a persistent problem at Wolds and that staff suspected that the problem was due to the private company's profit motive rather than a strategy to control inmates.

This particular ethnographic approach provided a rich documentary of the innovations that occurred at Wolds, from the perspective of both staff and inmates. To conduct their research, the authors spent a great deal of time observing the operations and interviewing inmates and staff. The interviews revealed that most of the inmates were much more experienced than the staff. Although there were a few experienced former public employees, the great majority of staff and almost all of the line staff were chosen because they did not have prior public prison experience. This was intended to dramatically change the staff culture. The prison system of England had "been rocked by the most serious and widespread disturbances ever experienced" (James et al., 1997: 58). Following these disturbances, a review of the entire system was published (Woolf and Tumim, 1991). Some of the most egregious problems occurred at the remand prisons. According to the Woolf report, there were problems endemic to the very nature of how the prison system was being run. One of those problems was how staff treated prisoners. The blame for this problem was directed at both management and staff. The government was searching for ways to implement a system that was safe and secure but that was also more just. In this context, the private company that won the contract to manage Wolds, Group 4, was allowed to experiment with a new management approach and a new orientation for their staff. The Group 4 strategy was to start with a "naïve" workforce and train staff in a more positive orientation to prisoners, particularly remand prisoners.

The regime changes at Wolds allowed some experienced and sophisticated prisoners to take advantage of the relaxed prison atmosphere. This in turn led to a reaction by staff and management to harden the prison regimes. The prisoner reactions to the greater freedom provided at Wolds was generally positive; however, while Wolds afforded more freedom, many prisoners did not take advantage of the opportunities provided to them. In varying degrees, inmates felt that there was quite a bit of idleness; that the openness of the units and lack of staff allowed bullying to take place; that it was easy to get drugs into the prison; and it was easy to make drug deals.

James et al. described how inmate-staff relationships were more positive at Wolds than at similar public remand prisons. Prisoners regarded the Group 4 staff as more willing to listen and address inmate problems and as more respectful of inmates. Staff expressed a concern that the openness of the prison made them rely on inmates too much to maintain order and control.

When Wolds first opened, there were only five staff members (managers) who had any experience in operating a prison. While James et al. describe a litany of problems resulting from staff inexperience, it is quite amazing that the situation was not chaotic. While the new management philosophy seemed to be positive for the inmates at Wolds, the staff felt isolated and vulnerable in the units. Wolds was also receiving bad publicity in the local newspapers. Whether or not that publicity was warranted, staff morale at Wolds deteriorated over time.

One of the important dimensions in evaluating prison performance is accurate assessment of how the first few years of operation set the "culture" of that prison and how the management philosophy changes over time in response to internal and external pressures. The James et al. ethnography vividly reveals the influence of ongoing pressures. Over time, the Wolds environment gave way to the pressure of internal and external forces common to all prisons under jurisdiction of HM Prison Service. As James et al. describe the situation, the original contract with Group 4 enabled the government to allow the private sector to experiment with a different management philosophy, to protect the prison from the endemic crowding within the public sector, and to introduce minimum prison standards in a systematic way. As the author's fieldwork was coming to an end, the external and internal pressures began to move the Wolds environment away from its original design to one much more similar to the public sector prison environment.

> These and some of the other factors which led to compromises being made to the original Wolds philosophy and pressures to resort to more familiar public-sector practices (such as the increasing restrictions over prisoners' movements, the introduction of more sanctions for non-cooperation, tightening up the Segregation Unit and the regime, and reducing some of the standards already set, such as lengths of visits, which had exceeded the minimum contract requirements), serve to highlight issues which are intrinsic to the management of prisons rather than being a function of whether they are managed by the public or private sector. (James et al., 1997: 97)

Soon after the contract was awarded to Group 4 to operate Wolds, the Prison Service built several other new generation prisons, and most of those were operated by the public sector. James et al. were able to include the publicly operated HMP Woodhill in their study and additional information from some of the other new generation prisons. Woodhill was similar to a local jail in the United States, housing remand, newly convicted, and short-duration sentenced prisoners. Woodhill was considered a post-Woolf generation prison. In other words, the operation of the prison was supposed to ameliorate conditions cited in the Woolf report condemning the conditions under which prisoners, particularly remand prisoners, were housed throughout the Prison Service. Thus, the management team at Woodhill began with a "new generation design" prison, and a management philosophy designed by the Prison Service based upon respect for the inmate.

> The establishment's statement of purpose was "to provide a secure and caring environment with a positive regime; to encourage the development of all staff and inmates and provide support within a safe, civilized and orderly work culture; to provide support to the families of staff and inmates; to assist inmates to make a positive contribution to their community; and to look to the community and share mutual resources and develop a greater understanding of the work we do" (HM Prison Service 1992). (James et al., 1997: 102)

Thus, the Woodhill philosophy was more like Wolds and those two prisons had an ethos unlike the majority of the establishments under the authority of the Prison Service. In their description of staff morale, inmate time out-of-cell, inmate-staff relationships, inmate bullying, inmate drug use, the organization of management and staff, the Woodhill experience parallels the Wolds experience. There were subtle distinctions between the two prisons— the private slightly outperforming the public on certain dimensions, the public performing better than the private on other dimensions. Their comparative analysis emphasized the commonalities among the "new generation" prisons, both public and private, that were associated with a well-managed prison: an overarching ethos based on humane and equitable treatment, endorsement of that philosophy from the highest level of the Prison Service, and a management team that endorsed the philosophy and that had the experience and talent to imbue those convictions in line staff.

The Prison Service used both the contract prisons and the new generation prisons to introduce extended periods of out-of-cell time. Apparently, HM Prison Service institutions had historically used lockdown procedures to safeguard inmates, staff, and the public. Introducing extended out-of-cell time created problems for the public and private sector operations. There was a lot of inmate idleness because there was little for inmates to do. The out-of-cell time gave inmates, so inclined, a chance to bully other inmates or carry on illicit activities (dealing drugs, theft). This created inmate management problems unknown to the Prison Service prior to this change in policy. Although it appears that the policy change was a net benefit to inmates and staff, both the private and public sector

CHAPTER THREE

prisons were struggling to develop new approaches for occupying prisoners' out-of-cell experiences.

James et al. conclude that the Wolds experience was clearly a net benefit to inmates and staff; however, those achievements were not unique to the private operation. The public sector prisons given the opportunity to innovate and create a new ethos and management philosophy were equally successful in carrying out these new regimes. James et al.'s greatest concern was the manner in which the private contractor brought in new staff at Wolds. Ninety-five percent of the staff had no previous correctional experience, and the experience gap between newly activated private and public prisons was particularly acute at the level of middle management. This created a management vacuum, especially in the initial months of operation. Public sector prisons under the "new regime" were still able to draw from a pool of experienced managers and new recruits who had been through extensive training. James et al. conclude that "from the staff perspective, the achievement of Wolds and other private sector prisons may be at the cost of higher levels of stress and greater job insecurity for many of those recruited to work in them" (James et al., 1997: 137).

The context provided in the James, Bottomley, Liebling, and Clare ethnography is essential to understanding the way in which Wolds and Woodhill began and continued to operate. This kind of context is often missing from studies that are portrayed as more objective. In fact, in an effort to be "objective," many researchers have put an institution under a microscope, examining details without understanding the broader context of prison operations.

A Second Qualitative Example— Prison Privatization in Texas

Another important example of this kind of contextual understanding of prison performance comes from the public administration literature. C. Elaine Cummins (2001) completed a study of the development and growth of prison privatization in the state of Texas. Her analysis is an important contribution not only to our understanding of the political, economic, and legal conditions prevailing in Texas during the growth in prison privatization, but to our understanding of the context in which prison performance must be understood. Cummins's analysis unveils the motives and interests of the parties involved in the prison privatization debate in Texas. Her analysis cautions us that, to understand the context of prison performance, sometimes we must also take into account the interests and motives of the parties who shape the debate.

Cummins's approach was to analyze the Texas privatization experience from 1987 to 2000 from a policy implementation perspective. Thus, her essential interest was to "determine why private prisons flourished in Texas and why the outcome varied so much from the policymakers' intent" (Cummins, 2001: ii). Using her background in public administration, Cummins employed implementation theory to dissect the Texas privatization experience. Implementation theory guides us to ask specific kinds of questions that may not occur to social scientists unfamiliar with the public administration literature. To what extent did the intended and actual outcomes of a policy differ (Pressman and Wildavsky, 1984)? How have the different interests of the various parties to the process affected the outcomes (Allison, 1969)? To what extent was the privatization of Texas prisons consistent with Edwards's (1980) assessment that policy implementation often goes awry when it is new, decentralized, controversial, complex, crises-related, and established by the courts? How did the interests of leaders at different levels of the policy implementation process, who may have had different viewpoints, affect the communication of policy interests and ultimately policy application (Goggin, Bowman, Lester, and O'Toole, 1990)? Cummins makes a case that most of the implementation factors raised by these questions were operating during the development of privatized prisons in Texas.

According to Cummins, what started off as a modest policy initiative to house about two thousand pre-release prisoners evolved into a system encompassing one-third of all private prison beds in the United States. By 1999, the state—under the authority of the adult division of the Texas Department of Criminal Justice (TDCJ)—had 4,078 inmates under contract to private vendors. TDCJ used private prison beds for its other components as well. The TDCJ Parole Division used 3,907 private beds, and the TDCJ State Jail authority used 7,786 privately operated prison beds. In addition, local city and county authorities housed 17,516 inmates and had subcontracted the operations of their facilities to private companies. Many of these latter inmates were under the jurisdiction of other states or the federal government. The authority to house these inmates was based upon an intergovernmental agreement between the local Texas jurisdictions and the sundry state and federal authorities. For these inmates, the originating jurisdiction transferred responsibility to the locality, which then delegated oversight to the private contractor. At the end of 1999, there were over thirty-three thousand inmates confined in privately operated prisons in Texas.

Several influences converged to escalate the growth of private prisons. Texas was under court order to increase its prison bed capacity as a result of the *Ruiz* case. Unfortunately, the state was experiencing a simultaneous economic downturn. After battling the federal judge, William Wayne Justice, for over a decade on the constitutionality of Texas prisons, Governor Mark Clements adopted a more conciliatory posture toward the court. However, because prison beds were so costly, the governor backed a legislative proposal to have private vendors construct and operate prison pre-release centers.

County jail overcrowding was exacerbated by a population cap the federal court placed on the Texas Department of Corrections. The jails had to hold sentenced felons until there was room in a state prison. The jails became very crowded, and a number of suits emerged from those conditions. This prompted counties to increase their jail capacities at the same time the state was under court order to expand capacity. Especially in the rural counties, there was also economic pressure to find jobs and sources of revenue for the local jurisdictions. The counties became "public proprietors" of prisons to generate revenues and jobs for its citizens. Cummins notes that the communities

> used various means to get the attention of state officials including having their state representative seek to gain a prison for their local jurisdictions. As noted, this heavy lobbying went on in the legislature as well as before the Board of Corrections, and has continued. As time went on, communities became bolder and bolder, offering incentives like country club memberships for wardens and longhorn cattle for prison grounds. (Cummins, 2001: 103)

If they could not get TDCJ inmates, communities sought out-of-state or federal inmates. There was nothing in state law to prohibit localities from building prisons prior to having agreements to house prisoners. As Cummins describes it, there was an almost frenzied climate in these rural, impoverished areas to compete for prison beds regardless of the speculative nature of some of the prison construction. Given this climate of crisis, the private corrections companies were encouraged. As a result, they increased their lobbying efforts to persuade the Texas legislature and local counties that prison privatization would allow jurisdictions to build prisons faster, build them cheaper, build them with private financing, operate them at a lower cost, and increase the level of services. Did the private sector deliver on these promises? Cummins's answer to this question is a narration of problems and incidents that she culled from newspapers, interviews she conducted among many of the notable policy makers, and public audits of the prisons. Her interest was not so much in comparing public and private prisons, but in demonstrating the extent to which the private prison industry failed to live up to its own promises.

The first failure of the private corrections companies was their inability to obtain performance bonds and funding for construction of the four pre-release centers that were the first to be authorized by the Texas legislature. Wackenhut Corrections Corporation (WCC) and the Corrections Corporation of America (CCA) were awarded the initial contracts. Public financing was eventually acquired, but it required Texas to pass enabling legislation that permitted certain cities and counties to issue bonds to finance the construction of correctional facilities. A second unintended consequence was that Wackenhut built all four pre-release centers, although originally it was hoped that CCA would be responsible for two of the facilities, promoting competition between the two companies.

Chapter 4 of Cummins's thesis is a chronological litany of the problems encountered by privately operated prisons in Texas throughout the 1990s. Early on, the pre-release centers did not meet expectations. "The intensive prison programs were non-existent and basic aspects of prison management like health care and mail handling also were found lacking" (Cummins, 2001: 202). The state had to tighten its controls and increase its oversight to bring the pre-release centers up to the contract requirements. Most of the problems in Texas, however, have been located in the public proprietary prisons—those facilities under the jurisdiction of a local government that have subcontracted with private companies. There have been escapes, riots, and murders. Cummins notes recent problems in two prisons under the authority of TDCJ. These involved sexual misconduct among employees and resulted in a state audit of all privately operated prisons in Texas. This internal audit had not been completed at the time of Cummins's dissertation.

Since Cummins did not have data to test whether these problems occur at a rate higher than the TDCJ publicly run prisons, it is not clear what the relative differences were between state and privately operated prisons. Nevertheless, her analysis of the different interests of the parties demonstrates why one must be cautious about the kinds of data one would collect to assess prison performance. Multiple data and information sources ought to be used to insure that conclusions do not depend on only a few sources, since some of those sources may be biased or misleading. Make no mistake, both the government and the corporation may have their own conflicting interests. Private prison companies must keep their costs low, but they must also make a profit. They must provide a good product to keep their contracts, but to make a profit they may have to pay lower wages and suffer from increased staff turnover. Government managers may want to use the threat of privatization to control union power; however, public administrators may also have an allegiance to their public workforce. Even within a prison system composed exclusively of public employees, the wardens and their administrative staff may have different interests than the other employees. Understanding these issues makes the task of assessing prison performance more difficult; however, it should also make it more meaningful.

Although it is unlikely that prison administrators have the resources or time to have staff or outsiders conduct qualitative assessments of their system, there are times when such a study may be important to understand all of the dimensions of a particular issue. Even "mini-studies" of a particular prison function, such as health care, may be important to capture the full context of changes in performance measures over time. We envision a system in which managers are monitoring changes in performance measurements over time, say for example, infectious disease incidence. When dramatic changes occur with little or no explanation, then a mini-investigation similar to sound field research may uncover the sources of previously unexplained changes in the data. In the next chapter, we introduce a more systematic way of analyzing and monitoring data.

CHAPTER FOUR
MULTILEVEL MODELS AND BEHAVIORAL PERFORMANCE MEASURES

I n this chapter, we discuss the benefits and limitations of behavioral data. We also introduce a methodology, multilevel modeling (also called hierarchical modeling), that has been used to analyze data in other research domains to evaluate the performance of institutions and organizations such as hospitals and schools. In our own research, we have applied these models to prisons. Since our main objective in this book is to evaluate the performance of the prison, an organizational unit, it is also important to recognize some of the traps an analyst may fall into when he or she groups data and interprets those groupings. We introduce these traps in a section on the "Perils of Summary Measures." Many of these perils are avoided when we use multilevel models.

While many researchers would argue that behavioral data are the most objective, we must recognize the limitations of these kinds of data by understanding what they signify and how they are collected. In our discussion of this topic, we discuss some of the possible biases and problems with these data. Behavioral performance measures are data that represent the actions of people. While we focus on inmates, it is also necessary to capture the actions of staff. Often social scientists will measure inmate behavior by reviewing the records and files of information collected by prison officials. In many jurisdictions, a lot of this information has been automated; however, there is still a lot of data that can only be obtained by reviewing inmate's "central files." These kinds of data have often been called operational data, because they have been collected to track and evaluate an individual inmate's behavior in relation to goals and objectives earmarked by counselors, case managers, health professionals, and other prison employees who interact with the individual on a daily basis. The use of the term *behavioral* does not imply that there is no discretion involved in recording this type of data. Instead, *behavioral* refers to the nature of the data. Generally speaking, behavioral data are collected as a by-product of daily prison activities. We distinguish this kind of measurement, primarily recorded by prison employees, from the survey data that is collected through face-to-face interviews or responses to written or automated surveys. We discuss those measures in the next chapter. Comprehensive studies that have empirically examined private and public prisons have relied upon operational data to a lesser or greater extent (Archambeault and Deis, 1996; Logan, 1992; Tennessee Select Oversight Committee on Corrections, 1995; Thomas, 1997; Urban Institute, 1989). Some analysts have used other sources of data to supplement the operational data. While the most common type of behavioral data analyzed to date has been records of inmate misconduct, behavioral data can also include records of program participation, work involvement, and other inmate activities.

Behavioral data can and do contain sources of variation other than the behavior that the information is believed to capture. Often, the data are taken from either paper or electronic files that record program participation, misconduct, and related information for individual inmates. While the data are often aggregated to either totals or rates for specific prisons, the data were not collected originally for this purpose. Consequently, the data may not consistently reflect the incidence of the behavior at different prisons, at different times, or even within a single institution. Using inmate misconduct as an example, some prison employees are simply more efficient in obtaining inmate compliance without resorting to written "tickets" for insubordination. Likewise, some employees are more effective in gathering intelligence to identify and disrupt illegal activities like gambling, making and drinking alcohol, or using illicit drugs. The more discretion there is in the recording of these data, the more opportunity there is for error or bias when reporting summary results across prisons or jurisdictions.

Identifying factors that influence what information actually makes its way into inmate records is a difficult proposition. In fact, we are not even sure that the factors can be completely identified. Nonetheless, it is necessary to try to control for these factors before comparing such indicators as the rates of misconduct or GED completion for different prisons. With inmate misconduct, it might be reasonable to assume that experienced and trained employees are better at obtaining inmate cooperation or uncovering illicit activities. As such, comparing prisons on rates of inmate misconduct should control for variations in staff experience and levels of training. The studies should also control for the characteristics of the inmates themselves, as we discuss below. Unfortunately, to date, in most of the existing studies of behavioral data, such controls have been nonexistent. It would be very interesting to conduct an evaluation of the process of inmate misconduct by evaluating characteristics of the victim (if the misconduct involves a victim), characteristics of the perpetrator, and *characteristics of the event recorder* for specific domains of misconduct. This could lead to an understanding about the discretionary nature of recording misconduct as well as have practical import for corrections officials. If it is discovered, for example, that an experienced staff member writes more serious "shots" and an inexperienced staff member writes more "shots" involving nuisance behavior such as being out of bounds, this information could be used to train staff on efficient and appropriate approaches to controlling inmate behavior.

The main focus of the discussion in this chapter is twofold. First, we want to demonstrate how the conclusions drawn in previous prison privatization studies that have used behavioral data may be very misleading because of conceptual and methodological problems with these evaluations (Camp and Gaes, 2001; Gaes et al., 1998). Second, we want to present a conceptual outline of how behavioral data can be analyzed in such a way that some of these concerns and other kinds of analytical traps are addressed. To help illustrate this latter point, we draw attention to work that has been conducted on analyzing the performance of hospitals, as well as work we have done evaluating prisons by studying inmate misconduct.

Prison Privatization Studies Employing Behavioral Data

Archambeault and Deis (1996) presented one of the most comprehensive comparisons of private and public prisons that primarily relied upon behavioral data. The authors reviewed numerous operational measures, many of which they converted into rates for individual prisons and then compared the prisons with statistical tests. While the statistical analysis gave the Archambeault and Deis study the appearance of scientific rigor, the approach was fundamentally flawed by an errant assumption. Comparing prisons with unadjusted rates assumes that a naive comparison is warranted. This is naive because the substantive assumption was that prisons do not differ in ways other than the ability of management to generate incentives to encourage good behavior from inmates, or disincentives that discourage inappropriate behavior. The assumption of prison equality, except for differences in management effectiveness, is most likely not true. Prisons hold different types of inmates, even when they are purportedly inmates of the same security level. Good inmate risk classification systems differentiate the risks posed by inmates (for misconduct, and to a lesser extent escape) in greater detail than the three or four categories typically used to assign inmates to prisons. This allows researchers to evaluate the composition of security risk posed by inmates even though they may be assigned to different prisons having the same institutional security level. Furthermore, there can be subtle differences in age, race, and ethnic composition, all of which can influence prison institution performance measures.

Given the competing goals that come into play when making actual inmate assignments (risk management, need to maintain community ties, etc.), it is unlikely that the inmates at one prison are pretty much like the inmates at another prison, as would occur if assignment within security level was random. The inmates, even within a given security level, probably differ in terms of age, criminal history, and race, just to name a few factors. Prisons may vary in their physical plant, their location to urban centers, and a host of other important dimensions. As discussed above, the characteristics of the staff may have important influences upon detecting inmate misconduct. It is also extremely unlikely that prisons are equivalent in staffing composition. Older prisons will have more seasoned staff. Minorities will most likely be underrepresented at prisons in rural areas. While Archambeault and Deis primarily focused upon three low-security prisons with similar architectural designs, they also used prisons with different architectural designs to make comparisons between the public and private sectors, and they even compared prisons of different security levels (for a detailed review, see Gaes et al., 1998).

It hardly seems fair to compare prisons on factors such as rates of inmate misconduct and call this "prison performance" if there has been no attempt to control for differences in the inmates, staff, or physical plant at the various prisons. This is exactly what was done in the Archambeault and Deis study, as well as many other studies that have compared prisons on different performance indicators.

To make a fair apples-to-apples comparison of prisons the differences in inmate, staff, and institution characteristics must be "equalized" simultaneously (Gaes et al., 1998). In our previous review of this research, we showed how many studies were technically misspecified and how the Archambeault and Deis type of approach can break down, producing misleading results. In the paper, we demonstrate how a commonly used statistical technique, known as multilevel or hierarchical linear modeling (HLM), allows analysts to control for differences between inmates, as well as the characteristics of prisons and staff, when making comparisons. In appendix A, we provide a technical discussion of the problems with the Archambeault and Deis approach, as well as an HLM solution. Since we refer to multilevel models throughout the remainder of this book, we take a short diversion in the next section of this chapter to explain the basic concepts behind this analytical approach. We symbolically demonstrate how these models work. Afterward, we discuss the pitfalls that await the naive and even sophisticated analyst who uses data that have been summarized from individuals within each institution, or from other kinds of groupings. This is important in the context of this book, because this is often how comparisons are made among prisons. We conclude this chapter by showing how analysts have used multilevel models to rate hospital performance, and by portraying the work we have done to rank prison performance.

Multilevel Models

This discussion introduces the fundamental concepts of multilevel models without delving into the mathematics or statistical requirements. It is mostly intended for readers who want to understand how these models are different from other typical approaches to data analysis. To add substance to this demonstration, we have chosen variables that may help us understand prison violence. While most of this section has been written for readers without a background in applied statistics, there are parts of this discussion that depend on familiarity with regression models. This is especially relevant in the section "Using the Results of Random Intercept Models to Rank Prison Quality." In figure 4.1a, we show two levels of data analysis; level 2, represented above the dashed line, and level 1 below it. Level 2 represents the organization, or what is called the clustering unit of analysis. These organizational units can be prisons, hospitals, schools, census tracts, and other spatial or temporal units of analysis.[1] Clustering units may also have factors that describe their different characteristics. In this figure, there is a level-2 factor representing the security level of the institution. Clearly, this is a characteristic of the custody practices at the prisons where inmates are incarcerated, not some individual characteristic of the inmates themselves. At this point, the variable is not being used to evaluate the analysis of inmate violence portrayed in the diagram, since there is no arrow between institution security level and violent misconduct. How institution security level influences violent misconduct is demonstrated shortly.

Instead, at level 1 of figure 4.1a, we show a circle with an arrow pointing to a triangle. The circle is labeled "Individual Security Scores" and the triangle is labeled "Violent Misconduct." In figure 4.1a, we have a simple model, which shows the relationship between the security scores of inmates and the amount of violence they commit in the year after they have been assigned to a prison. Most prison systems use a scale to measure an inmate's propensity to violent misconduct, and this is captured in the security score. Even though the inmates in this analysis are located in different security levels in different institutions, this facet of the data is ignored for now. This analysis, which could be an ordinary least squares regression analysis, is "indifferent" to the clustered organization of the data. If we "run" the implied model on the data, we would probably find the result indicated in figure 4.1b. This shows that inmates with higher security scores are more likely to commit violent misconduct in the year after their prison assignment.

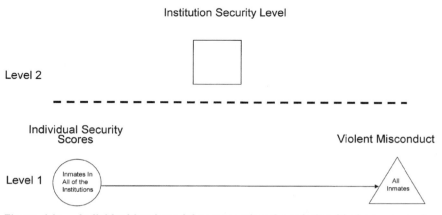

Figure 4.1a. Individual level model representing the relationship between an inmate's security score and level of violent misconduct with no assessment of the particular prisoner's institution.

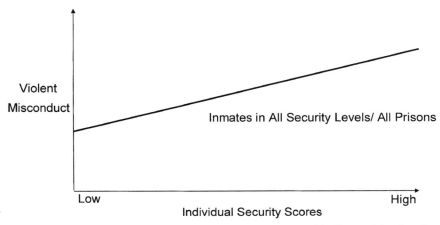

Figure 4.1b. **Theoretical results of the analysis indicated in figure 4.1a showing the higher the individual security score, the higher the rate of inmate violence.**

Now consider figure 4.2a. We have introduced two features into the analytical diagram. First of all, below the dashed line we explicitly recognize that inmates are in different institutions. We have only indicated two prisons, but this could have been any number of prisons. Thus, we are explicitly organizing the data so that we look at the relationship between security scores and violence within each institution in our analysis. In this case, we are recognizing that each prison may have a different average level of violent misconduct. In the vernacular of multilevel modeling, allowing the institution averages to vary is known as a random-intercepts model. Second, we also recognize in this figure that the level-2 variable (located within the square) has an impact upon violent misconduct, as there is now an arrow linking the two. In this case, the level-2 variable is the security level of the institution. The dashed lines indicate that institution security level affects the *average* amount of violence in a given institution, but institution security level has no effect in this instance upon the individual-level relationship between individual security scores and violent misconduct.

One reasonable outcome of the analytical approach represented in figure 4.2a is shown in figure 4.2b. Each line represents the relationship between individual security scores and violent misconduct within a particular prison. The graph presents lines for six separate prisons as well as a line

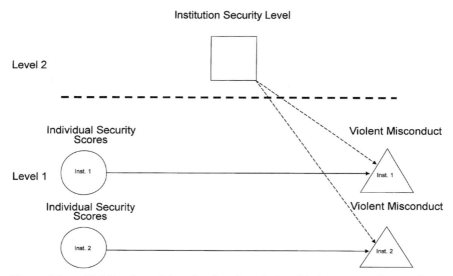

Figure 4.2a. **Multilevel model evaluating the relationship between an inmate's security score and rate of violence within a given institution and the impact of a level-2 variable, institution security level, on the average level of violence in each.**

representing the overall average value for all prisons. As one might expect, even though there is a relationship between security score and violence in every institution, the prisons with higher security levels have higher average violent misconduct. Thus, in one multilevel model, we are able to examine both the effect of a level-1 variable (individual security score) and a level-2 variable (institutional security level) at the same time.

Using the Results of Random Intercept Models to Rank Prison Quality

The type of model represented in figure 4.2a, the random intercepts model, is one we have used in many of the analyses we have conducted to evaluate prison performance. In later sections and chapters, we refer to expected Bayes residuals (EB residuals) as a way of ranking individual prisons. The EB residual analysis is based on the model represented in figure 4.2a. An analysis is conducted on a measure of prison performance, for example, inmate violence. We use individual level predictors at level 1, such as security score, and institutional predictors at level 2, such as institution security level. Based on the final results, such as those indicated in figure 4.2b, an analyst can compute

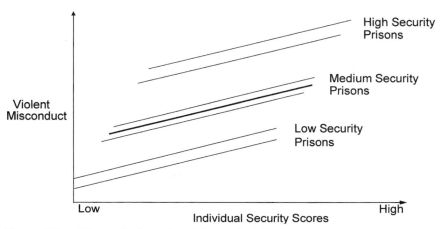

Figure 4.2b.   Theoretical results of the analysis indicated in figure 4.2a showing: (a) the higher the individual security score, the higher the rate of inmate violence within a prison; (b) the higher the institution security level, the higher the average level of violence within a prison.

how close the prisons' actual average level of violence (unadjusted mean) is, compared to what the random effects model predicts (adjusted). The difference (unadjusted minus adjusted) between these two is called the residual. There are many synonyms used in this book and other treatments of residual analysis. Unadjusted values can also be called observed or actual. Adjusted measures are also often called predicted, expected, or projected values. As a summary measure of the institution's performance, to compute the residual, the adjusted measure is subtracted from the unadjusted value. Obviously, if the adjusted value is larger, then the residual (unadjusted minus adjusted) will be a negative value. If the unadjusted measure is larger, the residual will be a positive value. Depending on the context of the analysis, better prison performance could be dependent on either larger positive or larger negative residuals. If, for example, an analyst is modeling predictors of per capita costs, when unadjusted values are higher than adjusted values, the residual will be positive. This implies that the prison is performing worse than expected because the actual (unadjusted) cost is higher than the expected (adjusted) cost. However, if an analyst is modeling inmate perceptions of their safety from attack, then if their unadjusted perceptions of safety are higher than adjusted perceptions, the prison is performing better than expected–actual perceptions of safety are better than expected perceptions. The larger the discrepancy between the predicted and the actual value the better (or worse) the prison is performing. "Expected Bayes residuals" refer to the type of estimation that is being used to calculate the adjusted values. The estimation method is particularly appropriate if some of the prisons have a relatively low number of inmates. Since these residuals vary in size and direction, an analyst can rank prisons based on the values. We use many examples throughout this book, showing different ways the rankings can be depicted.

The primary reason this type of analysis is so compelling is that it leads to an apples-to-apples comparison of prisons, equating prisons on the characteristics of inmates in the different prisons as well as characteristics of the prisons themselves. Raudenbush and Bryk (2002) discuss this type of analysis as a quasi-experiment, where you think of each prison as a treatment group. When random assignment to these groups is not possible, such as is typically the case in a prison system, then there are threats to the validity of the results. As Raudenbush and Bryk point out, one can never be absolutely sure that all of the appropriate variables have been chosen to "level the playing field." Raudenbush and Bryk also argue that "The more dramatically different the groups are on background characteristics, the more sensitive inferences are likely to be to different methods of adjustment and the less credible the resulting inferences" (Raudenbush and Bryk, 2002: 155). These authors give an exaggerated example comparing two groups of schools. One group of schools has very low average socioeconomic backgrounds (SES) of the students. The second group of schools has high average socioeconomic backgrounds. In fact, to demonstrate the point, Raudenbush and Bryk suppose that every student in the second set of schools has higher SES scores than any student in the first group of schools. In the example they present, they first analyze the data ignoring the average school SES as a contextual effect. In this case, the data show that all of the group 2 schools that have higher SES perform better than all of the group 1 schools with lower average SES. When the model incorporates both the student's level of SES and the school's average level of SES this essentially compares students within their schools holding constant the average school SES. With such a model there is no difference between group 1 and group 2 schools. As Raudenbush and Bryk argue:

> This strategy may seem fairer than the first, but is it? Suppose that the group 2 schools have more effective staff and that staff quality, not student composition, causes the elevated test scores. The results [described

above] could occur, for example, if the school district assigned its best principals and teachers to the more affluent schools. If so, the second strategy would give no credit to these leaders for their effective practices.

The key concern is that without having formulated an explicit model of school quality, we can never be sure that we have disentangled the effect of school composition from other school factors with which composition is often correlated. (Raudenbush and Bryk, 2002: 156)

Thus, leveling the playing field may, in fact, mute leadership and management strategies correlated with a compositional difference between the schools, or in our case prisons. Our experience with models of prison performance leads us to believe that there is a great deal of overlap in compositional characteristics among prisons within an institutional security level whether the prison is publicly or privately operated. It is not obvious to us that there are differences in the composition of inmate characteristics that would be correlated with management differences between publicly and privately operated prisons. If there are a sufficient number of prisons that are either privately or publicly operated, the random effects model can include a level-2 factor that explicitly tests the difference between private and public institutions while accounting for compositional differences. At this point, we think the ranking of institutions based on the EB residuals is the best method for comparing prisons, although we acknowledge the possibility, however unlikely, that compositional effects could be correlated with management influences.

However, when we develop the random effects models we should be careful not to include level-2 variables that might represent management initiatives, private or public, that could influence the rankings based on the differences in expected and actual outcomes. A concrete example may serve to explain this dilemma. We want to study the impact of privatization on prison violence. Let's say that compositional characteristics of inmates within a security level have overlapping distributions among privately and publicly operated prisons. Thus, inmates have about the same level of criminal histories, age composition, and prior record of institution violence. The level-2 composition effects and level-1 inmate characteristics are used in a random intercepts model similar to figures 4.2a and 4.2b. The major difference between the privately and publicly operated prisons is inmate-to-staff ratios. Let's assume public prisons use more corrections officers—a lower inmate-to-corrections officer ratio. We run this model and we find that prisons with lower inmate-to-staff ratios have lower violence. However, by equating the prisons on inmate-to-staff ratios, the rankings of private prisons are equivalent to public prisons.

This is a possible scenario. We believe the correct approach to this problem is to use inmate-to-staff ratios in the model and if it is significant, then run other models to see if the inmate-to-staff ratio mediates the effect of comparing private versus public prisons. This is done by using a factor (dummy code) at level 2 to represent public versus private prisons. If this variable is significant in the absence of the variable inmate-to-staff ratio and not significant in the presence of inmate-to-staff ratio, then we can conclude that indeed inmate-to-staff ratio is decisive in reducing violence by the publicly operated prisons. We can, however, still rank the prisons based on the residuals of a model that includes inmate-to-staff ratio and draw conclusions about whether publicly and privately operated prisons have more effective management despite the differences in inmate-to-staff ratios. Since we know inmate-to-staff ratios affect the projected violence level (low inmate-to-staff ratios lower the projected violence levels), we can actually compare the residuals with and without that variable. This would allow us to draw conclusions about how important this variable is to ranking prisons on prison violence. In our experience, the most dramatic differences in level-2 compositional variables are not the result of public/private initiatives. The differences are more likely to be among characteristics of inmates that predispose them to differences in outcomes.

More Complicated Multilevel Models

In figure 4.3a, we represent a different multilevel model. As in the random-intercept model represented in figure 4.2a, the level-2 variable, institutional security level, affects the average amount of violence in any given institution (the dashed lines from the square to the triangles). What is new in figure 4.3a is recognition of the relationship between institution security level and the level-1 *relationship* between security score and violent misconduct in each institution (the dashed lines drawn from the level-2 variable to the level-1 arrow between the circles and triangles). The latter relationship, where the level-2 variable affects the individual relationship, is known in multilevel circles as a random-slopes model. In practice, random-slopes models are less often seen in the literature than random-intercepts models, but they have proved to be very effective in analyzing school achievement.

One possible outcome of the type of model portrayed in figure 4.3a is shown in figure 4.3b. The level-2 variable is again related to increases in the average level of violent misconduct; higher security level institutions have higher average levels of violent misconduct. However, the level-2 variable also affects the *relationships* between individual security scores and violence within each institution. The lines are much steeper as we go from low to high security level prisons. This indicates that the relationship between security scores and violence is much stronger in higher security prisons than it is in lower security prisons. The relationships expressed in figure 4.3b represent a complicated multilevel model, but one can envision even more complicated models where there are many level-1 and level-2 factors. For example, if we were interested in the factors that influenced the individual level of violent misconduct within a prison, in addition to security score, we would probably want to measure the prisoner's age, sex, and history of gang

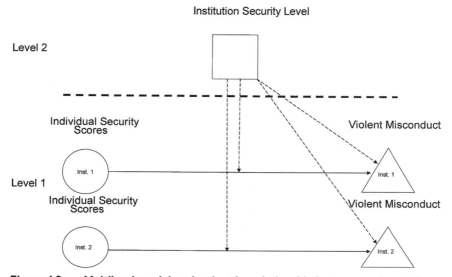

Figure 4.3a. Multilevel model evaluating the relationship between an inmate's security score and rate of violence within a given institution, and the impact of a level-2 variable, institution security level, on the average level of violence in each prison, and its effect on the relationship between security score and violence within each prison.

involvement. At level 2, we might want to measure the impact of institutional crowding, the staff-to-inmate ratio, the average age of the inmate population, and the percentage of the inmate population that was involved with gangs. Then, we would have to model, hopefully after review of strong theoretical writings, whether only the average levels of violent misconduct at each institution were affected by the level-2 factors (random-intercept model) or whether some or all of the individual-level relationships between level-1 factors and violent misconduct were also affected by level-2 variables. The latter alternative can lead to extremely complicated statistical models that are often hard to estimate with real world data.

Multilevel models can be very "busy" both conceptually and statistically. The analyst must sort out the level-1 and level-2 effects after conducting his or her analysis. There can be, however, a large payoff for this complicated analysis, as we try to show later in this chapter. For now, let us note that level-2 variables can be true global measures that describe some characteristic of the institution. In our example, the security level (as determined by custody practices) is such a true global measure. It does not derive from an aggregation of the individual-level units of analysis. Level-2 measures, though, are often composite variables of individual-level measures, such as age. Age can be included in a multilevel model as a characteristic of level-1

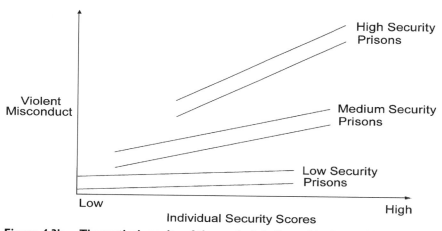

Figure 4.3b. Theoretical results of the analysis indicated in figure 4.3a, showing: (a) the higher the individual security score, the higher the rate of inmate violence within a prison; (b) the higher the institution security level, the higher the average level of violence within a prison; (c) the higher the institution security level, the steeper the relationship between security scores and violence within each prison.

individuals or as an average age for level-2 units, such as prisons. The question arises, though, why measure age at both level 1 and level 2? Won't both measures produce the same results? In fact, the two measures are conceptually distinct and can produce apparently conflicting results, and this leads us into a discussion of the meaning and analysis of summary measures.

The Perils of Summary Measures

People unfamiliar with data analysis often make the mistake of assuming that by aggregating or summarizing individual-level data within some group or institution, such as computing an average or a proportion, they are portraying characteristics of those groups or institutions. Then it is further assumed that one can look at aggregated relationships, such as the average socioeconomic status of students in a school in relation to the school's average math achievement scores, and make sense of those relationships. Statisticians and data analysts recognize the limitations of these kinds of analyses and the mistakes of inference one can make. First, we describe the essential reason why these data may not be what they initially appear to be within the discussion of clustered data. Second, we discuss why summary data of an attribute may mean something very different than what the attribute means at the individual level. This is called aggregation bias or the atomistic fallacy. Third, we show how the atomistic fallacy is related to a more commonly understood problem called the ecological fallacy. Finally, we introduce yet another aggregation error that even many data analysts commit called Simpson's Paradox.

Clustered Data

A researcher cannot assume that when he or she is studying institutional performance that the characteristics of individuals within that organizational unit are not, in some way, related to the specific institution in which they are behaving. The institution represents a clustering of individuals and the result of clustering may have an impact on measuring the institution's performance. For example, you cannot assume that patient characteristics are independent or unrelated to the hospitals in which they are receiving care. Individuals in institutions and other social and economic units tend to congregate for reasons that are related to the function of the institution. This is true of schools, prisons, hospitals, and other institutions that are designed for a specific purpose. The behavior of a patient receiving treatment in Hospital A may be quite different than if he were receiving treatment in Hospital B, even if the hospitals were identical in every way. As Bryk and Raudenbush (1992) note, either because of the shared experiences of individuals within a specific institution, or because of the way in which patients, students, or prisoners were drawn to the particular hospital, school, or prison, individuals in these settings are likely to behave as if they are dependent in some way (Goldstein, 1995). This dependence in behavior can lead to inferential mistakes about whether, or the extent to which, the hospital or any institution performs better or worse than other institutions that are being evaluated.[2]

The Atomistic and Ecological Fallacies

Second, there are two components to the variability of an individual's outcomes. The first source is the individual; the second source is the institution or clustering unit. If the analyst uses averaged or aggregated individual-level data to make inferences about the hospital, this can result in aggregation bias (also called the atomistic fallacy). Aggregation bias has been explained by Bryk and Raudenbush (1992) in the context of schools.

> In brief, aggregation bias can occur when a variable takes on different meanings and therefore may have different effects at different organizational levels. In educational research, for example, the average social class of a school may have an effect on student achievement above and beyond the effects of the individual child's social class. At the student level, social class provides a measure of the intellectual and tangible resources in a child's home environment. At the school level, it is a proxy measure of a school's resources and normative environment. (Bryk and Raudenbush, 1992: 83)

Aggregation bias is the antithesis of the ecological fallacy (Lazarsfeld and Menzel, 1972; Lincoln and Zeitz, 1980; Robinson, 1950). The ecological fallacy, coined by Robinson (1950), refers to the inappropriate use of an aggregated statistic to make inferences about an individual. For example, the relationship between the average socioeconomic status of a census tract and the average education level may be interpreted to apply to the relationship between individual level incomes and socioeconomic status. To make this relevant to the prison setting, consider an analyst who may incorrectly assume that the relation between the average security level of inmates in a prison and the rate of drug abuse can be interpreted to mean that an individual inmate's security level is related to his or her drug use. Often such relationships do not reflect the behavior of individuals within the clustering unit. Aggregation bias works the other way. Individual data is aggregated to make an inference about the clustering unit, like a prison or hospital. However, the aggregated statistic has a different implication at the level of the clustering unit than it does at the level of the individual.

Simpson's Paradox

There is also one other land mine awaiting the analyst who uses aggregate data to draw conclusions. It is called Simpson's Paradox. This occurs when data are grouped in a way that leads to misinterpretation. This happens when you group data according to some characteristics of the individuals and portray the data in different ways. The following example comes from a *Washington Post* article entitled "How Honest Data Can Mislead" (Rensberger, 1997). The average salary of the 145 women working at the Widget Inc. is $60,000. The 100 men in the company make, on average, $95,000. Yet, in every job category, the average salary Widget pays is higher for women than for men. How is this possible? It is possible because Widget employs very few women in management, the job category with the highest pay. Even though women clerks earn more than their male counterparts, the average company salary of men is higher because of the high salaries of Widget men in management. If you had looked only at the total average salaries of men and women, you might have mistakenly concluded there was wage discrimination. Thus, the complexity of the data is lost when an analyst presents simplified results, and those results may be quite misleading. Simplification of the data covers up a feature of the data that will lead you to quite different conclusions. The missing feature is sometimes called a "lurking variable." In the case of Widget Inc., the lurking variable was the categorization of men and women into job categories. In addition, you must be aware of the implication of the distribution of men and women in each of the job categories. By computing an average for men and women across job categories (collapsing the lurking variable), this weighted, gender-based average would look quite different than the average salaries for men and women within each job category.

To avoid all of these pitfalls one needs to look at individual and grouped data simultaneously, as we demonstrate in our explanation of multilevel models. Unless you account for the separate effects of the individual within each clustering unit (e.g., prison, school, or hospital) and the clustering unit itself, you will not know the relative impact of each. More importantly, the analyst will not be able to uncover the true variability of performance of the prison, school, or hospital relative to the variability attributable to the composition of the inmates, students, or patients. This last point is quite important. By using information at both levels—prison/inmate, school/student, hospital/patient—an analyst can measure the impact of each on some outcome such as prison violence, school achievement, or illness. The analyst can also avoid most of the perils of summary data.

Measuring Hospital Performance and Inmate Misconduct Using Multilevel Models

The performance of organizations and institutions may be no more important in any field than in the provision of medical care. Multilevel or hierarchical models have been used in the development of hospital "report cards" (Normand, Glickman, and Gatsonis, 1997). In 1987, the Health Care Financing Administration (HCFA) launched a major initiative to evaluate hospital performance by comparing observed and expected mortality rates for Medicare patients. HCFA suspended the release of this information in 1994, according to Normand, Glickman, and Gatsonis (1997), primarily because the data HCFA was using were inadequate in its detail and failed to account for patient compliance to instructions given to them by health care providers. To remedy these problems, HCFA began collecting disease-specific information. The article by Normand, Glickman, and Gatsonis capitalized on this new data collection and addressed several other methodological problems congruent with the issues we have raised about clustered data. To solve these analytical problems, Normand, Glickman, and Gatsonis used multilevel models.

In their paper, Normand et al. compare mortality rates across hospitals for patients treated for acute myocardial infarctia (AMI). By adjusting the hospital mortality rates based upon the risk of the patient complement at each hospital, Normand et al. found that the risk of dying at each hospital within thirty days of treatment for AMI was 12 to 44 percent. The analysts noted that it was extremely important to adjust for the illness severity differences of the patients at each hospital. For example, one hospital's unadjusted mortality was 29 percent, but the adjusted mortality was 37 percent. These analysts used two measures of hospital performance based upon hierarchical models. The first adjusted measure indicated whether a particular hospital's mortality was one and one-half times the median mortality of the ninety-six hospitals accounting for similarities and differences among patients in each of the hospitals. The second method used the model to represent the difference between observed and expected mortality using hospital characteristics such as location, academic affiliation, and size in addition to the person-specific risk levels. Thus, a given hospital was compared to the expected levels of mortality of all hospitals with similar characteristics. This is the kind of residual analysis described in previous sections of this chapter. The two measures did not always agree, however, as the authors point out they imply slightly different information. However, using HCFA's original metric, one that does not take into account differences among patients and hospitals simultaneously, nine hospitals of the ninety-six would have been flagged as having high mortality rates. Using the latter two indices developed by Normand et al., three hospitals would have been flagged as having a quality problem. It is clear that a researcher cannot ignore the implications of the composition of the patients and the relationships among them when evaluating institutions.

In their article, Normand, Glickman, and Gatsonis also discuss whether hospitals should be evaluated with a relative or an absolute measure of performance. Normand et al. argue that a relative measure of hospital performance is inadequate because "even if all mortality rates were low and close to each other, a profiling approach such as HCFA's would still classify some hospitals as aberrant" (Normand et al. 1997: 804). This has implications for prison performance levels. To establish an absolute performance level threshold, one has to be willing to state the minimum level of performance that is acceptable. How do we ascertain such thresholds? Is one prison homicide too much? What level of HIV transmission within prison rises to the level of concern? These are obviously complex public policy choices beyond the scope of this book. Clearly, the choice of the measurement approach is an important

decision in evaluating hospitals and, we expect, prisons as well. Our preliminary work supports that assertion.

In a recent paper (Camp, Gaes, Langan, and Saylor, 2003), we used an
approach similar to the one adopted by Norman, Glickman, and Gatsonis
to assess the contribution of specific prison environments to inmate misconduct. Using multilevel models, we tested the extent to which the
prison environment contributed to the level of inmate misconduct. The
analysis demonstrated a number of key points. We showed that proper
model specification, having the right combination of explanatory variables
at the institution level, makes a difference when comparing prisons in
terms of their relative contribution to inmate misconduct. For example, we
replicated a study by Woolredge, Griffin, and Pratt (2001) that showed
higher levels of prison crowding were related to higher levels of overall
prison misconduct. When we added other important dimensions to our
models reflecting the security-level composition and demographic
makeup of the inmate population, there was no longer a prison crowding
effect. We also classified misconduct into different kinds of categories
such as violent, sexual, and property. By doing this, we were able to
demonstrate that the different institutional factors that we used in our
models had different implications for different types of misconduct, although some factors had consistent effects. Finally, the paper demonstrated the ease with which results of multilevel models can be used to
compare the performance of prisons. We expand upon this last point here.

We examined the correspondence between the relative rankings of the
prisons produced by using unadjusted and adjusted rates of inmate misconduct. The unadjusted rate was the simple proportion of inmates involved in
misconduct for the one-month time period. While not often conceived as
such, an unadjusted rate implies a statistical model where no other explanatory factors (covariates) are necessary, either because the covariates do not
influence inmate misconduct or because the covariates are identically dis-
tributed across the prisons under examination. Since we did not believe that
either condition held in our analysis, we included other factors in multilevel
models to create adjusted rates. The factors at the inmate level depicted their
criminal history and socio-demographics characteristics. The prison-level
covariates represented aggregated characteristics of the inmates and staff.

There were large differences between the rankings of the prisons
based on the unadjusted and adjusted rates. To highlight the differences

between these two measures of prison performance, we used the Spearman correlation between the respective rankings. For the different classifications of misconduct, the correlations varied between a low value of 0.497 (for violent misconduct) and a high value of 0.855 (for property-related misconduct). Obviously, a correlation of 1 would have indicated that the different methods of ranking the prisons produced identical rankings, and a score of 0 would have indicated no correspondence at all.

Another way to calculate the degree of similarity between the adjusted and unadjusted measures is to compare how many places in the ranking an institution moves when comparing the two rank orderings. For example, if the unadjusted ranking of prison A is 50th out of 165 and the adjusted ranking is 40th, then it changes 10 places. This displacement can change up or down, but we indicate here the amount of change without indicating the direction. It is obvious that for every institution moving up, another moves down. Using property misconduct as the criterion, 50 percent of all 156 prisons moved at least 12 places. For violent misconduct, 50 percent of all the 156 prisons moved at least 34 places. It is clear from these results that by using multilevel models and the residual analysis one can discover very different substantive interpretations of prison performance. Based on work by Raudenbush and Bryk, Norman, Glickman, and Gatsonis, and many others, the multilevel-model-based residual analysis provides a sounder and more substantively meaningful policy conclusion.

One way of representing the results of a multilevel-model-based residual analysis in order to judge the contribution a prison makes to inmate misconduct, or any other outcome, is to use "caterpillar" graphs. The EB residuals are ordered from lowest to highest. A confidence interval can be constructed for the EB residual to show how much statistical confidence we have in the estimate. When the different prisons are ordered on the EB residual and plotted with its corresponding confidence interval, the graph typically resembles a crawling caterpillar.

An example of a caterpillar graph, taken from our analysis of total inmate misconduct, is presented in figure 4.4. The empty circle indicates the EB residual value for a particular institution. The vertical lines extending up and down from that empty circle terminating in the horizontal lines indicate the upper and lower values (bounds) of the confidence intervals for each institution. Confidence intervals indicate the extent to which we statistically believe that the EB residual, representing the institution's achievement, is what we estimate it to be. There are many useful pieces of information in the graph. First, it is easy to determine whether a particular prison falls significantly above or below the level expected for that prison. If the confidence interval crosses the horizontal line in the graph, indicating that the confidence interval contains the value 0, then it is not possible to reject the null hypothesis that the institution is performing as expected. As noted on the graph, there are several prisons in the center of the graph for which this condition is true. On the other hand, there are more prisons whose confidence interval falls either above or below the horizontal line, indicating the prison falls above or below its expected level of performance. For example, the prisons identified as FOR (FCI Forrest City), YAZ (FCI Yazoo City), and ELK (FCI Elkton) all fall below their expected value. These prisons have been designated as comparison prisons for an evaluation of a private prison operated for the Federal Bureau of Prisons at Taft, California. In this substantive example, a value below the expected level of performance is actually desired, since it indicates that inmates housed at these prisons were less likely to become involved in misconduct than what we would expect based on the adjusted score. The expected levels are determined from the models

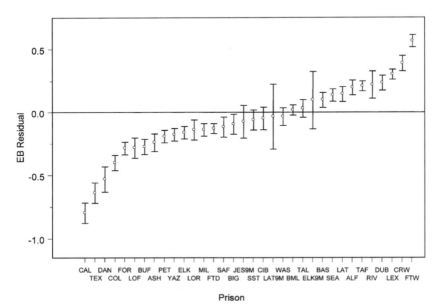

Figure 4.4. Caterpillar plot of the relative performance of prisons in managing inmate misconduct.

that incorporate the individual-level characteristics of the inmates as well as prison-level features. On the other hand, as one can see in figure 4.4, institutional performance at TAF (Taft Correctional Institution) was less positive. Inmates at Taft were more likely to become involved in misconduct than one would have expected based on the characteristics of inmates imprisoned there, as well as the features of the prison.

Another piece of information that can be easily derived from figure 4.4 is a comparison of any two prisons. If prison confidence intervals overlap, then it is not possible to claim that one institution is performing better than the other or vice versa. For example, YAZ has a lower EB residual than ELK, suggesting better performance in reducing inmate misconduct, but the difference is not statistically significant since the confidence intervals clearly overlap one another. On the other hand, there is no overlap between the confidence intervals for YAZ and TAF. With this comparison, it would be safe to infer that YAZ is doing a better job in discouraging inmate misconduct than TAF.[3]

A less obvious piece of information is also conveyed in figure 4.4. In the graph, the confidence intervals are fairly tightly clustered around the estimates of institutional performance. This means one can discriminate more of the differences in performance levels of the prisons than would be the case if the confidence intervals were wider. This feature of the graph implies that the rankings of inmate misconduct based on prison performance are reliable, and that is indeed the case.

While multilevel models may not solve all of the inferential problems we have noted in this chapter, they do directly address problems associated with clustered data, the atomistic and ecological fallacies, and Simpson's Paradox. They do so because when the analyst uses a multilevel model technique, he or she is explicitly examining the individual and institutional data separately and simultaneously. It is done separately, because the models allow you to interpret how individual responses are affected by individual characteristics, and how institutional factors affect the average response for the institution. It is done simultaneously, because the multilevel models are designed to evaluate how institutional characteristics also affect individual behavior.

Multilevel models are appearing more frequently in corrections research. A recently published book has used multilevel models to investigate whether inmate prisonization (a culture unique to prisons) varied across prisons (Gillespie, 2003). Gillespie used self-report data to examine whether inmate behavior is influenced by organizational level (prison) processes as well as by individual differences among inmates. The results of the analysis did not support a contextual effect for the different prisons once individual-level factors were included in the statistical models. Beyond this lack of a substantive finding, the ability to draw any conclusions in the study was limited because the data were of questionable value. The response rates for the inmates surveyed for this study were extremely low (18.2 percent in Kentucky, 10.5 percent in Tennessee, and there was an unknown response rate in Ohio since statistical sampling was not employed). Nevertheless, as more analysts use multilevel models to assess the impact of prison organization on individual inmate behavior, we will begin to get a more precise understanding of the interactions between these two levels.

Whether used in hospitals, prisons, or schools, modern analysis techniques now allow us to make more precise statements of the extent to which these institutions perform better than their counterparts. The techniques also inform the policy maker of the important determinants of institutional performance, insuring that these conclusions are not mistakenly based upon differences in the composition of the clients—whether they may be patients, students, or prisoners. Although we introduce these analysis techniques in this chapter, they can be applied to any kind of data, including audit data that can be categorized into nominal, ordinal, or continuous measures. In the next chapter, we discuss how to use multilevel models to analyze staff and inmate surveys.

STAFF AND INMATE SURVEYS AS PERFORMANCE MEASURES

Another way of measuring prison performance is to analyze staff and inmate responses to surveys. Surveys can be used to gather self-reported behavior, or they can be used to gather opinions about a specific subject matter. Although one should always be concerned about the tools used to gather data, when the focus of these measurement systems is to record illicit or embarrassing events (HIV infection, homosexual activity, rape encounters), it is even more crucial to compare the limitations and strengths of the different systems. A discussion of the relationship between behavioral and self-reported behavior is beyond the scope of this book. There is a large literature on this topic.[1] A discussion would get us into tangents about modes of collecting sensitive and stigmatized behavior, proper survey construction, methods of enhancing accurate recall, and underreporting in official records. While our focus is on the measurement of prison performance, there has been a great deal of theoretical and methodological discussion on the relative merits of self-reported and officially recorded indicators of crime, misconduct, and risky behavior.

In this chapter, we continue our discussion of the benefits of multi-level modeling, demonstrating how to use these techniques to analyze survey data. A great deal of the discussion in this chapter involves studies that have been conducted to compare public and private prisons, or studies that demonstrate how important it is to account for the characteristics of inmates, staff, and institutions to make equitable comparisons. Another purpose of this chapter is to further demonstrate alternative methods of representing the results of these multilevel models with graphical techniques. These illustrations have a twofold purpose. They demonstrate how it is relatively easy to translate complex statistical models into straightforward representations of prison performance. Second, they indicate how a prison system (or any government agency) can begin to convey to any interested audience a kind of graphical report card composed of many different outcome measures. Since much of the work we cite in this chapter involves analyses intended to compare public and private prisons, we summarize these findings at the end of this chapter.

The Bureau of Prisons (BOP) has administered an annual survey of staff and an occasional survey of inmates (in conjunction with specific research projects) for the last eleven years. These "Social Climate" surveys (Saylor, 1984) have been used to evaluate long- and short-term strategies and policy changes implemented by the BOP. The studies we cite in this chapter by Camp and his colleagues that use survey data are all based on the Social Climate survey results. We believe survey data can be a rich source of information to calculate indicators of prison quality, but we are critical of the way most social scientists who contribute to the prison privatization literature have analyzed survey data. This is a continuation of the argument we make in the preceding chapter about separating the influence of the organization from the individuals within each clustering unit of the organization.

A Critique of Prior Studies

Surveys of the perceptions and attitudes of staff and inmates have been used in previous studies to compare the operations of public and private prisons (Greene, 1999, 2002; Logan, 1991, 1992; Sechrest and Shichor, 1994, 1996; Urban Institute, 1989). To indicate how these surveys have been used, we briefly review the work of Greene and Logan. Greene (1999, 2002) used a structured interview of inmates in one privately and three publicly operated prisons in Minnesota (as well as operational records). Greene selected a subsample of the respondents from each sector based on matching characteristics. She found that inmates from publicly operated prisons were more favorable toward the public prisons when they were asked about educational and vocational training, chemical dependency treatment, instructions on general health issues, release planning, and safety. Inmates perceived that levels of medical care delivery were equivalent; however, public sector inmates received better dental care. In contrast, private sector inmates reported they had more access to case managers. One major difference between the public and private facilities in this study was that private sector inmates were employed by a local firm to earn a real wage. This type of employment was unavailable in the public sector prisons.

Logan also used staff survey responses in his study of prison privatization. He also collected inmate survey responses; however, because of their possible bias, he discounted these data when he concluded that the privately operated prison for women in Grants, New Mexico, was superior in almost every way to its public sector counterpart. To make his comparison, Logan collected data twice from staff and inmates, the first time when most of the same women were still housed in a public facility, the second time after the contract with Corrections Corporation of America to build and manage the new, privately operated prison was completed.

The shortcomings of many of these prior studies have been critiqued previously (Camp et al., 2003; Gaes et al., 1998). Rather than rehash those specific criticisms, we want to focus on the fundamental difficulty with these studies. Whether the responses came from inmates or staff, analysts in previous studies treated the survey respondents as though they had been randomly assigned to the prisons (Camp, 1999; Camp, Gaes, and Saylor, 2002). Working from this unstated assumption, analysts have computed aggregate measures of prison performance of staff responses to survey questions. These aggregate measures can take the form of averages or percentages, and may involve individual survey questions or scales constructed from these items. These summary measures were presumed to either represent a characteristic of the prison directly, or to be influenced by organizational practices at the prison, and therefore represented differences in employees' appraisal of the quality of prison operations. By conducting statistical tests of these summary measures, these researchers were recognizing that they had to account for sampling variation in their assessment. What was missing in these analyses was the inclusion of individual and organizational-level variables that could account for the differences in the performance of prisons independent of management strategies intended to improve the quality of prison operations.

The assumption that the assignment of staff or inmates to different prisons is a random process is untenable and seriously threatens the validity of the findings presented in earlier studies. Prisons do differ in the types of staff who work at them and the types of inmates incarcerated. Previous analyses have demonstrated that individual-level characteristics influence how staff evaluate their working conditions in prisons (Britton, 1997; Wright, Saylor, Gilman, and Camp, 1997). For example, staff with greater amounts of tenure answer many questions less favorably (Camp, 1999; Camp, Saylor, and Harer, 1997; Camp, Saylor, and Wright, 1999; Camp and Steiger, 1995) than staff with lesser amounts of tenure. The implication is that any comparison of two or more prisons that did not account for discrepancies in the tenure of the staff responding to the surveys at the different prisons could produce misleading results. What may appear to be differences in organizational performance may be the result of varying amounts of employee tenure. The purpose of the analysis is important. If the researcher is interested in comparing job satisfaction across prisons that may result from administrative policies, then staff tenure is a kind of "nuisance" factor that one should control for because of its relationship to the evaluation. If, on the other hand, an analyst is interested in the suppression of serious prison misconduct, then staff tenure may pose an important advantage to a prison, assuming more seasoned employees are more capable of controlling inmate behavior. In this case, the variable is no longer a nuisance and its effect should not only be taken into account in the multilevel analysis, we should recognize and report the extent to which staff tenure is important in suppressing violence.

In addition to controlling for individual-level factors that influence staff evaluations recorded in surveys, it is necessary to use statistical methods that directly address the interdependence (clustering) of observations within the prisons. Analyzing these responses represents the same problem as analyzing behavioral measures we discussed in the previous chapter. Multilevel methods, such as those advocated by Bryk and Raudenbush (1992) and Goldstein (1995), were developed specifically to address these types of problems. Multilevel methods have been effectively utilized to demonstrate that survey data collected from both staff and inmates can be used to compare prisons on selected dimensions of prison operations.

How Multilevel Modeled Results Differ from Simple Summary Measures

The differences between the simple aggregation of survey responses and results based on multilevel models have both theoretical and policy oriented consequences. Camp and his colleagues have demonstrated with multilevel techniques that measures that were completely acceptable at the individual level in terms of their measurement properties were not acceptable as organizational-level measures. The measures that Camp and colleagues (1997, 1999) singled out were respondents' job satisfaction and satisfaction with supervision. When aggregated to the level of the institution, the average ratings of job satisfaction and satisfaction with supervision simply did not vary between institutions in a statistically or substantively meaningful manner. These were scales that had high internal reliability, implying that they were good candidates for institution-level indicators. This is analogous to saying that the measurement tool was a good one, but that there was no difference in the units being compared. So that even though the survey-based satisfaction responses could be used to distinguish differences in individual staff behavior, as a summary indicator, they could not be used to differentiate prison performance. Researchers who fail to account for the multilevel implications of an analysis will mistakenly draw conclusions about differences in the average job satisfaction levels of institutions, when these differences may be entirely due to the composition of employees who work there.

Camp, Gaes, and Saylor (2002) also examined several measures of management effectiveness and prison safety based on survey data that had also been used by Logan in his analysis of privatization in New Mexico (Logan, 1991, 1992), seventeen measures in all. These measures were aggregations of the individual survey responses. They found that only four of the seventeen should be used to discriminate prison performance even though these were perfectly acceptable indicators of an individual's response. Only one of the measures, in fact, had measurement properties that were unequivocal at the organizational level (prison level). This may seem counterintuitive; however, as we note in the previous chapter, when you summarize individual data, the aggregate statistic may have a different meaning and therefore a different impact on the outcome variable.

Camp, Saylor, and Wright (1999) demonstrated the practical consequences of not employing multilevel techniques in evaluating prison performance with survey responses. They examined the performance of eighty federal prisons in 1995 based on the levels of institutional commitment reported by workers at the institutions. They found that institutional commitment was an adequate measure for making comparisons between prisons. However, whether those comparisons were made on adjusted measures or unadjusted measures made a large difference. As we explain in chapter 4, an adjusted measure accounts for the characteristics of individuals and institutions in the multilevel model. An unadjusted measure is simply the "raw" aggregate such as average level of commitment by the employees at a particular institution. On the unadjusted measure of institutional commitment, Camp et al. (1999) reported one institution that was ranked twenty-first out of the eighty prisons. In other words, about 75 percent of the institutions generated higher levels of institutional commitment. However, when an adjusted measure was created with multilevel techniques, this same institution was ranked seventy-second out of eighty. Only 10 percent of the prisons had a higher level of institutional commitment. While admittedly this was the most dramatic of the findings reported by Camp et al. (1999), it once again points to the importance of multilevel modeling.

One of the reasons analysts have not used multilevel techniques previously is that their evaluation has been based on too few prisons. In many cases, prior analyses have involved two or three prisons. Multilevel techniques usually require at least ten prisons and sometimes more. In those cases, where too few prisons are available, analysts should at least recognize the problem of aggregation bias when summing individual measures to make inferences about the institutions.

Graphical Presentations of Multilevel Models of Survey Responses

Camp, Gaes, and Saylor (2002) demonstrated how multilevel techniques can be used to compare the operational capabilities of public and private prisons. Generally speaking, Camp et al. advocate a method that employs three steps. First, it is necessary to model the outcome measures with multilevel models to demonstrate whether these measures are appropriate for comparing prisons and to control for nuisance sources of variance in the models. Second, graphs should be constructed to show prison rankings. The rankings are based upon the empirical Bayes residuals we have referred to several times summarizing actual versus expected performance. Finally, the relationships between these prison-level measures should be represented graphically. Camp et. al used an example where they modeled all low-security prisons, even though the primary research question involved one privately and three publicly operated, low-security prisons.

Figures 5.1 and 5.2 were taken from the Camp, Gaes, and Saylor (2002) paper and demonstrate how complex model results can be presented in an easily understandable manner. In figure 5.1, information on employees' assessment of the quality of institutional operations is presented. Each set of bars represents the average responses for different prisons. WCC-TCI (Taft Correctional Institute operated by Wackenhut Corrections Corporation) and CCA-ELY are two private prisons operated for the Federal Bureau of Prisons. The other three prisons in figure 5.1 are BOP-operated prisons. These three prisons have been chosen as the primary comparison prisons to evaluate WCC-TCI operations, because they were built with the same architectural "footprint" and began their operations at about the same time. All of the prisons in figure 5.1 are considered low-security. The CCA-ELY facility has an entirely different mission and therefore is not part of the privatization study. It is included in these graphs to illustrate the technique.

As we note in chapter 4, multilevel modeling allows the analyst to produce "expected" values or expected levels of performance for each prison. We have already referred to this as the adjusted value based on the distinguishing features of inmates and institutions. Institutional features

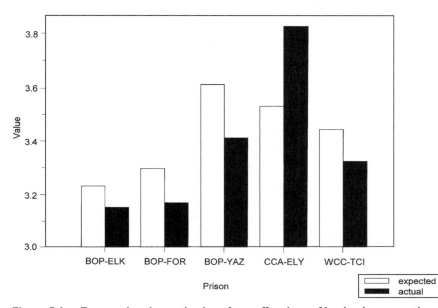

Figure 5.1. Expected and actual values for staff ratings of institution operations.

include aggregate measures of inmate and staff characteristics such as averages of inmate age, and staff tenure. Given the different profiles of staff at the respective prisons, there were differences in the expected values for the average evaluation of institutional operations. FCI Yazoo City was expected to have the highest average evaluation. The black bars in figure 5.1 present information on the actual evaluations provided at the different prisons—the average level without modeling inmate and institution factors. The white bars represent the expected ratings. As can be seen in figure 5.1, all of the prisons received slightly lower evaluations than expected, with the exception of CCA-ELY where the actual evaluation was higher than expected. This graph gives correctional administrators a quick visual reference to determine whether the staff evaluations of institutional operations are about where they should be, below where they should be, or above where they should be. In this case, four of the five institutions had lower than expected ratings. Of course, the analyst must ensure that the correctional administrator fully understands the meaning of expected and actual levels of performance.

Figure 5.2 also presents information on institutional operations, but in a slightly different fashion. In this graph, the intent is to present information about relative performance of prisons. In figure 5.2, the bars on the chart indicate the difference between the expected value and the value actually observed at the respective prisons. In this graph, the prisons are ranked by the value of this difference. The worst institutions appear on the left and better performing institutions are on the right side of the graph. This is similar to the caterpillar graph but devoid of the confidence intervals. Other low-security prisons are represented in figure 5.2, but on this graph we have only identified the individual prisons appearing in figure 5.1. CCA-ELY from figure 5.1 is depicted as prison PP2 on figure 5.2, and WCC-TCI on figure 5.1 is depicted as Taft on figure 5.2.

Based on staff evaluations of the quality of institutional operations, figure 5.2 shows FCI Yazoo City rated the lowest of all low-security prisons. Forrest City and Taft were about the same, and FCI Elkton was slightly higher than the other targeted prisons in this graph. All of the targeted prisons, as also indicated in figure 5.1, had ratings that were lower than expected. In figure 5.2, this is indicated by the fact that the bars fall below the horizontal line representing no difference between expected and actual performance. PP2, on the other hand, was the highest rated prison

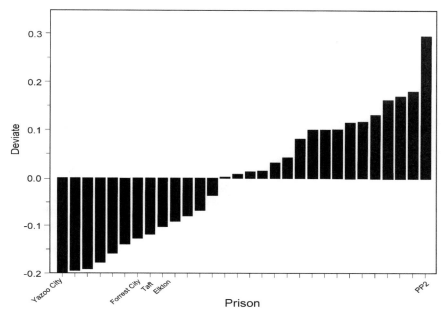

Figure 5.2.   Staff ratings of institution operations for all low security prisons.

on this measure of the quality of institutional operations, even though because of its unique mission, it was not part of the privatization study.

To demonstrate how to graphically depict more than one multilevel derived performance indicator at a time, we refer to Camp, Gaes, Klein-Saffran, Daggett, and Saylor (2002). In that study, the researchers examined survey information collected from inmates at ten low-security prisons. One of the prisons was TCI (Taft), and the others were BOP-operated and included FCI Elkton, FCI Forrest City, and FCI Yazoo City, the same comparison sites represented in figures 5.1 and 5.2. In this analysis, they took the empirical Bayes residuals for several, conceptually related measures and presented them in the same graph with a technique known as parallel coordinates display (Inselburg and Dimsdale, 1990) as implemented by Howell (2001).

Figure 5.3 presents the parallel coordinate display of information on gang-related questions that came from the inmate version of the Social Climate Survey and is reported in Camp et al. (2002). The questions on the survey probe inmates about whether gang activity is present at their prison, whether gang members are in danger, and whether non-gang members are in danger. The gang activity question was modeled with nonlinear techniques since the only possible responses were yes and no. Each line of the horizontal parallel lines represents one of the gang-related survey questions. The vertical lines crossing the parallel lines represent the difference between the expected and observed average value for the institution based on the hierarchical model. Thus, this is simply another way of representing the institutional results where all of the survey questions can be depicted graphically in one display. As can be seen in the graph, the expected values from these models have been converted to the proportion of inmates indicating gang activity. For the other two measures, the responses were converted to a scale that takes into account the relative position of this institution to other institutions.[2] The points on the vertical lines in the graph indicate how far above or below the expected value the institution's response fell.

The purpose of the technique used in figure 5.3 is to demonstrate how prisons compare across related measures. The graph also shows whether there is consistency among the ratings. If there is consistency, then the lines drawn to join the points for the different prisons on the different measures should be parallel to one another. If there is inconsistency, on the

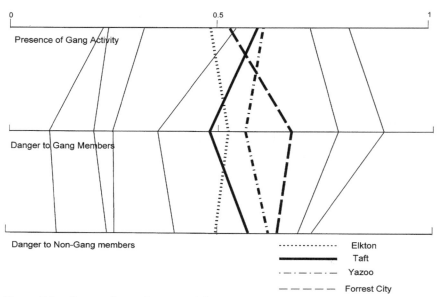

Figure 5.3. Perceptions of gang activity.

other hand, then the vertical lines will cross each other, making the graph look more like spaghetti.

As can be seen in figure 5.3, there is considerable consistency in the opinions of inmates for these three measures. In these graphs, a low score is favorable, and typically, an institution rated favorably on one measure was also rated favorably on the other measures. As can be seen in figure 5.3, Taft and the BOP comparison prisons tend to fall in the middle of inmate evaluations of gang-related questions. Clearly, the parallel coordinates display provides an alternative for providing information to correctional administrators to the techniques used in figures 4.4, 5.1, and 5.2. None of the methods is inherently superior to another. It is simply the case that each technique emphasizes different aspects of the information derived from the results of multilevel models.

Summary of the Multilevel Analyses of Survey Responses Comparing Private and Public Prisons

Although the primary purpose of this chapter was to demonstrate how multilevel models improve our understanding of prison performance, many of the studies cited in this chapter by Camp and his colleagues have used this approach to compare publicly and privately operated prisons. Has a consistent pattern emerged indicating the advantage of one sector over the other? Generally speaking, the studies by Camp and colleagues have not found a consistent pattern in inmate and staff evaluations of private and public prisons. It appears that the private sector does better in some areas than others, and the same can be said about the public sector. TCI, for example, was rated very low on inmate evaluations of food services. The BOP comparison prisons, on the other hand, were rated very low on inmate evaluation of whether there was enough staff to provide for inmate safety, and whether inmates felt safe from being attacked (Camp, Gaes et al. 2002). Similar results were noted with staff surveys. Staff at the BOP comparison prisons rated organizational commitment and fire safety in the housing units more highly than TCI staff, but the private prison clearly provided higher indications of commitment to the institution.[3]

The best conclusion we can offer about the information that has been gathered from properly conducted studies using survey data is that there are many survey performance criteria that analysts can use to distinguish different levels of performance in the different prisons. However, no clear pattern has emerged favoring one sector over the other. As more and more analysts incorporate well-constructed multilevel models into their research of prison performance, a clearer picture of the relative performance of public and private prisons will emerge. This will not only advance our knowledge about prison privatization, but our understanding of the dimensions of prison performance as well.

CHAPTER SIX
COST ANALYSES

T he prison privatization debate, more than any other influence, has elevated cost as a key measure of prison performance. Early proponents of the private prison industry, and the industry itself, claimed that private prisons would be 10 to 20 percent cheaper than their public counterparts. More recent advocates (Moore, 1998) also make the same claim. Nelson (1998) provides a critical appraisal of much of the work found in Moore (1998). Her analysis suggests why these claims do not have merit. A recent American Federation of State, County, and Municipal Employees (AFSCME) report, "The Evidence is Clear: Crime Shouldn't Pay," provides a summary of several more recent studies. This report, available on-line (AFSCME, 2001), is also critical of other cost assessments; however, AFSCME could be considered an advocate on the opposite side of the debate. A recent study suggests that the anticipated cost savings are either considerably lower than implied by the advocates of privatization, or nonexistent (Pratt and Maahs, 1999). In some cases the private sector has been shown to be more expensive.

While the evidence is mixed as to whether the private sector is a less costly alternative, much of the confusion arising out of competing claims of efficiency is due to inadequate or outright incorrect costing methods. In this chapter, we explore some of the most vexing problems. Nelson (2002) has proposed a framework for comparing costs of public and private prisons. We rely on that paper to sort out some of the confusion arising from misconceptions about how to do a proper cost analysis of prison privatization. Her method, however, is generic enough to be applied to the costing of any government service. There is a great deal of literature on cost benefit analysis (Kahn, 1988; Kelley, 1984; Martin, 1993) in the fields of microeconomics, public administration, cost accounting, regulation, and public finance that can be used to build a solid analysis framework. Nelson (2002) has used that literature to explicate a set of principles that, if followed, can provide a fair assessment for decision makers who want to evaluate the potential outsourcing of government services, or who are interested in retrospectively comparing private versus public operations. In our discussion, we highlight those areas of cost analysis that are the most controversial and also most likely to be manipulated by the various parties whose interests are at risk. We then explore some of the theoretical reasons underlying the privatization debate on cost. We offer competing explanations that arrive at different conclusions as to whether the public or private sector could provide quality prison programs at a lower cost.

We divided the cost discussion into two chapters. In the following chapter on costs, we draw the link between quality and cost and propose a method to analyze cost as it relates to quality. In that chapter, we also devote a subsection to the role of labor in the cost argument. Labor costs are typically 60 to 75 percent of the total per diem cost of a prison. If there are to be cost savings, they will probably come primarily from reductions in labor costs. In the section of chapter 7 labeled, "The McDonaldization Argument for Efficiency," we consider whether restructuring labor will lead to lower costs while at the same time providing the same level of quality. "McDonaldization" refers to the rationalization and routinization of prison tasks as first described with respect to fast food restaurants (Ritzer, 1993, 1998).

The mechanics of cost comparisons can be boiled down to two fundamental questions: "How many taxpayer dollars are currently spent?" and, "How many taxpayer dollars would be devoted when the services are provided through a contract?" These general principles apply to virtually all government outsourcing. For readers who are interested in critically thinking about the outsourcing of other government services, we believe that by providing a great deal of detail on prisons, we lay the groundwork for understanding other privatization decisions. However, we attend to the details of prison privatization because it raises unique theoretical and substantive problems, and because we have collectively spent a great deal of time analyzing the issue. Understanding these cost and evaluation concepts can enhance the efficiency of public services. If an alternative scenario appears to be less expensive than the status quo (and of acceptable quality), the money saved could be returned to citizens for other uses.

While these questions appear simple, attempts to answer them can lead to vehement disagreements. Before we review some of the principles of cost comparisons, it is instructive to consider three examples of what happens when parties with competing interests are involved in costing out equivalent government and private services. These examples also provide an insight into some of the most contentious issues.

Past Debates over Cost Measures

Recent privatization debates in Texas and Florida, as well as the history of the guidelines used by the federal government to make the outsourcing decision, serve to illustrate that when vendor contracts and union jobs are at stake, parties with different interests are likely to offer competing cost assessments.

Prison Privatization in Texas

The Cummins (2001) study, cited above in the context of qualitative measures, provides a detailed account of the cost questions that arise during the planning, development, and execution of a contract for prison beds. Cummins recounts the history of the S. B. 251 legislation passed in Texas in 1987 that made it possible to privatize some of the state prison system.

As we noted, Cummins's portrayal points to an economic downturn in Texas as the primary motivating factor for prison privatization. S. B. 251 required private vendors to provide programs similar to those available in state facilities at a savings of at least 10 percent over the cost of comparable state facilities. To meet the requirements of S. B. 251, there had to be a precise estimate of the Texas prison per diem costs. As time to award the contract grew near, Jim Lynaugh, deputy for finance and administration for the Texas Department of Criminal Justice (TDCJ), provided the Legislative Budget Board (LBB) with a cost estimate of $27.62 per diem based on salary and other operating expenses for state prisons. Using this estimate and allowing for a 10 percent savings, the private vendors could expect to receive $24.86 per inmate day for salaries and operating expenses.

The LBB amended Lynaugh's figures to include the following per diem adjustments: $2.27 for *Ruiz* costs that the state would also have to face to come into compliance with an existing court order; $4.51 for the building cost, since the vendors were to fund the facilities; $1.63 for additional personnel costs to provide more intensive programs; $.32 for additional personnel for increased salary and operating expenses; $1.07 for the additional facility space required by these program personnel; and $4.25 more for staff, construction, and startup costs not calculated by TDCJ. The final LBB estimate was $41.67 per inmate day. An accounting firm gave yet another estimate. When Governor Clements became aware of the differences in the expected per diem costs between the TDCJ and LBB estimates, he reportedly "hit the ceiling" (Cummins, 2001: 171). When the initial Texas contracts were finally awarded, the vendors were given $35.25 per diem for all four pre-release centers.

As Cummins points out, Lynaugh's original estimates may have been vindicated. After a decade of private prisons in Texas, per diem awards from TDCJ in 1999 ranged between $28.72 and $33.80. Whether the relative decline was attributable to the specter of competition, or the ability of TDCJ to manage their contracts better, it is clear that the original estimates were much higher than they should have been. TDCJ has assumed a decisive bargaining position with the private prison sector because it owns the prison realty. Thus, when there are negotiations for the contract award, TDCJ is in a position to easily change vendors or take over the prison itself.

One might have expected that it would have been relatively easy to determine the actual TDCJ costs to set a benchmark for bids from private vendors. Instead, there was as much as a $14 per diem difference between the TDCJ and LBB estimates, an annual discrepancy of $5,110 dollars for each inmate. It is not clear from Cummins's study whose policy interests were being represented by the LBB. The governor's office and key members of the legislature saw an opportunity to build prisons without bearing the cost of financing them, and to operate them more cheaply. However, lobbyists for the private sector and local jurisdictions seeing an opportunity to bring in revenues and create jobs had an incentive to increase the public sector per diem cost estimates. Whether or not the LBB was influenced by the latter groups is unclear. What is clear, however, is that while almost all of the parties favored the principle of cost cutting through privatization, competing interests became increasingly important as the actual contract costs were negotiated at a rate higher than would have occurred in a competitive market. Whether or not these are true markets is a theme we discuss later.

Prison Privatization in Florida

The controversy over actual operating costs in Florida prisons also reveals how hard it is to get all sides to agree on whether or not privatization saves money.[1] Florida state law determines the four major participants to this dispute: the state Department of Corrections (DOC), the Correctional Privatization Commission (CPC), the Florida Corrections Commission (FCC), and the Office of Program Policy Analysis and Government Accountability (OPPAGA). Chapter 89-526 of the Florida state statutes, enacted in 1989, first authorized the Department of Corrections to enter into contracts with private prison management companies. Chapter 93-406, adopted in 1994, created the Correctional Privatization Commission (CPC) to expedite prison privatization. CPC is housed in the state Department of Management Services and operates independently of the Department of Corrections. Chapter 957.05 of Florida law requires the CPC to demonstrate—before any contract is signed—that private prison management will result in at least a 7 percent savings, relative to the cost of allowing the state Department of Corrections (DOC) to run the prison. Chapter 957.07 also empowers the state auditor general to decide whether or not this condition has been satisfied before any contract with a vendor has been signed.

To provide for ongoing, independent oversight, Florida state law also requires the Office of Program Policy Analysis and Government Accountability (OPPAGA)[2] to review the performance of all management companies that operate private prison facilities in Florida, either vendors under contract to CPC or the DOC. A separate oversight board, the Florida Corrections Commission, established in 1994, is "charged with reviewing the effectiveness and efficiency of [Florida's] correctional efforts, recommending policies, and evaluating the implementation of approved policies."[3]

Not surprisingly, these different oversight units do not always favor the same measure of privatization benefits. For example, the DOC argued in its *1996–97 Annual Report* that the three privately managed adult prison facilities then in operation were more expensive than similar, publicly run facilities would have been.[4] Using a somewhat different approach, the OPPAGA (Office of Program Policy Analysis and Government Accountability, 1998) reached a similar conclusion. Nevertheless, the OPPAGA report included responses from the Correctional Privatization Commission, the Corrections Corporation of America, and

Wackenhut Corrections Corporation proposing alternative cost methodologies—ones that led to conclusions directly opposed to those reported by the DOC and the OPPAGA.

The Department of Corrections estimates were somewhat suspect. The per diem rate for the men's publicly managed prison was derived as the *average* of nine other facilities. However, all but one of these public facilities was substantially larger than any of the private facilities being analyzed (Office of Program Policy Analysis and Government Accountability, 1998). Given the economies of scale in prison operation, this approach probably understated the public sector cost of running a prison comparable in size to Bay or Moore Haven, two of the privately operated prisons.

Nevertheless, OPPAGA reached a similar conclusion from a different starting place. OPPAGA compared two private men's facilities, Bay and Moore Haven, with a single, comparably sized public facility (Office of Program Policy Analysis and Government Accountability, 1998). In its analysis, the OPPAGA started with the management fee due to CCA and Wackenhut (for running Bay and Moore Haven, respectively); and then made adjustments for monitoring costs paid by the management companies, unpaid property taxes, and medical insurance co-payments collected from prisoners and retained by the prison operators. These monies were deducted from the cost of the contract because they were returned to the state. For example, unpaid property taxes were deducted because the state had anticipated that the private prisons would owe those taxes. The state provided those monies in its contract award, but when the taxes did not have to be paid, the monies were given back to the government. For the publicly managed Lawtey prison, the OPPAGA used the annual cost of operations, health services, and education programs reported for this facility by the Department of Corrections in its *Annual Report* for FY 1996/97. All three cost estimates were then adjusted for differences in scale economies, the scope of management responsibilities, and the quality of services provided.

The OPPAGA inferred from its calculations that Bay was slightly more expensive to operate than its public sector equivalent; and that the Moore Haven facility was only 3.9 percent cheaper. The OPPAGA nevertheless rated the performance of both CCA (at Bay) and Wackenhut (at Moore Haven) as "satisfactory," while noting in passing that neither private facility achieved the 7 percent cost savings required by law.

CCA provided yet another cost assessment. Adjustments proposed by CCA substantially changed the interpretation of the data. CCA found that private management of Bay and Moore Haven resulted in an 8.3 and 6.0 percent savings. The discrepancy between these and the OPPAGA estimates arose primarily from three simple changes: an increase in CCA's credit for taxes paid to the state; an increase in CCA's credit for the "Inmate Welfare Trust Fund Net Revenue"[5]; and a decrease in the state's adjustment for "medical costs for higher medical grade inmates at Lawtey" (Office of Program Policy Analysis and Government Accountability, 1998: 38).[6] The OPPAGA had rejected these three CCA amendments, observing (1) that CCA sought to claim credit for more tax revenue than was properly attributable to its Bay facility,[7] (2) that the state retained custody over Inmate Welfare Trust Fund balances,[8] and (3) that Lawtey inmates had considerably more medical needs than those at the Bay facility.

A more recent OPPAGA report shows that the debate continues over the potential cost savings to be realized from prison privatization in Florida. OPPAGA (Office of Program Policy Analysis and Government Accountability, 2000) reported that Bay continued to be more expensive to operate than Moore Haven and that a modification to the CCA contract for the Bay facility was likely to aggravate the problem.

This kind of detailed cost accounting may seem arcane to the naive observer; however, it is a prerequisite to understanding reasonable alternative cost scenarios that can be used to compare public and private costs. Despite the fact that there was a discrepancy between the DOC, the OPPAGA, and the private sector assessment of costs, there was sufficient detail in each analysis to allow analysts to challenge the assumptions and conclusions of each, as well as to judge which might be the most appropriate representation. It is also important to note how subtle changes in interpretation of facts can make a large difference in cost comparisons. While the Florida privatization experience has been an interesting example of a dispute in the details, the next example describes a dispute in the rules that guide cost comparisons.

Privatization at the Federal Level: OMB Circular A-76

Even the general rules used to make cost comparisons can become the subject of partisan lobbying efforts. At the federal level, the Office of Management and Budget (1996) has issued formal instructions on how to make comparisons between public and private sector operations. In principle, these guidelines are intended to help analysts identify the most efficient means of providing government services. However, even though Circular A-76 has been updated frequently since 1966, it remains a subject of controversy. According to the GAO,

> government officials have been concerned about the cost and length of time required to complete the procurement process associated with A-76 studies, and employees have been concerned about the potential loss of jobs. Private sector representatives, on the other hand, believed that the A-76 process favored the government. They have contended that the government did not include all costs of operations in its A-76 competitions. In particular, they believed the government excluded proportional shares of indirect and administrative costs such as facility maintenance and upkeep, payroll, and personnel services. (General Accounting Office, 1998: 2)

Some of the conflicts over Circular A-76 can be traced to the political process that created the guidelines themselves. Other difficulties arise from inconsistencies in the current version of the document itself.

Choosing an Overhead Rate

Overhead, in the context of prisons, can be defined as that portion of the total cost allocated to shared services and functions. Thus, the salary of central office staff is an overhead cost. The history of the overhead rate currently used to estimate the cost of public sector services illustrates the impact of the political process. In response to complaints that the A-76 methodology favored the government at the expense of taxpayers, OMB staff met with public and private sector officials to define a government-wide overhead cost rate.

Among practitioners, there was no broad consensus on the appropriate rate to be used. The rates proposed by public and private officials contacted by OMB ranged from 0 to 30 percent. Instead of testing these rates for appropriateness, OMB implemented a compromise. The rate chosen was 12 percent—roughly the midpoint of the range of plausible proposals (General Accounting Office, 1998: 6). However, as the GAO observes, this rate lacks an analytical basis, could understate or overstate overhead costs and unfairly shift the competition results to either the government or private sector. (General Accounting Office, 1998: 30)

According to the OMB A-76 handbook, the study of comparative costs can include an agency-specific or sector-specific cost factor for overhead, but the analysis has to be approved by OMB. In a later section we examine these potential sources of "unfairness" in the context of prison privatization in greater detail.

Divergent Interpretations

The text of Circular A-76 provides another potential source of disagreements over cost principles. For example, exhibit 1 in chapter 1 of the current version of the guidelines stipulates that

> Conversion to contract is required if a cost comparison indicates that contract performance is the *lower cost* alternative. (Office of Management and Budget, 1996: 7) (italics added)

In other words, if the private sector is cheaper, let the private sector do it. However, the actual cost comparison process substantially amends this stated goal. Chapter 2 of the A-76 guidelines establishes that

> [a]n activity will not be converted to or from in-house, contract or ISSA performance on the basis of a cost comparison unless the minimum cost differential is met. The minimum cost differential is the lesser of 10 percent of in-house personnel-related costs (Line 1) or $10 million over the performance period. (Office of Management and Budget, 1996: 19)

Thus, the amendment states that the private sector has to be 10 percent cheaper. Many would argue that a 10 percent cost differential is too stringent a test to establish an opportunity for meaningful savings for taxpayers.[9]

The current version of Circular A-76 authorizes processes designed to mitigate some of the shortcomings in the guidelines. For example, the guidelines allow for agency-specific, governmentwide cost factors. In part II, chapter 2, OMB states:

[a]gencies are encouraged to collect agency or sector-specific data to update and improve upon the standard cost factors provided herein. The official in paragraph 9.a of the Circular, or designee, may develop alternative agency-wide or sector-specific cost factors including overhead, for approval by OMB. (Office of Management and Budget, 1996: 18)

This allows the agency to make a reasonable argument about factors that exaggerate or mitigate cost comparisons. OMB guidelines also allow for contracts to be awarded on the basis of quality rather than cost (Office of Management and Budget, 1996: 5).[10] Nevertheless, it is not clear that these alternative processes have had an impact on current practice. In its 1998 review of the use of A-76 guidelines, the GAO found no federal agencies that had chosen to establish their own overhead rates. The air force reportedly considered doing so but decided against it (General Accounting Office, 1998: 6). The GAO also found that the "best value" approach to procurement—cost plus quality—had received only "limited use" within the Defense Department (General Accounting Office, 1998: 13). As a result, there is no guarantee that the current OMB guidelines are accomplishing their stated purpose—"empowering Federal managers to make sound and justifiable business decisions." In the following sections, we propose guidelines for making cost comparisons that promote a rational system for making such a decision.

A Proposed General Approach

In this section, we summarize Nelson's (2002) framework for making cost comparisons between public and private prisons by developing a scenario of the tasks to be performed by the private contractor, and then costing that scenario correctly. Typically the scenario will depict private and public provision of the same service. While this may seem to be an unambiguous task, the execution of a sound cost comparison is rife with problems. The "devil in the details" is partly because of the different ways public and private bureaucracies do cost accounting.

While the details of cost comparisons are perhaps best left to economists and procurement specialists, controversies and common mistakes characterize quite a few previous cost analyses. Those unfamiliar with the premises of cost analysis may not be aware of how subtle and not-so-subtle differences in assumptions can lead to radically different conclusions about the relative costs of alternatives. We review some of the more difficult issues; however, more detail is provided in Nelson (2002). We begin with basic principles, then we underscore the most important factors, and we conclude this analysis with an example of "overhead" calculations. The following sections cover the most basic cost comparison principles advocated by Nelson.

Within Each Policy Scenario Identify Only Those Expenditures that Are Borne by *Taxpayers*

Since the purpose of the cost comparison is to use taxpayer money as efficiently as possible, it makes sense to frame the issue in terms of *government* expenditures—and *not* in terms of spending decisions made by contractors and other vendors. Some previous prison privatization analyses have compared costs by listing the line item expenditures of the public and private entities separately.[11] Ultimately, it does not matter how contractors spend their money as long as quality meets an acceptable level. Some analysts do not favor this approach, especially those representing the government, since it hides the contractor's expenses for specific prison functions such as medical care, staff overhead, and food service. We amend this rule ourselves below when we broach the problem of assessing cost and quality simultaneously.

Work to Capture All Expenditures that *Do* Change—The Concept of Avoidable Costs

When money is paid to a contractor to perform a service, the cost is termed an *avoided* cost. It is avoided in the sense that it is no longer an in-house government expense. *Unavoidable* costs are government costs that are still present even after a contractor has been paid for the work. Thus, avoided costs are associated with that part of the service that will be done by the contractor.

To determine potential savings using the avoidable cost approach, you subtract the *full cost of contracting* (i.e., all payments to the vendor as well as the cost of monitoring contract performance) from the *avoidable cost of in-house operations*. This latter cost is typically one that is estimated by calculating how much it costs the government to provide a service making sure that the costs that are unavoidable (those that still remain after paying a contractor) are excluded from the estimation. The *difference* between these two cost measures represents the potential savings to be realized by taxpayers.[12]

While this sounds simple, determining the avoided costs may not always be easy. In practice, it is often difficult to develop appropriate estimates of these costs. For example, to identify the effect of privatization on shared "central office" support services, the exercise is to determine that part of the shared "central office" function that will no longer be necessary once a contractor is providing the service. It is tempting to assume that all of the central office support costs will be assumed by the contractor. However, this is unlikely. If one or only a few prisons are to be operated by contractors, most of the central office overhead will still be necessary to operate the prison system. Assuming all of the support costs will be borne by the contractor would overstate taxpayer savings.[13] The allocation of shared support costs is probably the most difficult aspect of the avoidable cost methodology, the least understood, the most likely to raise controversy, and one of the most likely to tip the cost comparison in favor of one sector over the other. In the next section of this chapter, "Avoidable Cost in Practice—Devilish Details," we give a concrete example.

Another difficulty is that costs are not always assigned to the departments, institutions, or regions that actually incur them. For example, unemployment insurance for prison staff, as well as liability insurance, inmate health care, and employer contributions toward staff retirement savings, are all "direct" costs of prison operation, part of the avoidable cost of in-house operations. Nevertheless, government accounting systems do not regularly allocate these expenditures to the institutions or divisions that incur them but may include them as part of the central office budget or possibly the state budget. For example, in some states inmate medical care is handled by the state public health agency, so this direct cost lies buried in another agency's budget. These costs are allocated at the end of the year, and it takes a discerning accounting eye to make sure these costs are assigned to the prison direct costs. Because of this accounting convention, analysts may inadvertently understate the direct cost of public provision of services.

Other cost issues include debates over the appropriate treatment of property, sales, and/or income taxes paid by vendors; profits from inmate phone calls and commissary purchases; revenues from inmate co-pays for health care; appropriate adjustments for differences in inmate populations (number of inmates, their security level, age, sex, tendencies toward violence, health conditions, etc.); appropriate adjustments for differences in programs and ancillary functions at an institution (in-take facility, pre-release facility, in-house rehabilitation programs, hospice or long-term health care programs, etc.); appropriate adjustments for differences in the age and design of comparison facilities; and appropriate allowances for construction costs, capital expenditures, and other nonrecurring expenditures.

Ignore Costs that *Do Not* Change from One Scenario to the Next

If a proposed policy change has no impact on a cost, then that cost is *not* relevant to the analysis at hand. In the context of prison privatization, costs that do not change between scenarios should either be added to the expenditures for *all* scenarios or added to none. Once again, this accounting problem is particularly serious when it comes to handling overhead or support costs that are shared among several services. The shared nature of these costs makes it difficult to attribute them to any one activity.

Instructions issued in 1995 by the Defense Department illustrate the basic difficulty in using this approach:

> for the cost comparison study, only calculate support costs which would be eliminated in the event the function is contracted. This decision is based on the conclusion that costs involved in funding, policy-making, long-range planning and direction would continue and be equally applicable to both in-house or contract operation.[14]

In other words, if the potential for *cost savings* is the issue at hand, then only those support expenditures that are to be eliminated need be considered. Many functions will have to be supported into the future as an overhead cost that will *not be avoided* in the event of a contract.

Be Certain that Cost Measures Are Consistent over Time

It is essential to ensure that costs are measured consistently when comparisons are made across years. Adjusting costs over time for inflation ensures that comparisons are made in terms of "constant dollars." Multiyear comparisons of official cost reports should be adjusted to reflect changes in any accounting treatment. If a particular expense is moved from one account or budget to another, it will be important to adjust for this change when years before and after the event are compared.

Avoidable Cost in Practice—Devilish Details

The accounting calculations for this type of analysis require either someone familiar with the nuances of an agency's books, or accounting processes that are extremely transparent. Operating budgets for prisons are often in the range of $30 million, or more, per fiscal year. A mistake in the calculation of costs based on accounting nuances, or based on equity formulas intended to level the playing field, can easily push the cost comparison in favor of one sector over another. And these mistakes can misleadingly indicate that millions of dollars will be saved (or lost). In this section, we list some of the most common dimensions that should be accounted for when doing a cost comparison. We also discuss an exemplary analysis of overhead costs conducted by the Oklahoma Department of Corrections.

The analyst must be able to separate anticipated budget expenditures into avoidable and unavoidable costs. He or she must use equity formulae or analyses to level the playing field. For example, it is important to insure comparability between the public and private providers by making adjustments for differences in the sizes of the inmate populations (economy of scale differences), local cost of living, level of inmate programming, and operations assumed by the private and public provider. Finally, the analysis should also include appropriate adjustments for revenues earned by the contractors, and state and local taxes paid by the contractor that are revenue streams that would not occur if the institution were being publicly managed.

As a hypothetical scenario, the private provider may have more inmates, lower expenses due to its location in a lower cost of living area, and fewer inmate programming opportunities than a public comparison site. If an analyst does not account for the economic implications of this scenario, the private provider has a cost advantage, but one based on an inequitable comparison. Furthermore, if the public sector continues to manage some of the penal functions such as sentence computation and disciplinary process for the privately operated prison, these operational costs should be considered part of the cost of private provision, or they should be deducted from the public expense to insure comparability. If the private company pays taxes to the state or local government, this should lower the cost of the privately operated facility, since part of the government expense is returned to the taxpayer. Again, all of these examples are considered in much greater detail in Nelson's (2002) paper, including an exposition of how to treat health care co-payments and commissary profits equitably. Typically, the most problematic area of comparability concerns the treatment of overhead costs. We consider that problem in greater detail.

Overhead Cost Allocations

As we have already noted, in a cost comparison between the public and private sector, one should expect to save money only on the *avoidable* portion of the overhead cost. The breakdown used by the Oklahoma State Department of Corrections furnishes a helpful example of the differences between avoidable and total support costs. Table 6.1 reproduces the breakdown of Oklahoma overhead expenditures for FY 2000 and indicates which of these costs are properly allocated to public and private prison operations.[15] If a "No" appears in the column labeled "Allocated to Private Operation," it means that this part of the central office overhead will be avoided because the contractor will take responsibility for this function and cost. If a "Yes" appears, this means the state must still provide and pay for the service. This cost is therefore unavoidable. Examples of *unavoidable* cost in table 6.1 are transportation, information technology, director's office, finance and accounting, general administration, internal affairs, legal services, and other administrative functions.

We are using the Oklahoma example to lay out a template on how the avoidable portion of the overhead cost should be calculated. This does not mean that every jurisdiction will have the same percentages of avoidable and unavoidable overhead costs. The percentages will depend on the size of the privatization effort in any given jurisdiction and on the nature of the contract—generally, the smaller the privatization effort in a jurisdiction, the lower the percentage of overhead costs that will be avoided. In fact, as a proportion of their total inmate population, Oklahoma has had one of the largest privatization efforts of state and federal jurisdiction in the United States. For that reason, we would expect that the avoidable proportion of central office overhead expenditures should be larger for Oklahoma than it is for most other jurisdictions that have privately operated prisons. At the bottom of table 6.1, the total central office overhead expense is almost $26 million, but the unavoidable share is still large, about $16 million.

Although the *avoidable* portion of support costs in table 6.1 is large, it amounts to only 38 percent of *total* overhead costs. The remaining

Table 6.1. Overhead Cost Allocation for Oklahoma

Unit	Amount (Dollars)	Allocated to State Operations	Allocated to Private Operations	Amount (Dollars)
Administrative Services	356,869	Yes	No	
Adult Basic Education	64,000	Yes	No	
Building Maintenance	474,896	Yes	No	
Center for Correctional Officer Studies	653,017	Yes	No	
Central Transportation	1,453,223	Yes	Yes	1,453,223
Chief of Operations	430,245	Yes	Yes	430,245
Information Technology	2,736,643	Yes	Yes	2,736,643
Construction & Maintenance	1,432,987	Yes	No	
Curriculum Development	13,100	Yes	No	
Day Reporting	124,000	Yes	No	
Director's Office	554,242	Yes	Yes	554,242
Education Administration	342,908	Yes	No	
Electric Monitoring	586,000	Yes	No	
Finance & Accounting	1,482,278	Yes	Yes	1,482,278
General Administration	3,864,918	Yes	Yes	3,864,918
Internal Affairs	531,442	Yes	Yes	531,442
Legal Services	1,143,344	Yes	Yes	1,143,344
Offender Program Monitor	607,933	Yes	Yes	607,933
Office Technology	560,651	Yes	Yes	560,651
Oklahoma State Industries	3,001,683	Yes	No	
Personnel	1,100,458	Yes	No	
Population Management	1,542,864	Yes	Yes	1,542,864
Probation & Parole Equipment	500,000	Yes	No	
Public Relations	168,631	Yes	Yes	168,631
Research & Evaluation	698,830	Yes	Yes	698,830
Safety	22,100	Yes	No	
Sentence Administration	323,534	Yes	Yes	323,534
Staff Development Center	848,991	Yes	No	
Statewide & Regional Cognitive Skills	73,700	Yes	No	
Tulsa Female Offender Care	66,666	Yes	No	
TOTAL	$25,760,153			$16,098,778

amount, 62 percent, is assumed to be unaffected by privatization. The avoidable cost approach requires that these *un*avoidable overhead costs should either be totally ignored or assigned equitably to all comparison sites.

To see how this works in practice, suppose first that the per diem cost calculations for state-run facilities include *both* avoidable and unavoidable costs—in other words, overhead costs are "fully allocated." This could be accomplished in a variety of ways, including the use of a uniform overhead rate to be applied to some definition of direct costs. If, for example, we assume a rate of 12 percent were to be applied to operating costs, then the overhead cost at a publicly managed facility would be computed as

Fully allocated public sector overhead cost = (.12) × (operating costs).

In jurisdictions where the breakdown between avoidable and unavoidable overhead costs is similar to the one observed in Oklahoma, estimates for privately run facilities should be allocated a share of overhead costs equal to 62 percent of the amount assigned to the public facilities. In other words, if the overhead rate for the publicly managed facilities were equal to 12 percent (.12), then the private sector overhead rate would be (.12)×(.62)=.0744 or 7.44 percent. The level of overhead costs assigned to the privately managed facility would then be

Private sector overhead cost = (.0744) × (operating costs).

The above approach allocated unavoidable overhead costs to *both* public and private facilities. The other basic alternative consistent with this cost methodology would be to assign only avoidable overhead costs to public facilities (i.e., 38 percent of all overhead costs) and to assign no overhead costs to privately managed ones. In either case, the *difference* between the public and private sector cost estimates would be equal to avoidable overhead costs.

The treatment of overhead cost appears to be one of the major sources of controversy in the Florida prison privatization imbroglio we note above. It is unlikely that OPPAGA adopted the type of avoidable cost methodology we are advocating when analyzing privately managed prisons in this state. The general share of overhead assigned to the privately managed facilities was significantly smaller than the Oklahoma analysis suggests. Private facilities in Florida were assigned a DOC overhead amount that was only a quarter to a third of the amount assigned to publicly run prisons. Given that overhead costs appear to be fully allocated to the public sector facilities, this approach probably *understates* the amount of private sector overhead costs. Unless it can be shown that the private sector is assuming a greater burden of shared overhead services, or the economics in Florida are much different than those in Oklahoma, the Oklahoma analysis suggests the private overhead costs should be roughly 62 percent of the total public overhead costs, not the 25 to 33 percent share allocated by OPPAGA.

As a result, OPPAGA probably *over*stated the privatization savings, a common mistake in public-private cost comparisons. Shared public overhead costs are only partially reduced through privatization. Until we have a system that is entirely operated by a private vendor, there will always be some level of administrative oversight and that overhead will be borne by the taxpayers. Even if a system were entirely operated by a contractor, it will probably always be necessary to have the public sector involved in administrative oversight and strategic functions.

Other Adjustments to Ensure Consistency—Even More Devilish Details

A variety of other adjustments may be necessary to ensure the consistency of comparisons across facilities. "Unfunded" public sector liabilities represent one such category of expenses. Many states have such liabilities because they have not fully funded their retirement systems. It is tempting, but incorrect, to assign public facilities a share of such liabilities already incurred, but to exclude this cost from private sector estimates. The privatization debate in Florida provides an example. In FY 96/97, an OPPAGA report comparing the privately managed Moore Haven and Bay facilities with the publicly managed Lawtey prison failed to adjust appropriately for the unfunded liability of the State Retirement System. An amount equal to 5.78 percent of payroll costs was included in the costs reported at Lawtey, but no corresponding amount was added to contractor costs at Moore Haven and Bay. The OPPAGA justified this exclusion by claiming that the liability was still a state cost to the taxpayers, but that "privates do not pay this and thus should be able to reduce costs in comparison to the state by at least 5.78% of payroll" (Office of Program Policy Analysis and Government Accountability, 1998). However, this reasoning is flawed unless privatization actually changes the amount of the *existing* unfunded liability. If, for example, the private company offered to defer some of its profits to reduce the unfunded public liability, then these would be revenues back to the taxpayer. Of course that would be an unlikely scenario, and the state would probably expect a lower contract bid instead.

OPPAGA later adopted an approach consistent with the avoidable cost analysis advocated by Nelson. The OPPAGA report comparing Okeechobee and South Bay facilities for FY 97/98 and FY 98/99 reduces the per diem cost estimate for the publicly managed Okeechobee facility by $.88 per inmate day to "reduce costs of Okeechobee for contributions to repay prior year's unfunded debt of the Retirement System."

While the calculations we have discussed may seem esoteric to someone unfamiliar with the details of cost comparisons, it should be obvious that these calculations can be very complex. Given these complexities, we believe it is impossible to draw any conclusions about the quality of prior cost comparisons unless all of the details have been provided such as those in the OPPAGA examples. This has implications for summary analyses of prior cost comparisons studies, which we discuss in the next section.

A Meta-analysis of Private/Public Cost Differentials

There has been one attempt to provide a synthesis of the existing literature on cost comparisons between publicly and privately operated prisons by conducting a meta-analysis of the extant cost studies. Pratt and Maahs (1999) converted the per diem costs reported in twenty-four published studies into z-scores. These scores allow an analyst to compare units of analysis that may not be ordinarily comparable. Then they coded the following variables for each study: ownership of the facility, number of inmates, age of the facility in years, security level of the institution, and the year of the study. They then analyzed the z-score as a function of the coded variables.

Whether or not this study represents a real meta-analysis is questionable. Since the per diem metric is already a standardized metric, it was unnecessary to convert it into a z-score. In meta-analyses, studies that measure an effect in different metrics must be converted into a common metric to allow meaningful comparisons among the studies. Furthermore, the authors did not follow conventional methods to analyze data with known variance, the primary assumption of meta-analysis. For example, there was no test of heterogeneity of variance to assess whether all of the effect sizes represented the same population. Finally, there is no real sample size in any given study to represent how a particular study should be weighted in the analysis. Nevertheless, the results of a multiple regression analysis indicated the following: the number of inmates was related to a decrease in cost—the economy of scale finding; higher security levels were less expensive—a finding that seems to raise problems with the analysis, since it is almost always the case that higher security levels are more costly, even when controlling for the types of variables used by Pratt and Maahs; and finally, there was no effect of public versus private ownership on cost.

Given the problems we have noted above with one of the better cost assessments (the OPPAGA analysis of private prisons in Florida), we are less sanguine than Pratt and Maahs about the usefulness of meta-analysis in this context. Our sense is that a meta-analysis is premature until we have settled on a coherent method of measuring the relative costs of publicly and privately managed institutions. Failure to standardize on inmate population can cause a swing of 10 percent or more in the cost differentials. Failure to properly compute the avoidable portion of overhead cost can easily add 4 percent or more to reported public sector costs. These miscalculations can result in estimation errors amounting to millions of dollars over the life of a contract with a private provider of corrections services.

Different authors deal with these analytical problems in different ways. In a recent review of the literature on the cost of incarceration, Segal and Moore (2002) chose not to adjust for the methodological differences found in published studies. Instead, they surveyed the results reported in twenty-eight separate cost studies and conclude that "virtually all" authors find that private prisons are cheaper. Unfortunately, this analysis was even less rigorous than the study by Pratt and Maahs (1999), with the result that the strength of the conclusions presented by Segal and Moore is open to question.

The Relationship between Market Structure and Potential Savings of Privatization

Some proponents of prison privatization have argued for choosing between public and private providers on the basis of "market structure." For these advocates, the economic assumptions alone should insure greater efficiencies achieved by the private sector. They assert that the private sector is generally more efficient than the public sector because of the competition inherent in a market relationship. For example, Volokh (2002) has written, "Comparative studies on the cost and quality of private and public prisons give reason to be cautiously pleased with private prison performance. The empirical evidence is consistent with economic theory, which predicts that with privatization, costs will fall and quality (however defined) may rise" (Volokh, 2002: 1870). As an extreme example of a market-based enthusiasm for privatization of criminal justice, Gilbert (2001) discusses the proposals of The National Center for Policy Analysis (NCPA), which lobbies for such privatization. The NCPA advocates the privatization of prosecution, the private management of imprisonment, and the integration of criminal and civil law to enhance economic penalties for crimes.

At least within the prison privatization debate, theorists such as Volokh have had a louder voice than those who may hold a contrary view. For such an oppositional viewpoint, Paul Starr, writing for the Economic Policy Institute (Starr, 1987), has argued for mixed public and private structures without the presumption that privatization always improves the service. He distinguishes between privatization, the shift from public to private production, and liberalization, "the opening up of any industry to competitive pressures" (Starr, 1987: 2). There are instances where government has simply transferred ownership of industry or services to the private sector without subjecting them to competition. He cites the Thatcher government's sale of British Telecom and British Gas as examples of the latter. Starr also challenges the assumption that there is a zero sum relationship between the government and the economy—where it is assumed the private economy gets smaller when government grows.

Under the heading of partial privatization, Starr argues that government outsourcing may not dismantle coalitions that advocate for greater spending in a particular area. He cites the private production of defense equipment, the construction of roads, and delivery of Medicare services by private doctors and hospitals as examples of privatization that do not necessarily lead to lower spending. As he eloquently writes about defense, "The defense companies and their employees are quite capable of determining their stake in higher military expenditures" (Starr, 1987: 5). Starr does advocate mixed private-public economies for the postal service, and even public housing, as two examples of rational policy decision making. But these are examples where the restructuring has to be comprehensive and specific. Starr notes that there is an "illusory appeal of privatization . . . to provide a single solution for many complex problems" (Starr, 1987: 16). His assessment of the record is quite different from the privatization proponents. They are more likely to:

> read the record as showing conclusively the superiority of private providers, but this is an act of heroically selective attention. Given the American experience with defense production, construction projects, and health care—all mostly produced privately with public dollars—it is remarkable that anyone could see a path toward budgetary salvation simply by shifting the locus of service production from the public sector to the

private sector. Advocates of privatization show an undue tenderness toward private contractors and an undue hostility toward public employees. They indulge private contractors their history of cost overruns; they rebuke public employees for their history of wage increases. But their preference for private provision actually reflects a deep underestimate of the skills that private firms can deploy. They underestimate the capacity of contractors to manipulate to their own advantage the incentives that are held out to them for better performance. And they underestimate the contractors' capacity to influence political decisions, either illegitimately through bribery or legally through campaign contributions and lobbying. Missing from the case for privatization is any clear sense of feedback effects—the influence on government of the enlarged class of private contractors and other providers dependent on public money. (Starr, 1987: 6)

Paul Starr's essay underscores the importance of understanding the implications of privatization arguments as applied to the broad arena of public policy. We next review a paper that was written to directly consider the arguments for the privatization of prisons.

Hart, Shleifer, and Vishny (1997) identify the nature of the contract as the key to the inherent efficiencies produced through privatization. They claim that the private "owners" have a greater incentive to innovate because they directly reap the benefits of cost reduction or increases in productivity. Government employees do not reap rewards from cost reductions or productivity increases in the same direct fashion. Hart, Shleifer, and Vishny argue that in most cases, the incentive to innovate leads to higher levels of productivity in the private sector.

Nevertheless, there are circumstances in which the incentives to reduce costs produce undesirable outcomes for the recipients of the contracted services. If acceptable performance levels are not or cannot be explicitly delineated in a contract, then the vendor can exercise discretion in reducing costs even if performance suffers. Hart et al. attribute this problem to ownership of "residual rights of control." They observe that in contracting for a service having complex determinants of performance (such as the operation of prisons), there may be aspects of the service that are not covered by the contract. Using our terminology, performance standards for prison operations are sufficiently ambiguous and vague that comprehensive and precise performance expectations cannot be delineated by the government in a contract. Under these conditions, Hart, Shleifer, and Vishny (1997) argue that the private sector's incentive to cut costs could lead to compromises in the quality of prison operations.

In another paper, Shleifer (2001) makes a strong argument for private ownership over government ownership in most situations. Shleifer examines the conditions that lead the government to "make" or "buy" services, and he concludes that the government should buy services from the private sector *unless* a narrow set of conditions is met. "These are the situations in which: 1) opportunities for cost reductions that lead to non-contractible deterioration of quality are significant; 2) innovation is relatively unimportant; 3) competition is weak and consumer choice is ineffective; and 4) reputational mechanisms are also weak" (Shleifer, 2001: 11).

It is likely that these conditions *are* often satisfied in a corrections environment. Hart, Shleifer, and Vishny (1997) already demonstrated that the first principle may apply in the operation of a prison. The quality of prisoner treatment may be difficult to monitor, and the incentives to reduce costs through such means as paying lower staff wages may have adverse effects on inmates (Camp and Gaes, 2002).

Regarding the second condition cited by Shleifer, it is not clear how important innovation is in prison operations. Since most of the noncapital expense of prison operations derives from staff salaries, the strongest incentive to innovate comes from substituting either lower-paid employees or technological innovations for the higher-paid employees found in the public sector. We have not found any study that documents technological or organizational innovations that are employed in the private sector but not in the public sector. Camp and Gaes (2000) have documented how jurisdictions have moved to greater standardization of the prison management contracts. Under these circumstances, there is no competitive edge or incentive to innovate by private companies.

As to the third condition, there really is no direct consumer demand for prison services as there might be for schools or medical care. Private citizens may be viewed as the ultimate consumers of public safety, but citizens lack a direct ability to make that purchase. The community's consumption of safety is indirectly "purchased" with taxpayer dollars, but the actual buyers are legislators and government executives whose behavior is supposed to represent the taxpayers' interests. Under this scenario, the taxpaying citizenry cannot "vote with their feet" as is possible in choosing schools or medical care in a market of schools and medical care providers. There is competition in the prison marketplace, but it is mostly between the public and private provision of prison operations within a jurisdiction. There are still only two dominant providers in the prison marketplace, Corrections Corporation of America and Wackenhut Corrections Corporation. Gilbert (2001) also has a discussion of whether criminal justice markets are genuine markets. From his perspective, the consumer of the service is the prisoner; however, "[P]rivate contractors are likely to view elected and appointed public officials as their customers and regard offenders as simply a commodity" (Gilbert, 2001: 71). In economical terms, even if there were sufficient suppliers, the demand side of the market is missing.

The last condition presented by Shleifer, reputational mechanisms, may currently be limiting the growth of prison privatization. Companies do not want to tarnish their reputations for fear of losing bids on contracts that rely on past performance. In the United States, both WCC and CCA have had well-publicized problems that may be limiting their ability to penetrate the adult prison market any further than they have. There is also recent evidence that privates are losing some of the market share of adult prisoners (Austin and Coventry, 2003).

It is important to recognize one possible implication of the public/private competition deriving from the Hart, Shleifer, Vishny analysis of residual rights of control. If private vendors are cutting costs by reducing quality because the contract does not explicitly cover specific performance benchmarks, this may also drive the public sector to lower costs to be price competitive. However, the public sector may also have to reduce the quality of its services to stay competitive in the "market." Thus, in some jurisdictions, as the privatized share increases, the overall level of prison quality may decline as the average cost declines. Second, if the real impact of lowered services inside of prison is an increase in post-release criminality, then unless a jurisdiction tracks this result it will be unaware of the long-term increases in criminal justice expenses. We realize this argument is completely antithetical to the reigning belief that privatization and liberalization in Starr's terminology will produce a more efficient production of prison services at the same or better level of quality. We propose this alternative viewpoint because it elevates the importance of performance and accountability. Prison performance measurement is the key to our understanding of not only the relative performance of private and public management, but it is also the key to monitoring the absolute performance of the costs and benefits of the prison system over time.

CHAPTER SEVEN
THE RELATIONSHIP BETWEEN COST AND PERFORMANCE AND THE ROLE OF PRISON LABOR

While the theory of the economics of prison privatization is important in understanding why the private or public sector may be more efficient or why quality may increase or decrease, the nuts and bolts of cost comparisons has been the main objective of our discussion of prison performance. Up to this point, we have focused on how to do a cost comparison, but as the previous theoretical discussion suggested, it is important to evaluate quality at the same time. To this point, we have been concerned about a level playing field. In that context, quality is brought in to make sure that cost differentials take account of the type of service being delivered. For example, if two prisons are being compared, and one requires drug treatment and specialized mental health treatment, while the other does not, this difference in mission must be explicitly brought into the cost differential. The prison required to deliver special services will be, by its mandate, more expensive, all else being equal.

The argument made by proponents of privatization is that private prisons can deliver the same services more efficiently. One approach to measuring efficiency is to make all of the adjustments we have proposed in the previous chapters to level the playing field, and then assess the difference in cost that remains facility by facility. We must also be cognizant of differences in quality, facility by facility. One of the most straightforward ways to assess cost and quality simultaneously is to analyze the different institutions on cost and quality measures function by function. This violates our earlier prescription that we should not be concerned about the disaggregation of private sector costs. The price of the contract is all we need be concerned about. However, we did qualify that principle when it came to a consideration of assessing quality in the context of cost. If the major difference between the public and private sector cost differential is due to money spent on health care, it would be important to know whether the cost differential results in a quality disadvantage. Or, has one sector figured out a way to deliver health care more efficiently without compromising health care quality?

If there are only a few institutions, then one could make a side-by-side comparison of cost and measures of quality after adjusting for any additional factors that might bias our understanding of the relationship. Sticking with health care, we can compare the per capita costs of medical services at each institution and compare these institutions on measures of the quality of health care delivery. However, we should make sure that one institution has no special advantage over another as a result of the underlying potential for morbidity or mortality. Age, sex, pre-existing conditions, either infectious (e.g., HIV infections rates) or chronic (e.g., heart disease), can all tip the balance in favor of one prison or another. This same analysis can be done for any prison function. For example, if a facility spends more on security than other prisons, does that produce a lower rate of violent or nonviolent inmate victimization?

If there are a sufficient number of prisons, then one could also approach the problem the same way we have advocated for other prison performance measures—using models that allow us to disentangle prison effects from inmate effects much the same as the hospital report card example. Using per capita cost as the dependent variable, the analyst would model individual and institutional predictors of that cost. Using the expected Bayes residuals of this model would allow an analyst to rank the prison on relative efficiency. This could be done for the overall per capita costs; however, an analysis of the separate prison functions—health care, program services, security—would be more revealing. Each of these analyses would yield an expected versus observed per capita cost for health care, security, program delivery, and other important dimensions of prison services.

Another approach would be to use the per capita cost for, say, health care as a predictor of measures of morbidity and mortality. This would inform prison management whether costs within the narrow range that is being studied have an impact on health indicators.

As an example of such analysis, prison managers may be interested in the health care per capita expenditures on the quality of health. The multilevel models could be set up to examine inmate- and institution-level factors that would be expected to be related to indicators of health, such as the prevalence or incidence of chronic and infectious disease. One might examine the incidence (new occurrences) of HIV infection, tuberculosis, and hepatitis C, even though these would be relatively infrequent. One might examine the prevalence of acute episodes of chronic disease such as high blood pressure, diabetes, and asthma. In each model, at the level of the inmate, the equation would include inmate factors that would insure that differences in institutions would not be the result of predisposing correlates of disease such as age, race, and prior medical histories. At the institution level, prison composition factors would also be included to insure an equitable comparison. Per capita medical expenses would also be entered as a prison-level variable. Several kinds of inference can be made from these models. One could first examine whether per capita expense does, in fact, make a difference in the medical outcomes. Assuming more money means lower rates of health problems, what are the per capita rates of private and public prisons? Is prison privatization implicated in this analysis? If there is no effect of per capita health expenditures on the health outcomes, it would still be interesting to compute the residuals for all of the indicators and simultaneously graph the "caterpillar" plots of all these residuals to see where the different private and public institutions fall. In this case, the level playing field also includes a leveling of per capita expenses. Let's assume that per capita expenditures have no impact on health outcomes; however, the private prisons do well relative to their public counterparts. This indicates that the private managers of prisons have achieved efficiencies in their delivery of medical care. These kinds of models should also incorporate patient satisfaction surveys to insure that the analyst is not missing something in the evaluation.

In the prison privatization literature, there has been no systematic assessment linking inmate and prison factors to cost, or using cost as an indicator of outcome. In the absence of such a link, prior claims of private efficiency may not hold up when the analysis is completed.

Prison Labor—The McDonaldization Argument for Efficiency

Implicit in many of the cost arguments about prison privatization and prison performance is whether we can save money by lowering the cost of labor. Most of these discussions, however, do not specify how labor costs will be reduced. Instead, there are often vague references to the enhanced use of technology. One approach implicit in these arguments involves re-engineering the structure of correctional work. In this section, we try to shed light on the argument about the appropriate approach to prison labor by capitalizing on recent organizational sociology literature.

A natural social experiment is underway, an experiment in the social organization and management of prisons, to wit, a test of whether McDonaldization can be extended to the field of corrections. Previous scholars have used the term *McDonaldization* as a reference to work practices that are structured to make workers more easily replaceable (Ritzer, 1993, 1998). The McDonalds chain of fast-food restaurants, faced with the economic realities of providing low-cost food in small restaurants, designed work practices that allowed it to succeed with generally unskilled, part-time workers, who were paid at, or near, the minimum wage. By being able to draw upon an unskilled pool of labor, McDonalds was able to realize its goals by effectively utilizing employees who traditionally sought short-term employment opportunities, most often teenage workers attending school, but increasingly other segments such as quasi-retired workers and immigrants.

The work practices at McDonalds were designed, in a manner reminiscent of Adam Smith's pin factory, so that tasks were broken down into individual steps that were routinized and standardized, and thus easily learned. Technology was employed in the process, as in the well-known example of replacing ordinary cash registers that have numbered keys with cash registers that have little icons of McDonalds' products. Traditional cash registers require knowledge of the prices of McDonalds' products, but with the latter type of register, cashiers simply had to locate the "Big Mac" key. Other assembly line strategies were employed, such as selling only standardized products that generally were not personalized to customers' specifications. McDonalds has since adapted to another market force from a competitor and allows customers to "have it your way." As envisioned by Adam Smith, not only were efficiencies achieved with this design, the restructuring allowed workers to quickly develop the requisite skills to take on new job functions, and workers were more easily expendable. In short, McDonalds developed strategies that allowed it to efficiently use a workforce that was less costly, especially compared to traditional diners and restaurants, where either higher wages were paid to retain trained staff, or greater inefficiencies resulted from staff turnover. At McDonalds, staff turnover still carries a price, but it is more easily managed.

No private-sector prison operator has ever publicly stated that they believe the management of corrections is a government function ripe for Mc-Donaldization techniques. What they have claimed, though, is that public-sector workers are too protected and overpaid (Crants, 1991), and/or that the government pays wages that are higher than market wages.[1] One of two principles, or possibly both, is implied in these statements. Either the government hires corrections workers who are overqualified for their jobs, and who thus receive wages that are comparable to their skills but not their job demands; or workers simply are paid wages that are greater than their skill levels. Regardless of which scenario holds, the private-sector prison firms consistently claim that they can operate prisons at much lower costs, primarily by paying correctional workers less.[2]

Both public and private corrections officials typically claim that workers are their most valuable resource, and we do not mean to imply that private prison operators feel that they can reduce corrections jobs in a manner directly comparable to the development of routinized tasks in the typical McDonalds restaurant. However, it is fair to claim that private prison operators must feel that they can realize greater efficiencies in the use of less-skilled labor, at least moving toward something of a McDonalds model. First, private-sector operators claim that public-sector workers are not being paid at market rates and that cost reductions can result from paying lower wage/benefits packages. Second, private operators claim that they can design efficiencies into prisons that require fewer corrections workers than are used in the public sector, primarily with organizational innovations, the greater use of technology, and improved facility design. Third, the private sector has developed their operational practices with a workforce unskilled or lacking corrections experience. McDonald, Fournier, Russell-Einhourn, and Crawford (1998) reported that a typical federal prison would activate with approximately half of the staff coming into the new prison that had experience at other federal prisons. WCC, on the other hand, opened the Taft Correctional Institution with only 10 percent of the workforce having any correctional experience. Furthermore, turnover of correctional staff in the private sector is much higher than that normally encountered in the public sector. Camp and Gaes (2000: 14, 47) found that nearly half of all private prisons in the United States experienced a turnover rate of at least 50 percent in a six-month period between February and July 1999. Given these factors, the claim that the private sector can use less costly and fewer workers, and the unstated claim that they are able to operate prisons with less experienced line staff that are more likely to turn over, we feel we are justified in using the McDonaldization analogy. What we call the McDonalds formula is simply the ability to successfully utilize a workforce composed of fewer and less costly workers, and the implementation of techniques that allow the firm to succeed in the face of high levels of worker turnover.

Clearly, the most controversial part of the formula is the turnover of staff. The private prison operators do not make public statements about their ability to deal with high rates of turnover. In fact, they largely say nothing about turnover rates at their facilities. Camp and Gaes (2000) surveyed the contract administrators for all private prisons operating in the United States or in a U.S. territory. With respect to staff separations among custody staff, they found that turnover was much greater on average in the private sector than in the public sector. Part of the high turnover rate in the private sector was attributable to the large number of new prisons that had opened, largely with new staff. New corrections staff, especially in their first year of employment, quit their jobs at higher rates than more experienced staff. However, even at private prisons that had been in operation for more than one year, the turnover rates were still high. Camp and Gaes (2000: 47) reported that 22.5 percent of "older" private prisons had turnover rates of 50 percent or more in a six-month period. Another 15 percent had a turnover rate between 40 and 49.9 percent, 22.5 percent had a turnover rate between 30 and 39.9 percent, and 20 percent had a turnover rate between 20 and 29.9 percent. In short, among the operating (not activating) private prisons, 80 percent of the facilities had a turnover rate in excess of 20 percent during a six-month period. Clearly, this means that private prisons constantly have to retrain staff. Many of these employees presumably come to this field with no prior corrections experience. Given these circumstances, the private sector faced with high turnover rates and inexperienced staff will have to innovate or suffer problems in prison performance.

The overriding question, then, is whether this organizational experiment in corrections is working to protect the interests of public safety for inmates and the general public as well as the economic interests of stockholders. Secondary issues include specifying the actual nature of the innovations in social organization, facility design, and the use of technology that have facilitated these changes. As noted elsewhere (Camp and Gaes, 2001), there has been little evidence presented, to date, to support the existence of meaningful innovations, although privatization proponents such as Adrian Moore make this claim repeatedly (Segal and Moore, 2002). However, the experiment in using cheaper labor with the resulting levels of turnover must be evaluated empirically, not rhetorically. There is a strong sentiment in the public sector that low rates of turnover, such as the 4.4 percent rate for the Bureau of Prisons reported by Camp and Gaes (2000) for the six months between February and July 1999, are a prerequisite to running good prisons. While intuitively appealing, this has not been rigorously demonstrated.

In summary, while a great deal has been written about the relative costs of publicly and privately operated prisons, most of the questions surrounding this issue are still unanswered. Most cost comparison studies are flawed. Reviews of the literature have not taken into account the inadequacy of the cost comparisons. The weight of the evidence has come from advocates of privatization who claim market forces should produce efficiencies. Claims not withstanding by market theorists, there are theoretical reasons to question why prison privatization will result in cost efficiencies or in better quality. Since prison labor is the largest component of cost, future studies need to be conducted to evaluate whether the costs of labor are related to the production of safety, security, health care, and other important prison functions. Since staff turnover seems to be endemic to the private management of prisons, what is its effect on prison performance?

CHAPTER EIGHT
SYSTEM LEVEL MEASUREMENT

The majority of our discussion has concentrated on an analysis of prison performance within a jurisdiction. While that unit of analysis is central to our understanding of the performance of different institutions, there are questions about prison performance that benefit from analyses that contrast prison systems. Interjurisdictional comparisons are interesting in their own right. They raise questions about broader contexts and environments. Since prison systems operate under different mission statements, even the overarching purpose of the system may be implicated in the way a jurisdiction performs. These differences may inform policy and management practices. Furthermore, some performance questions raise issues about rare events, so rare that it is possible that only crossjurisdictional comparisons will provide insight into causes and solutions. While crossjurisdictional comparisons are important, the methodological problems can be formidable. There has been a recent effort by the Association of State Correctional Administrators to develop jurisdictional performance measures that address some of the concerns arising from differences in measurement definitions across jurisdictions. We discuss that effort briefly. Then we consider how crossjurisdictional comparisons inform our understanding of rare events. We examine briefly one study by John DiIulio (1990) that used comparisons among three jurisdictions to try and draw policy generalizations about prison management. Finally, we list some of the methodological problems that one must consider when these comparisons are made.

The Association of State Correctional Administrators (ASCA) committee on prison performance indicators has developed a preliminary set of measures that can be used to compare and contrast the different jurisdictions (Wright, 2002). When we refer to jurisdictions in this context, we typically mean between and among states; however, ASCA also represents large city districts such as New York and Washington, D.C. Members of this committee were aware of some of the problems researchers, administrators, and policy makers encounter when performance indicia in one jurisdiction are used to make comparisons to another jurisdiction. There are publications (Camp and Camp, 1999; Maguire and Pastore, 1999) devoted to state-by-state statistics on all aspects of corrections. Publishing these compendia of data invites comparisons, and naive readers may incorrectly assume that side-by-side comparisons of suicides, escapes, homicides, HIV infection rates, and other indicators provide prima facie evidence of relative differences in state/jurisdictional performance. The story is much more complicated, as directors of corrections composing the ASCA membership know. Jurisdictions may define events differently. For example, an aggravated assault in one state may have different predicates than an aggravated assault in another state. The "counting rules" may also differ. Counting rules refer to both numerator (the number of instances of an indicator) and denominator decisions (the population base or at-risk pool of inmates). By defining the counting rules, these publications try to ensure uniformity in measurement; however, ASCA committee members felt these rules needed much more clarification and precision.

Another complication arises from the fact that the different jurisdictions may have custody of dissimilar criminal justice correctional populations. In one state, the department of corrections may have jurisdiction over inmates in jails and prison. Another may only have authority over the prison population. Jurisdictions use work camps and halfway house placements differently. States that extensively use halfway house placement "siphon off" their lowest-risk prisoners by placing them in other facilities. These jurisdictions may have higher rates of misconduct in their prisons simply as a result of that policy. To circumvent as many of these difficulties in comparison as possible, ASCA committee members and expert consultants are trying to develop indicia that have more precise definitions, and more complete standardization of counting rules. To circumvent some of the problems arising from jurisdictional differences in the kind of inmates under the authority of the state, criteria were established to minimize these discrepancies. For example, recidivism is only computed on inmates whose sentence is more than one year. Thus, only the recidivism rate of felons will be computed, mitigating the problem that currently exists because of systems that have responsibility for both felons and misdemeanants. The ASCA subcommittee will try to persuade the entire ASCA membership to adopt these definitions.

Homicides, escapes, and suicides are significant events and can tell us a lot about prison management. Because these events are infrequent, their occurrence at a small number of prisons, public or private, may mislead the researcher into false conclusions. To get a sense of the relative frequency of these events, an analyst may have to look across jurisdictions. Even though an escape from inside a secure perimeter or under armed escort is a relatively rare event, in most prison systems, if there is any goal of corrections that can be said to be endorsed unequivocally by all prison administrators, it is public safety. Because this goal is paramount, prison custody and security procedures are constantly monitored and improved by correctional agencies. An inmate escape typically represents the culmination of the failure of many procedures and practices. An escape often involves failures by more than one person, more than one system of control, and more than one set of procedures.

To make this point clear, let us suppose that the following safeguards have to fail for a prisoner to escape: a fence alarm does not work; staff improperly carry out an inmate count so that the prisoner has more time to escape; procedures to check on inmate escape contraband have not taken place; procedures to prevent inmate access to escape paraphernalia (tools, ropes, staff clothing) are lax; metal detectors are not working properly to detect escape tools; staff in the perimeter vehicles guarding the outside fence line are not vigilant; staff in the control room who monitor cameras are not attending to those cameras; a staff member has lost a vital key, and the system to monitor keys is haphazard. An inmate escape could be the failure of all of these systems or procedures. Many of these safeguards are redundant so that a failure in one or more is not fatal. Thus, an escape is a singular event in the sense that when it happens, it signals failures in more than one, if not many, systems of control involving many different people. Also implicated are prison administrators and midlevel managers whose job is to ensure that the controls are in place and that staff are trained and monitored.

While an escape in one prison probably signals a failure in procedures in that prison, it does not necessarily signal a systemic problem in the administration of the entire prison system. This point reinforces our first argument that system comparisons can be extremely important in their own right. Even in a decentralized prison system typical of most private prison companies, there must be systems in place to share knowledge, share best practices, capitalize on staff talent, learn from mistakes, and provide and reinforce a uniform corporate vision. Although it is difficult to measure the influence of corporate headquarters or the top levels of a government bureaucracy, there are systemic manifestations. Escape rates may be viewed as one of those manifestations. Just as an escape is an indicator of the failure of many systems of control in a prison, high escape rates for a prison system may be symbolic of management failures at the highest level of the agency. This raises many thorny theoretical and methodological questions. How do you conceptualize the organization and influence of the headquarters? How do you articulate the relationship between management at headquarters and the administration of the system? Nonetheless, comparisons at this level may be the only way to approach the systematic, empirical assessment of rare events.

Biles and Dalton (1999) provide a pertinent example. They compared death rates, both suicide and other, in their analysis of Australian private and public prisons. There was no statistical difference either in the total death rates or the suicide death rates for the two sectors. Camp and Gaes (2000, 2001) published a comparison of public and private prisons in the United States. They analyzed the escape rates, staff turnover rates, and urinalysis hit rates of privately operated prisons, comparing these institutions to institutions of similar security levels in the Federal Bureau of Prisons. In this case, an artificial jurisdiction was formed by conceptualizing all of the privately operated prisons as an entity despite the fact that the private prisons were located in many jurisdictions primarily in the south and southwest sectors of the United States. While there are some inferential problems with this kind of analysis, for escapes in particular, it may be the only way to draw any conclusion about the relative efficacy of privately and publicly managed prisons, especially for rare events such as escapes. Camp and Gaes (2001: 11) found "that privately operated prisons used more custody staff, had much higher separation rates for correctional officers, had much higher escape rates from secure institutions, and much higher random drug hit rates than the Bureau of Prisons. The homicide rate appeared to be comparable between the private prisons and the BOP, and assault rates could not be effectively compared."

A more policy driven perspective is provided by John DiIulio in his book *Governing Prisons: A Comparative Study of Correctional Management*

(DiIulio, 1990). DiIulio's comparative analysis of the prison systems in Texas, Michigan, and California drew upon data collected from the three prison systems in order to generate evidence to support conclusions about the impact of management on prison order. DiIulio supplemented this data with information collected through interviews, site visits, and policy documentation, drawing upon his understanding of differences in practices within a jurisdiction. DiIulio discusses many possible explanations for the differences in prison order found among the three systems. Among the factors he considered were inaccurate or biased data, characteristics of the inmate population, level of expenditures, crowding level, inmate-to-staff ratios, training level of staff, prison architecture, inmate social system, level of inmate treatment, inmate/staff race relations, and the level of repressive measures. All of these characteristics may have had the potential for affecting the level of prison order among these systems. DiIulio concludes, after a lengthy exposition of these factors, that none of them can completely explain the differences in prison violence in the three systems. DiIulio then discusses the management model of the three systems: the Texas control model, the Michigan responsibility model, and the California consensual model. To govern prisons, DiIulio concludes that the control model will produce the best results both for prison order as well as prison rehabilitation.

Whether or not DiIulio's analysis was correct is less important for this discussion than the fact that he compared and contrasted prison systems to gain insight into the relationship between prison management models and prison order, amenity, and service. DiIulio's analysis is important because he was trying to sort out data at three levels simultaneously: the prisoner, the prison, and the jurisdiction levels. While he probably had sufficient data to use hierarchical models to study differences in prisons within a jurisdiction, with only three prison systems, he would not have been able to construct a meaningful three-level multilevel model to compare the prison systems themselves. Instead, he did what he could, namely, try to make sense of differences in jurisdictional policies and practices that might explain why the Texas prison system had the lowest rate of prison violence. To accept DiIulio's argument, we have to be convinced that his dismissal of the differences in jurisdictions among its inmates and prisons could not account for the differences in the rates of prison violence and other indicators. Had he been able to construct a multilevel model, then we could also have looked at empirical analyses of the same set of hypotheses.

Many of the methodological problems we discussed in the context of measuring prison performance within a jurisdiction also apply to these crossjurisdictional analyses. If one were analyzing enough jurisdictions, instead of a two-level model, one could develop a three-level model— inmates, institutions, jurisdictions. At the jurisdictional level, one might construct indices that assess the management structure of the corrections systems. The jurisdictional model would benefit from organizational and public administration theory as well. We leave that theoretical development to the next researcher who tackles this problem. In this book, our interest is to develop a more modest two-level model. Nevertheless, with ASCA's interest in the future development of crossjurisdictional performance measures, there may come a time when analysts will have a much better set of criteria to begin to construct these models and address questions that cannot be answered without interjurisdictional comparisons.

CHAPTER NINE
A LIFE COURSE PERSPECTIVE
OF RECIDIVISM

W e return to the conceptualization and measurement of recidivism in this chapter. Why do we come back to this one dimension of prison performance as opposed to other ways to gauge accomplishment? As we argue in the first chapter, recidivism is implicated in the missions of prison systems that purport to offer inmates opportunities to change. In some systems, a stronger argument is made that reintegration and crime reduction are the primary goals of imprisonment. Given the formidable measurement issues noted in chapter 1, have these jurisdictions set the cross bar too high? Furthermore, why do we think of prison as a kind of last resort to insure public safety when many of society's other institutions—social welfare, family, and community—have already failed? To deepen our understanding of the role of prison in this chain of developmental events, we discuss the life course literature and the role of prison as but one institution in a criminal's developmental trajectory. This opens up the research questions to a wider horizon of issues, and we think it promotes a better understanding of both problems and potential solutions to the measurement of prison performance. Good theory is often lacking in many dimensions of criminology and criminal justice. This is especially true of a theoretically bereft domain such as prison performance. Embedding prison performance in this exciting new arena of criminological theory may promote knowledge for both those scholars who focus on life course work without comprehending the prison context, and those scholars who study prisons in isolation from this broader framework of criminal propensity.

The Life Course Perspective

Social scientists using the life course perspective study cohorts of individuals for long periods of time recording significant events and relationships from many different perspectives. There is ongoing research in Germany, for example, called the German Life History Study, in which eight thousand life histories have been collected spanning more than one hundred years of German history (Bruckner and Mayer, 1998). A criminological application of this approach focuses on events, institutions, and relationships that affect the individual's lifelong pattern of crime. One of the more famous American collections of crime-related life histories was the one initiated by the Gluecks in 1940 and recently extended by John Laub and Robert Sampson (1998). Criminologists study the factors over the life course that cause the onset of criminal activity, that elevate the rate or lower it perhaps to the point where we can say the individual has desisted from a life of crime. *Desistance* has become the term of choice for those researchers trying to understand why some individuals persist in a life of crime, and others stop—desist.

From this perspective, prison is one of many institutional experiences in the criminal life course. The rate of criminality over time is called a criminal trajectory by researchers who study these processes. There are different theoretical viewpoints about the life course of criminal behavior, and each of these variants suggests a different implication about the effect of prison on the criminal trajectory. The importance of the life course literature is that it provides a framework for understanding why criminal trajectories may change as a result of imprisonment. For prison systems that advocate reintegration and rehabilitation, prison performance translates into the impact of incarceration on lowering the criminal trajectory. This may be difficult since some researchers who specialize in life course analysis of crime suggest that incarceration itself may elevate criminal trajectories by limiting opportunities, especially work-related opportunities (see especially Bushway, Piquero, Broidy, Cauffman, and Mazerolle, 2001; Grogger, 1995; Kling, 1999; Sampson and Laub, 1993).

The life course perspective forces us to rethink the prison experience and its impact on post-release recidivism, framing questions in different ways. Does incarceration constrain criminal activity within the prison? In other words, does prison lower the criminal trajectory? If prison lowers the trajectory, is it because the institution affects criminal propensity or criminal opportunity? Does the prison experience impact post-release desistance? If it does, is it because the experience affects criminal propensity or are there also opportunity constraints imposed by increased post-release supervision? How do we disentangle any effects we observe either within prison or post-release from the process of aging (maturation)? How do we separate possible surveillance artifacts from actual desistance patterns? In other words, since inmates and supervised releasees are under increased surveillance, how do we evaluate the level of the criminal activity or misconduct trajectories in relation to a pattern that would exist in the absence of increased surveillance? How do we account for the criminal trajectory prior to imprisonment in our analysis of the individual's prison and post-release offending? The correctional specialist may not even pause to consider some of these issues unless he or she is familiar with the life course literature.

The literature on the life course of criminal behavior is abundant, and we claim no special expertise in this domain. However, there are papers that provide a summary of this literature, representing the major theoretical models, explicating the life course methods, and reviewing the empirical literature. We begin with a discussion of the paper by Bushway, Piquero, Broidy, Cauffman, and Mazerolle (2001) to introduce the fundamental constructs involved in defining desistance and criminal trajectories. We then examine the work of Uggen and Massoglia (2001) and Laub and Sampson (1998) to discuss the dominant theoretical approaches that have been used to explain how or why criminal trajectories differ from other trajectories and to investigate the basic constructs of the process. We then outline the relationships between this life course literature and prison performance.

Life Course Background

In the Bushway et al. (2001) article, the authors make an argument that desistance should be construed as a *process* by which an individual changes from offending to nonoffending and arrives at a permanent state of nonoffending. Bushway et al. distinguish between maturational theorists who claim aging is the only significant factor in desistance, and sociogenic theorists who claim desistance also involves factors drawn from theories of social control, social learning, and strain. These are processes that influence the probability of criminal behavior as people age. From this perspective, age is simply a dimension along which these processes change over time, but age itself should not be treated as a cause. Citing Blumstein, Cohen, Roth, and Visher (1986) and Gottfredson and Hirschi (1990), Bushway et al. refer to three components of criminality: propensity, opportunity, and a random component. Propensity is time varying and is affected by poor self-control, temperament, the strength of social bonds, negative labels, exposure to delinquent peers, and strain. Opportunity depends on available targets and the level of external controls that constrain the individual from committing crime. The last component is a random process[1] that introduces variability to the phenomenon.

Bushway et al. also note that even if we can assess propensity and opportunity, and we are aware of the possible randomness of criminal activity, we must also be concerned about potential biases in the way crime is measured and reported. For example, if African Americans and whites commit crime at the same rate, but there is a racial bias in arrest, then what might appear to be true underlying differences is actually an artifact of bias. Bushway et al. also present a technical discussion of ways by which criminal trajectories can be measured. One of the important points in that discussion is that the trajectories should yield important information about how the actual process of desistance occurs. Since both the maturation and sociogenic theorists believe that the trajectories change over time, it is important to discover the determinants of the beginning levels, ending levels, and shapes of these trajectories.

While the Bushway et al. exposition refers to the entire life course of criminal activity, there are clear implications for understanding criminal activity within prison and post-release for those offenders whose life course includes a prison term. Prison performance can be viewed from the perspective of how a period of incarceration impacts the criminal trajectory both within prison and subsequent to prison. Furthermore, theorists who believe strictly in the maturational perspective would be led to argue that the best way to lower the criminal trajectory during a prison stay and during a period of post-release supervision is to reduce opportunity. Sociogenic theorists, on the other hand, focus upon the strain of imprisonment, social learning opportunities, and social control mechanisms in addition to criminal opportunity. We adopt the latter perspective when we develop a model of prison performance.

Although the criminal life course paradigm is an exposition of individual criminal behavior, and prison performance is essentially an exposition of organizational behavior, we capitalize on the features of the multilevel models previously discussed because they allow us to conceptualize the organization and the behavior of individuals at the same time. As we have already noted, while institutions or prisons are composed of individual inmates, there is a unique contribution to individual behavior that is a product of the nature and qualities of the organization. A sociogenic perspective implies that a period of incarceration may either elevate and lengthen the trajectory of criminal offending, or reduce the trajectory, depending on how the prisoner adapts to the strain of imprisonment, how the prisoner develops pro-social skills and values, and how the prisoner is influenced by his or her antisocial peers. Confounding our understanding is the fact that custody practices may reduce criminal opportunity.

We represent some of the possible patterns of individual criminal trajectories in figure 9.1 using panels A, B, C, and D. Every panel has three parts: the rate of criminality prior to prison ("Pre-Prison"), the rate of misconduct and crime inside of prison or an equivalent period in the community

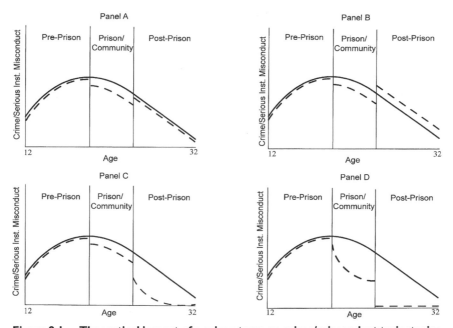

Figure 9.1.   Theoretical impact of a prison term on crime/misconduct trajectories.

127

("Prison/Community"), and the rate of crime after release from prison ("Post-Prison"). In all of the panels, we depict a criminal trajectory as if a person or a group defined by this trajectory either experienced a term of custody (the hashed bottom line) or did not (the solid top line). Thus, these two groups are considered to be equivalent other than their prison experience. Prior to prison, we assume the trajectories of the groups, whether or not they subsequently get a prison term, were the same. Furthermore, the top solid line during the "Prison/Community" period is the rate of criminality for people in the community who did not get a prison term, while the bottom hashed line represents serious misconduct and crime inside of prison.

In panel A, we assume that prison reduces opportunity but has no effect on propensity. Thus, the hashed line is lower for the people in prison than the solid line representing the people who are not in prison. When the individual is released from custody, he or she resumes the life course criminal trajectory at that lower level simply as a result of aging, but the trajectory is the same as the one for those who did not get a prison term. In panel B, we represent a "criminogenic" effect of prison. During the prison stay, an individual's level of criminality is suppressed because of custody practices that lower opportunity. However, during the prison stay, as a result of labeling, identifying with criminal norms, strain associated with labor force dislocation, family dysfunction, or other sociogenic factors, the individual's propensity to crime increases. Thus, the trajectory after release from custody is higher than it would have been in the absence of a term of prison. In panels C and D, we have two scenarios in which prison lowers the propensity to commit crime. Panel C indicates a suppression of crime in prison due to decreased opportunity and a lowering of propensity that is not apparent until the offender is released from custody. In panel D, crime decreases rapidly within prison both as a result of lack of opportunity and lower propensity, and this results in immediate post-release desistance. The ex-offender shows no evidence of post-release criminality.

These are idealized sketches of possible trajectories, and it will be difficult to separate opportunity effects from propensity effects both within prison and subsequent to prison. For example, one could surmise that intensive probation supervision decreases opportunity. At the same time, it has the effect of increasing the probability of detection. The end result is that our understanding of the changes in propensity is confounded. As we already noted, it is difficult to separate opportunity and propensity effects within prison. Almost all modern prison systems assess criminal propensity through classification assessment procedures. The result of this procedure is to place individuals with higher risk scores (higher propensities) into higher custody levels designed to reduce opportunity by restricting freedoms, increasing surveillance, and increasing regimentation. There is empirical evidence that increased custody does suppress misconduct of high risk (high criminal propensity) offenders below the level we would expect based on their risk scores (Berk and de Leeuw, 1999). If we measure propensity implications within a custody level, then we should theoretically be able to discover the effects of sociogenic factors independent of the suppressing effects of custody. Because the data requirements for a longitudinal assessment of the possibilities represented in figure 9.1 are quite demanding, we are not aware of any study that has tried to represent pre-prison criminality, prison official misconduct, and post-prison offending with the trajectory modeling that is now available (Jones, Nagin, and Roeder, 2001).[2]

A study by Piquero, Blumstein, Brame, Haapanen, Mulvey, and Nagin (2001) investigated the impact of incarceration on a sample of high risk California youth whose arrest records were gathered from ages eighteen to thirty-three after being released from the jurisdiction of the California Youth Authority. These researchers used a Poisson model and a latent class Poisson methodology found in Nagin and Land (1993) and Land, McCall, and Nagin (1996). The first model can be used to investigate differences in the rate of offending over time, and test the extent to which a period of incarceration impacts that rate. The second analysis extends this approach by also examining different patterns or trajectories of offending. The authors found that for a couple of distinct groups (nearly 28 percent of the sample) a period of incarceration is associated with increases and/or persistence in crime in their arrest rates. For the remaining subgroups, a period of incarceration had no impact on the crime trajectories.

Camp and Gaes (2004) have used data from an experiment conducted by Berk, Ladd, Graziano, and Baek (2003) to show that it is theoretically and empirically possible to separate the influences of criminal propensity, opportunity, and other characteristics of the prison regime to study whether prisons are criminogenic.

The experiment conducted by Berk et al. was used to test whether a new inmate classification system improved the prediction of misconduct. Inmate classification scores are a measure of criminal propensity. To assess the effect, the California Department of Corrections allowed the researchers to randomly assign inmates who had different security levels under the new and old classification schemes to institutions commensurate with the old and new classification scores. As a result, there were inmates who previously would have been placed in a level I prison who were placed at a level III prison instead. These inmates could be compared to those inmates who were still being assigned to the level I institution. Higher security level inmates are assigned to higher security prisons because there is a higher likelihood of criminal conduct. Higher security level institutions also use more procedures to limit opportunity and suppress crime and misconduct inside of prison. Camp and Gaes developed a theoretical model to show how the impact of criminal propensity, prison culture, and prison regime can be analytically separated and measured to test whether aspects of the prison environment have an impact on the trajectory of inmate misconduct during a prison term, as well as post-release. Prison culture can be conceptualized as the subculture that results from inmates of similar propensity living together. Prison regime is a global concept that covers all aspects of the prison environment, including the procedures prison administrators use to limit opportunity, and even the various prison programs designed to rehabilitate prisoners, as well as make the institution more habitable. By capitalizing on a subset of the Berk et al. data, Camp and Gaes demonstrated that propensity was more important than culture and regime in determining the institutional behavior of prisoners. Although the data covered low and intermediate security level institutions (California uses levels I, II, III, and IV), the same approach can be used in higher security prisons as well. In a follow-up study, Camp and Gaes are examining the impact of these processes on post-release behavior.

Criminal Life Course Theory

To inform our understanding of the prison performance measurement model, we briefly discuss the major theoretical perspectives that have been proposed to explain the criminal life course. These theories imply different models of prison performance.

Uggen and Massoglia (2001) briefly summarize the life course theories of desistance from crime. However, they consider a period of juvenile or adult imprisonment as an "'off-time' [period] with regard to important markers of the transition to adulthood" (Uggen and Massoglia, 2001: 2). Thus, custody delays or precludes the process of embedding the individual in normative institutions and roles such as marriage, work, and school. However, most prison systems support these normative institutions and roles within the fences and walls of the prison. Is there then a theoretical distinction to be made between the prison-based normative endorsement of these roles and those that are community-based? In general, this raises questions about how we view a period of custody during the life course. We turn to this question after we briefly present life course theories of desistance borrowing from the work of Uggen and Massoglia (2001).

Gottfredson and Hirschi (1990) propose a combination of propensity and aging to account for desistance. They argue that there are person-specific differences in the propensity to commit crime; however, the age distribution of crime, which they describe as invariant across many social conditions, cannot be explained by a single or combination of institutional or role-related markers. The decline in criminality, they assert, is attributable to aging rather than intervening life events such as work, education, or marriage. Moffit (1993) theorizes that there are two distinct life-course trajectories of criminality—adolescent limited and life course persistent. This is a developmental theory, and early childhood determinants launch the individual onto the different trajectories. Children with neuropsychological deficits and precarious home environments develop deficits at a very early age. As Uggen and Massoglia characterize Moffit's theory:

> Life course persistent offenders therefore develop both *cumulative* and *contemporary* disadvantages relative to their peers through a series of disrupted relationships, attachments, and academic failures. Life course persistent offenders have limited options as a result of these disadvantages, and their anti-social behavior affords them ever narrowing options to desist from anti-social behavior. (Uggen and Massoglia, 2001: 17)

Adolescent limited individuals are the much larger group of delinquents, and Moffit claims that they "suffer from a maturity gap . . . between [their] social and biological age. For example, many adolescents are able to engage in sexual relationships, but social controls restrict or inhibit such relationships" (Uggen and Massoglia, 2001: 16). Adolescent limited delinquents copy the antisocial activities of their life course persistent peers. Adolescent limited delinquents desist from crime because they have the skills to recognize the costs of crime and the benefits of prosocial activity. Life course persistent offenders are limited in these abilities.

Sampson and Laub (1993) have proposed an age-graded, informal social control theory of desistance that depends on both individual propensities and adult bonds to conventional roles and institutions. They posit that as people develop social bonds to these conventional institutions, they "gain social capital [and] they are more responsive to informal social controls that engender desistance from criminal activities" (Uggen and Massoglia, 2001: 18). The events are not as significant as the quality of the events.

Matsueda and Heimer (1997) propose a symbolic interactionist perspective on crime and desistance. This perspective emphasizes the dynamic process of the interaction between an individual's role and group identity. The more committed individuals are to prosocial groups, the more likely they will conform to informal social controls. Matsueda and Heimer (1997) view the life course "as branches in a time-ordered tree diagram, with past decisions impacting future options. Conventional role taking entails predominantly conforming behavior. Criminal roles include crime and role taking (e.g., drug dealing) that is sustained through criminal activity, as well as law-abiding behavior" (Uggen and Massoglia, 2001: 19). The life course transformation away from crime, consistent with the perspective of Sampson and Laub, depends on transition events such as marriage and work; however, Matsueda and Heimer underscore the importance of the changes in self-identity that result from new roles.

Hagan (1991, 1993) postulates a theory of criminal embeddedness. Early criminal activity with delinquent peers lowers the likelihood of later participation in legitimate adult institutions. Thus, youth are embedded at an early age in a life course trajectory of criminal activity that further isolates and precludes participation in more prosocial institutions and roles. In opposition to Sampson and Laub, Hagan's embeddedness hypothesis is less sanguine about altering the trajectories of early delinquency.

As Uggen and Massoglia (2001) point out, Sampson and Laub, Matsueda and Heimer, and Hagan all conceptualize desistance as a process of social integration and reintegration although they each emphasize different mechanisms. Uggen and Massoglia's contribution is to articulate reintegration as occurring in three domains: socioeconomic, familial, and civic. These domains are consistent with many of the interventions designed by prison administrators to reduce post-release reoffending. Socioeconomic reintegration refers to "labor force participation and educational and occupational attainment" (Uggen and Massoglia, 2001: 21). Familial reintegration refers to the quality of the marital union, the management of adult family roles of spouse and parent, and the particular problems posed by parents under criminal justice custody. Civic reintegration refers to the level of commitment of the individual as a member of his community. It can refer to the extent to which an individual identifies with civic norms such as volunteering, community service, voting, and membership in community groups and activities. This is an area of reintegration that has received little attention relative to the work on labor force participation and family.

The theoretical perspectives described by Uggen and Massoglia imply different orientations to prisons. The Gottfredson and Hirschi perspective implies a term of prison may only temporarily suppress criminality as a result of limited criminal opportunity. Any lowering of the trajectory after release can only be attributed to aging. Moffit's theory seems to suggest that adolescent limited individuals will desist prior to a period of adult incarceration. Since she theorizes that life-course persistent offenders have severe deficits that increase their criminal propensity, it would seem that criminal trajectories would be difficult to alter and that a period of prison may only lower the trajectory because of decreased opportunity. Sampson and Laub, Matsueda and Heimer, and Hagan all seem to suggest that propensity can be altered throughout the life course. Although they are not specific about the role of prison, anything that would increase (in Uggen and Massoglia's terminology) socioeconomic, familial, and civic reintegration ought to lower the trajectory independent of the effects of opportunity. However, prison also causes a discontinuity in the individual's participation in these normative institutions. Furthermore, prison has the additional detriment of marking (labeling) the offender and limiting his or her choices when released to the community. While it is beyond the scope of this book, psychological explanations and approaches such as Andrews and Bonta, *Psychology of Criminal Conduct* (1998), can also be incorporated into this broader framework. Their theory and research suggest that there are social learning opportunities to lower criminal trajectories and this orientation would be consistent with other sociogenic theories. The major difference between this psychological approach and the theories mentioned so far is the emphasis placed on learning theory. The psychologists argue that certain behaviors that are criminogenic, such as addictions and even crime itself, are learned and therefore can be "unlearned." The more sociological theorists do not dismiss this possibility; however, they also emphasize that institutional barriers that result from criminality make the "unlearning" process more difficult. Even the more psychological theories of Gottfredson and Hirschi and Moffit imply that for some groups learning to desist may be a very difficult, if not almost impossible task.

Laub and Sampson (2001) have summarized a great deal of research on criminal desistance. They distinguish between the termination of criminal behavior as the event signaling the end of criminal activity, and desistance, which they conceptualize as an underlying causal process that leads to and sustains criminal termination. Although it is difficult to do justice to their review in a limited space, they theorize that desistance depends on "turning points," those psychological or phenomenological processes that result from, and are determined by, life events such as marriage, work, and serving in the military. These institutions provide the individual an opportunity to exit their immediate criminogenic environment, a process Laub and Sampson refer to as "knifing off." Desistance is enhanced by "structured role stability." Thus, individuals adopt a daily routine that inhibits the return to crime and causes them to disassociate from their delinquent peers. Human agency is important. This entails "a new sense of self and a new identity as a desister from crime or, more aptly, as a family man, hard worker, good provider, and so forth" (Laub and Sampson, 2001: 50). Laub and Sampson also caution that "criminal sanctions—incarceration as a juvenile and as a young adult had a negative effect on later job stability, which in turn was negatively related to continued involvement in crime over the life course" (Laub and Sampson, 2001: 57). Based on the Gluecks' data (Glueck and Glueck, 1966), Laub and Sampson concluded that the impact of a long period of incarceration was most severe when it occurred in early adolescence.

Linking the Life Course Literature to Prison Performance

A model of prison performance can be linked to this broader literature on individual criminal trajectories by examining how prisons contribute to socioeconomic, familial, and civic reintegration and how they control criminal opportunity. We represent this model of prison performance as if the integration theorists such as Laub and Sampson and Uggen and Massoglia are correct. If Gottfredson and Hirschi and Moffit are correct, it may only make sense to monitor a prison's "ability" to limit opportunity while the process of aging slowly erodes the underlying compunction to criminality.

Although Uggen and Massoglia refer to prison as an off-time period, we prefer to open up the black box and view a period of incarceration as another community in which the life course of the individual is passing through. There are many other institutions and settings that envelop the individual during their life course. These institutions, such as the military, are not considered off time. Some of these institutions, as Goffman (1961) has described, are total institutions, but they are nevertheless settings in which many people experience part of their life course on their way to participation as members of a community. For the purpose of this discussion, we assume the prison setting is an opportunity to instill normative behaviors and lower the trajectory of criminality. At the same time, prisons must promote socioeconomic, familial, and civic reintegration while minimizing criminal opportunity. They must also minimize strain, counterbalance the effect of labeling, and disrupt social bonds among antisocial peers (gang members or others). This is clearly a tall order. By stating these goals at the level of the individual, in a sense we have created a new mission statement that articulates the functions of prison with the strategy to promote desistance in a more clearly defined and systematic way. This is by no means an argument for incarceration as a policy or strategy to promote integration. For many offenders, less punitive sanctions are more rational (Morris and Tonry, 1990).

Much of the empirical work on criminal trajectories summarized by Bushway et al. (2001) and Laub and Sampson (2001) roughly categorizes offenders into groups based on the characteristics of their criminal trajectories. There are persistently high rate offenders, offenders who have an intermittent pattern, those with a low rate of offending, those that have an onset late in their lifetime, and those that have an early onset. Recognizing and studying these trajectories in the context of prison interventions may inform our understanding of prison rehabilitation. Prison performance may depend on the ways programs are designed to handle prisoners who have different criminal trajectories.

In table 9.1, we characterize the connection between the individual level factors implied by the criminal life course literature and prison functions.

The prison functions that are intended to promote reintegration in the socioeconomic, familial, and civic domains are classically thought of as prison rehabilitation programs, and there is continuing evidence that programs can reduce recidivism (Gaes and Kendig, 2002). Education, work programs, and vocational training promote socioeconomic reintegration. Cognitive skills training, drug treatment, and sex offender treatment address important skill deficiencies and addictions. Familial integration is particularly difficult in a prison setting. Often prisoners are housed in remote areas far from their families. Nonetheless, prison systems have "parenting programs," and some states even have conjugal visiting privileges. Civic reintegration is also difficult because states often take away voting privileges as a result of a felony conviction, and this disenfranchisement probably reduces the offender's sense of community. Nonetheless, victim restitution programs and community service may help instill a sense of community membership in the offender. There are even opportunities within the prison system to promote civic reintegration. The New York State Department of Corrections has Inmate Liaison Committees. These promote a kind of internal civic responsibility. They allow inmates to have a "voice" and a process to express their individual and collective grievances.

There are many individual-level factors that can be thought of as related to strain. Any factor that makes prison life harsh, such as lack of good medical care or risk of assault, increases the strain of imprisonment. These have complementary prison functions that can make an institution more habitable and less stressful. The programs attend to the basic needs of the prisoner while providing a safe environment. The labeling phenomenon is a side effect of prison that cannot be circumvented. Perhaps the most that can be accomplished while someone is in prison is to provide the individual skills and training to meet the problem "head on." Lin (2000) has written that many inmates have unrealistic and elevated expectations about their abilities and post-release opportunities. On the other hand, Glaser (1969) has written about a defeatist attitude among prisoners with low expectations about their prospects of succeeding. Finding a balance between enthusiasm and diminished expectations is a difficult problem.

Criminal associations, especially gang affiliations, are particularly problematic. Much of the current strategy and thinking in corrections is to segregate and control gangs by suppressing their activities and transferring gang members to other prisons or jurisdictions (Fleisher and Decker,

Table 9.1.   Integrating the Criminal Life Course Literature with Prison Functions

Individual Level Factors	Prison Functions
Socioeconomic Reintegration	
Education	ABE, GED, Post-Secondary Education
Job Training	Industries, Work Programs, Vocational Training
Self Control / Impulse Control,	Cognitive Skills Training
Control of Addictions	Drug Treatment
	Sex Offender Treatment
Familial Reintegration	
Parenting	Parenting Programs
Promoting Family Ties	Visiting Room, Conjugal Visits
Civic Reintegration	
Community Service	Volunteer Work Inside of Prison
Victim Restoration	Victim Restitution, Restorative Justice Programs
Civic Responsibility Inside of Prison	Spirituality/Ethics Programs, Justice/Fairness within the Prison
Strain	
Health	Health Care
Mental Health	Mental Health Care
Diet	Nutrition
Safety (Occupational and Living)	Occupational, Living Standards
Risk of Assault, Other Victimization	Security-Custody Procedures
Labeling	
As a Result of an Incarceration	*Realistic Expectations*
Associations (Gangs)	
Gang Participation	Procedures, Programs to Minimize Gang Participation
Opportunity	
Criminal Opportunities within Prison	Risk Assessment / Classification Security-Custody Practices
Criminal Trajectories	
Pre-/Post-Institution Criminality, Institutional Crime and Misconduct	Procedures to Promote a Safe, Secure Environment

2001). Reducing criminal opportunity is the dominant theme in corrections. The hardware, technology, sanctions, and regimentation used by prison systems are designed to maintain prison order.

The pre-institution, institution, and post-institution criminal conduct factors that are depicted in table 9.1 are an explicit recognition of the differences in criminal trajectories of inmates. The key concept here is that the analyst must capture the rate of prior criminality, not just the amount. This is an important point.[3] Most recidivism studies use a prior measure of the amount of crime or prison misconduct when an analysis of recidivism is being conducted. It is more important to know the rate of prior criminality. For example, if we knew offender A committed ten crimes prior to his current release and offender B committed nine crimes prior to release, we might assume offender A had a more elevated prior level of crime. But if we also knew that offender A was thirty-five years old and his "criminal career" spanned twenty-five years, while offender B was only twenty-five years old and his criminal career spanned five years, that would certainly change our opinion about the relative risks of the two offenders. Likewise, it should change our analytical approach. This is why the rate of crime prior to the recidivism study is such an important dimension, and it is also why the offender's age and the amount of prior crime may not completely capture the underlying rate.

Bushway, Brame, and Paternoster (2003) have suggested that one way to approach this problem is to set up a model of the individual that incorporates the criminal trajectory as well as other individual factors or characteristics that would determine his or her subsequent rate of crime. This, of course, would include the prior rate and sociogenic factors such as having a spouse, drug addiction, education level, and socioeconomic status, to name a few. As Bushway et al. note, this could determine the expected future rate of criminality at the individual level—a kind of base rate. The extent to which prisoners last longer post-release than we would expect based on the base rate suggests a salutary impact of prison. The extent to which offenders do not last as long, on average, as expected suggests a pernicious effect of prison. Then an analyst can evaluate people with similar base rates and see the extent to which dynamic factors both inside and outside of prison affect the expected rate. To measure prison performance, we need an evaluation strategy that allows us to use the expected post-release base rates while taking into account prisoner movement during incarceration and changes in post-release jurisdiction.

One might expect that prisons are primarily composed of high rate, early onset offenders. However, given the very large prison populations in the United States, there are probably many low rate, late onset offenders as well. Since it is only recently that researchers have begun to link criminal life course theory and methods to recidivism (Bushway et al., 2003), it is premature to say how heterogeneous prison populations are in their criminal trajectories. Much of the work remains to be done. One of the first steps is to create a data source that represents conduct prior to, during, and after imprisonment. This will allow an analyst to examine the impact of prison on criminal trajectories, as well as begin to evaluate the extent to which these prison populations are heterogeneous. Since the ultimate goal of our proposal is to examine the performance of prisons, we are suggesting that we must first theoretically recognize the importance of understanding criminal trajectories of individual inmates. They have a certain momentum of their own. Then we must have an analytical strategy to measure the inertia of the trajectory, and summarize these trajectories to the prison level of analysis. Finally, we need a technique that allows us to evaluate the impact of the individual- and institution-level factors that may affect the rates of recidivism. It is difficult enough to theorize and analyze an individual-level model of criminal conduct. The models, both theoretical and analytical, become quite complicated when we combine the individual-level with the organizational-level effects.

There are already techniques that allow us to conceptualize and measure a hierarchical model of prison recidivism in which inmates move among prisons prior to their release. Mixed models of this sort are called multiple membership models (Hill and Goldstein, 1998; Rasbash et al., 2000). With these models, one can also test whether the release jurisdiction has an effect on recidivism, as well as the institution. Because some offenders from an institution will be released to more than one jurisdiction, the institution and jurisdiction are cross-classified. And because some offenders spend time in more than one prison, the level-1 units must be represented proportionally within the level-2 prisons. To model these data, a set of weights are used to apportion the different prison effects. The amount of time an inmate spends in a prison can be used to assign the weights. Alternatively, one could use some combination of time, program participation, and courses completed. We are unaware of any empirical work, to date, that has used these kinds of models to measure the effects of prisons on recidivism. These are quite sophisticated models and are not readily available in most software packages.

Although we have used the life course literature in this chapter to develop a deeper understanding of the nature of individual level desistance, the prison implications have yet to be tested. Even in prison systems that have no interest in reintegration, or whose mission emphasizes public safety, the criminal life course literature has implications for prison behavior and prison order. In prison systems that are focused on safety, policy makers may not hold them accountable for post-release recidivism; however, they will clearly hold them responsible for reducing criminal opportunity within prison. Recognizing that different prisons may contain inmates who have had different criminal trajectories will increase our understanding of how prisons suppress (or elevate) misconduct during incarceration.

We recognize that the criminal desistance literature is not the only relevant theoretical perspective we might have used to enhance our understanding of recidivism and ultimately our understanding of prison performance. Because we are invested in testing the limits of the impact of prison on post-release success and incorporating recidivism into our models of prison performance, we felt it was important to explore at least one way we can enrich our understanding of the recidivism process. The life course literature is one such way. Nevertheless, it should be obvious that by introducing recidivism into the prison performance measurement process, the analysis problems become more complicated.

PRISON PERFORMANCE TEMPLATES, USER-FRIENDLY PERFORMANCE MEASUREMENT TOOLS, AND CONTRACT COMPLIANCE

I n this chapter, we continue our discussion of performance measurement by giving an example of the types of factors one might consider in developing the multilevel model. We call this a prison performance template. These templates will vary among jurisdictions. Then we show how the work that has been done to gather and analyze the data can be put into user-friendly computer tools that allow administrators to get a view of a particular functional area such as per capita costs. Finally in this chapter, we have a discussion of contract compliance. Some proponents of prison privatization have argued that the contract between government and the provider of prison services is a breakthrough in holding prison managers accountable. We discuss the rationale for that claim.

Developing a Template

Chapter 9 is devoted to conceptualizing desistance as an indicator of prison performance. Those measurement models can get quite complicated. In this chapter, we propose a general template for the analysis of prison performance of the other major prison functions. Separate models should be developed for the major prison functions corresponding to the objectives of the prison mission. Thus, there should be a health care model, a mental health care model, a model for program delivery within the institution, a model for security custody practices, and so forth. Each model should be hierarchical. It should account for both individual-level and institution-level characteristics. The model should capitalize on the best information available, including prison audits, objective indicators, surveys of staff and inmates, and under some circumstances, narratives of the context in which the analysis is done. The model should also depend on the knowledge of corrections professionals within each functional area. These models are intended to represent the outcomes dependent on specific processes prison managers claim will meet their objectives.

We give an example of a template in table 10.1. This is an example of how to assess a prison's performance in maintaining a secure and safe en-

Table 10.1. A Hierarchical Model for Measuring Prison Security Performance

Institution Level

Independent Variables

Gang Concentration
Staff-to-Inmate Ratios
Staff Turnover Rates
Composite Measures of Strain such as
   Crowding, Size of Inmate Population
Institution Security Level
Security Labor Costs
Security Costs Other than Labor Costs
Overtime Costs for Security Officers
Composite Measures of:
   Age
   Race
   Ethnicity
Audit Measures of:
   Compliance with Post Orders
   Contraband Management
   Use of Force
   Searches
   Security Inspections
   Controlled Movement
Composite Measures of Surveys (Both
   Staff and Inmates):
   Efficacy of Shakedowns
   Aggregate Perceptions of Safety
   Perceptions of Security Procedures

Individual Level

Independent Variables	*Dependent Variables*
Specific Gang Affiliation	Official Records:
Classification/Risk Score	Violent Misconduct
Age	Sexual Misconduct
Race	Drug Misconduct
Ethnicity	Other Misconduct
Prior Criminal Trajectory	Victimization Surveys—Report of Victimization
Time Served	Staff/Inmate Surveys
Days at Risk	Perceptions of Staff Safety
	Perceptions of Inmate Safety

vironment. This is both a research and an evaluation template. There are two levels of independent variables, one at the individual level, and the other at the institutional level. The dependent variables are represented at the individual level; however, conceptually they exist at both levels. At the institutional level, they are averages. If there is sufficient interinstitutional variability remaining after controlling for the composition of inmates within institutions, then we can analyze and monitor a prison's performance. If all of the variability were explained or captured by the composition of the inmate population, then institution-to-institution variation would be solely dependent on the characteristics of inmates. Once again, we want to emphasize the importance of conceptualizing prison performance with this two-tiered approach. Analysts who study only the prison averages of inmate indicators such as violent misconduct may mistakenly conclude that differences they find among prisons are attributable to management practices at these institutions, when, in fact, these differences may be completely determined by the types of inmates housed there and have nothing to do with prison administration.

In the model represented in table 10.1, at the institutional level, there are composite measures of strain such as crowding and the size of the inmate population. There are cost indicators including security, labor, and overtime. There are composites of objective measures such as age, race, ethnicity, gang concentration, and staff-to-inmate ratios. We include audit measures: composite indicators of searches, security inspections, controlled movement, and contraband management. There are also composite measures derived from staff and inmate surveys that assess the extent to which people feel secure or believe security practices are working. Because the same indicators may not be available in every system, we propose table 10.1 as a template and not as a definitive list.

At the individual level, important variables that we expect to be related to misconduct are included to ensure that institutions will be evaluated on a level playing field. These variables include gang affiliation, the propensity to violence (classification score), demographic factors, prior criminal misconduct (as a rate), time served, and time at risk. Separate models can be developed for each important substantive area of prison performance. Each of these submodels will have its own unique set of individual and institutional variables. Similar to the hospital report card, one can develop a report card for each prison. The report card will be based on all of the areas of performance that are mandated and essential to the prison mission, rather than being based on a single indicator such as mortality. If reintegration is one of those mandates, then criminal desistance should be one of the grades.

Using these models, we can rank order institutions based on their relative performance in each of the functional areas important to prison operations, much the same way as was indicated in the chapters on inmate behavior and staff and inmate surveys. As these data and models are developed over time, we may be able to move from a concept of relative performance to one of absolute performance in some functional areas. Thus, rather than say institutions x, y, and z are in the lowest decile of health services performance, we may be able to say institutions x and y are performing below an acceptable level of performance. Furthermore, it is only through this type of modeling that we discover the most important process indicators. It will be particularly interesting to see how well audit information fares in relation to other indicia such as inmate and staff perceptions. For example, as predictors of the level of drug misconduct, how well do measures of inmate shakedowns and cell searches compare to staff and inmate survey responses to the perception of the level of drug use?

Logan (1992) analyzed scores of indicators and organized them by functional areas. The difference between our approach and his is that we recognize that some indicators are outcomes, some process. Prisons affect change in the former by monitoring and manipulating the latter. Second, we recognize the hierarchical relationship between inmates and institutions. Prisons may differ in their performance levels simply because they are composed of inmates with different backgrounds. Or, prisons may differ in their performance levels because they have more resources or more capable management. Finally, the approach is different because rather than speculate on what the relationship is between processes and outcomes, we test these causal links directly.

User-Friendly Performance Measurement Tools

Throughout this book, we have tried to demonstrate methods and techniques that can be used to develop models of prison performance. The template we just presented provides a concrete way to organize performance measures into domains of interest to prison administrators. These are the same domains that prison administrators typically monitor by program audits. We are not suggesting that administrators abandon program audits, but that they use the audit material in a more systematic way, as we suggest in chapter 2. Furthermore, the performance measures can become a part of the process of monitoring prisons on a day-to-day, month-to-month, or year-to-year basis.

We certainly do not expect that prison administrators, whether they are midlevel or high-level managers, would be saddled with the responsibility of generating the models and the statistical analyses necessary to create the performance measurement system we have been advocating. However, given the amount of continuous improvement in prison-automated data systems, many prison systems are now in a position to adopt a process similar to the one we are proposing. Many prison systems already have a great deal of automated information that could be used to generate the performance models in many different functional areas. If misconduct data were automated along with the results of random urinalyses, then it would be quite straightforward to use other inmate characteristics such as age, criminal history, prior drug use, and gang affiliation, as well as characteristics of the prisons, such as average inmate security level and average age, to generate a monthly ranking of the different prisons comparing expected to actual level of drug use performance. Prisons could easily be ranked on the basis of models of violent misconduct, drug "hit" rates, and total misconduct. The monthly trends in these data would be rather easy to graph. The modeling would be done "behind the scenes," and the results could be presented in a user-friendly format.

Given the advances in computer languages, prison jurisdictions could pool their resources and either develop the tools themselves, or contract with a vendor to help develop these tools. We provide an example of one such tool in figure 10.1 developed by Howell (1997). This is a display from an interactive computer program that allows an administrator to easily monitor per capita costs. The reader should, however, think of this as a generic screen, and substitute drug hits, serious violent misconduct, infectious disease incidence, and other such indicators for per capita costs. This is an interactive tool developed for the Federal Bureau of Prisons. Because it is interactive, it is difficult to demonstrate its versatility in a one-dimensional figure.

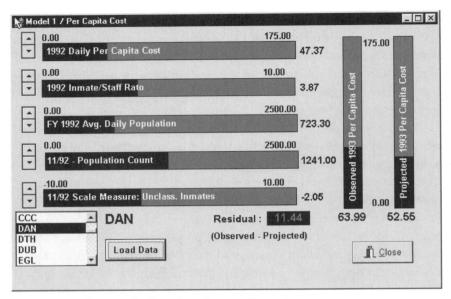

Figure 10.1. "Interactive" display of per capita costs.

In the bottom left corner of figure 10.1 is a "pick list" of institutions. In this case, the user has selected "DAN," appearing with a dark background. "DAN" is a mnemonic for a Bureau of Prisons institution. Above this selection are five horizontal bars labeled "1992 Daily Per Capita Cost," "1992 Inmate/Staff Ratio," "FY 1992 Avg. Daily Population," "11/92 - Population Count," and "11/92 Scale Measure: Unclass. Inmates." On the right side of the display are two vertical bars labeled "Observed 1993 Per Capita Cost" and "Projected 1993 Per Capita Cost." There is also a little bar labeled "Residual (Observed − Projected)." We are hopeful that, by now, the reader will immediately understand the implications of this display. The per capita costs for each institution in 1993 were modeled based on the factors appearing in the bars to the left. Each bar, whether vertical or horizontal, has the endpoint values located at either end of the bar. For example, the "1992 Daily Per capita Cost" bar is anchored by the values "0.00" and "175.00." This represents the range of values of all of the prisons in this analysis. The value for "DAN" on this particular display for 1992 daily per capita cost is $47.37, found to the right of the bar. As can be seen in this display based on the factors indicated in the leftmost bars, the model projects that the per capita cost for this prison for 1993 would be $52.55, and the actual cost was much above that projection, $63.99, demonstrating that this prison's actual daily per capita cost was $11.44 more than expected—not a good result. This display quickly shows an administrator—perhaps a budget analyst or a prison warden—that relative to the other prisons in this analysis, this institution's costs should be questioned further.

Because this is a grayscale display of a color screen, it is not obvious how different values can also be color coded. So, for example, if this institution's 1992 inmate-to-staff ratio was unusually high or unusually low, the label could appear in different colors, such as red for high and green for low. The residual values can also be color coded, indicating low, medium, or high per capita costs relative to the other institutions.

A graphical display of all of these institutions can also give the administrator a quick insight into all of the institutions at the same time. This is shown in figure 10.2 and comes from a report by Saylor (1997). This is called a trellis graph. It is really five different graphs that can be used to organize the prisons by their security level, since prison security level is such an important dimension of daily per capita cost. In the lower left plot, where Sec.Level=Low appears, is the graph depicting all of the low security level prisons, including "DAN." DAN is all the way to the right. On this graph the observed 1993 daily per capita costs are indicated with little "o's," and the projected 1993 daily per capita costs are indicated with little "+'s." The figure shows that the observed daily per capita cost for DAN in 1993 was one of the highest for low security prisons. The plot also indicates that the difference between the projected and observed daily per capita costs is the highest for DAN and should be investigated further. There are institutions depicted in figure 10.2 showing higher expected than observed per capita costs. Some of these have rather high observed costs. If a budget analyst had looked only at the observed per capita costs for these other institutions, he or she may have concluded that they were inefficient and fiscally unsound prisons. As a result of the model, quite the opposite conclusion is reached. If the model is a sound one, then it is more appropriate to draw conclusions about the fiscal effectiveness of these institutions from the residuals than from the observed values. Once the tools have been developed to depict trellis graphs and interactive displays, these types of tools require very little additional maintenance.

Per Capita Costs in 1993

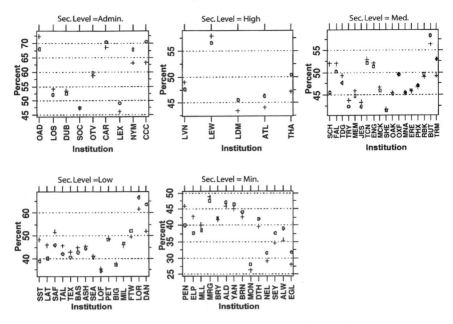

Figure 10.2. Trellis plot of per capita costs organized by institution security level.

While it is fairly straightforward to develop the analytical models and the tools, it is quite another matter to first persuade administrators to use these tools with the understanding that they are to be used as a supplement to the other procedures administrators have for managing a particular functional area. One way of co-opting administrators to use these tools is to engage them in the development of the underlying models. Table 10.2 is a list of questions that can be used to engage administrators in these tasks. These were developed by William Saylor to be used with Bureau of Prisons managers, and these questions seem to engage administrators in thinking through the task of developing performance measures. These questions step through listing objectives, defining outcomes, defining the outputs (processes affecting the outcomes), and thinking through the relationship between output and outcome. While it is important to have a process to engage managers and even line staff in performance measurement development, the key to a successful performance measurement system is

Table 10.2. Questions to Guide the Development of Operational Performance Models

Defining the Objectives

- How many objectives are there to achieve?
- What are these objectives?
- How can we determine whether (and when) each objective has been achieved?
- Is it possible to achieve the objective more than once?

Defining the Outcomes

- For each objective provide an outcome; that is, something that can be observed and is under the control, or influence, of local management.
- How can this outcome be measured?
- Does your organization maintain any operational data that would provide a correspondence to the objective that is to be achieved? If not, how can we obtain an understanding of whether the objective has been achieved? That is, how can we systematically collect this outcome measure when we can't rely on operational data?

Defining the Outputs

- For each outcome provide all the operational processes (outputs) that are expected to influence, or control the observed outcome.
- Does your organization maintain any operational data that would provide a correspondence to each operational process? If not, how can we obtain an understanding of each operational process? That is, how can we systematically collect each process indicator when we can't rely on operational data?
- For each output indicate whether the operational process can be influenced by local management, by regional management, by central management, or whether it is not under the control of management at all.
- For each output that is under the control of management, state how management can influence the process. That is, can management influence the volume, magnitude, or range of the process, and can management control the direction of the process?

Linking the Outputs to the Outcomes

- What kind of relationship do we believe exists between each operational process and the outcome it influences? That is, do we expect that an increase in a process (whether the increase is engineered by management or not) will result in an increase in the outcome? Or is there an inverse, or perhaps nonlinear, relationship? (We need to understand how each operational process influences the outcome even when management cannot control the process.)
- How can management manipulate those operational processes that they can control so as to optimize the outcome (that is, maximize or minimize the outcome, whichever is desirable based on our stated objective)?

accountability. The most senior administrators must actually hold subordinates accountable by using performance measures to gauge changes in prison functions and to seek further understanding of the mission, goals, and objectives of the prisons under their authority.

Contract Compliance

In this section, we briefly review the implications of contract compliance on the measurement of prison performance. The primary reason that we discuss this topic is to clear up some of the confusion that results from equating contract compliance with measuring prison performance. Since we advocate a model-based assessment of prison performance, we would not consider anything short of that standard to be adequate.

Richard Crane, an expert in writing prison operational contracts, has suggested that there are two approaches to monitoring contractor performance: measuring operations and measuring results. As an example of measuring operations, Crane gives the example of the number of inmates in a GED class. As an example of measuring results, he uses the illustration of "how many inmates received their GED in the last quarter" (Crane, 2001: 13). In our view neither is sufficient. We need both and we need to measure both, adjusting for the composition of the inmate population and the institution. Since no jurisdictions have achieved the level of measurement sophistication for which we are arguing, the best jurisdictions can do now is to develop a contract that is performance-based by setting standards for escapes, assaults, suicides, homicides, and other indicators. The premise in this approach is that the private institution's standard is the same as "similar" public institutions. Without a model, there is no way of knowing whether two institutions are, in fact, comparable. From our perspective, writing performance-based contract compliance is the correct way to proceed. Policy compliance and/or the measurement of institutional operations, as Crane describes them, are not sufficient. If the contract is written equating performance with policy compliance, then the contractor is justified in its sole obligation to meet that standard. That may mean the institution's performance will fall far short of meaningful performance standards. This is not the result corrections professionals want. At this point, the reader should be mindful of the Hart, Schleifer, and Vishny argument, discussed in chapter 6, about residual rights of control. Contracts may indeed be explicit; however, if they are not based on performance and well-constructed standards, they are no more likely to improve prison operations than other approaches.

Advocates of prison privatization argue that prison contracts provide a more explicit way of holding private prison operators more accountable than their public sector counterparts. There is no reason why administrators cannot make their expectations for performance explicit and hold both privately and publicly operated prisons equally accountable under the same standards. This is the only way meaningful comparisons between the two sectors can be made. Of course accountability means something much more than simply having performance standards. It also means that there are mechanisms that hold private and public administrators responsible for performance failures. But that is altogether a different discussion (Gilbert, 2001; Harding, 2001).

McDonald, Patten, Fournier, and Crawford (2003) have recently completed a report that covers the purpose, implementation, management, and monitoring of contracts for privately operated prison beds. In that report, they also make the claim that contracts are a way of providing an impetus for managers of public agencies to think about performance objectives. The act of writing the contract, they claim, forces the public agents to think through the process. McDonald et al. also raise another assumed advantage of the contract. They argue that "When structuring contracts, they [government managers] also have opportunities to create incentives and mechanisms for accountability that are more difficult to implement in existing public organizations" (McDonald et al., 2003: xxvii). We don't agree with either premise. Public managers are already devising ways to think through and implement objective performance measurement. There is certainly no reason why public administrators cannot award bonuses to the best performing public prison managers and their employees, while also demoting, firing, or transferring the managers who are substandard.

LESSONS FROM THE PUBLIC ADMINISTRATION LITERATURE

erformance measurement has received considerable attention in the public administration literature. While we do not offer a comprehensive survey of that domain, we found certain publications that resonate with our interest in prison performance measurement. It is especially interesting to see how public administration research adds to our understanding, converges on techniques similar to those we have proposed, or diverges in any significant way. While the substance of prison performance raises unique challenges, other public services have equally compelling missions and concomitant problems. A review of the public administration literature shows how important the development of performance measurement has become for all levels of government. In discussing this literature, it should also be apparent that the paradigm we have developed to measure prison performance could serve as a model for the evaluation of any government service. In the public administration literature, the impetus for performance measurement has also been associated with possible privatization of a government service and more generically with holding governments accountable. While a great deal of conceptualization of the problem has preceded the paradigm we propose in this book, the model we have developed for prison performance easily generalizes to the great majority of government services.

The earliest citation we found to performance measurement in the public administration literature was by Taylor in 1911. Despite its early entry into the literature, the level of attention increased dramatically in the 1990s. Two landmarks cited by Streib and Poister (1999) were resolutions passed by the National Academy of Public Administration (in 1991) and the American Society for Public Administration (in 1992) that called for the development and reporting of performance measures. Streib and

Poister also credit influential scholars such as Joseph Wholey and Harry Hatry (1992), David Osborne and Ted Gaebler (1992), who promoted the development of performance measurement. They also acknowledge Ammons (1996) and Hatry et al. (1992), who wrote books providing a foundation for developing sophisticated performance measurement techniques. There is also a relatively recent edited volume in the American Society for Public Administration's Classics series entitled *Public Sector Performance: Management, Motivation, and Measurement* (Kearney and Bergman, 1999).

In the following sections of this chapter, we cover how scholars writing in the public administration journals have organized theory, linked performance to privatization, promoted tools to hold governments accountable, empirically evaluated different government performance measurement systems, linked performance measurement to government contracts, demonstrated the use of multilevel models to evaluate jurisdictions, and explored the unintended consequences of these systems. The last section on unintended consequences provides a framework for administrators and policy makers that will allow them to anticipate the kinds of problems that can and will occur, when performance measurement systems are put in place.

Theory

In the public administration literature, there is a rich tradition of theory that explores and explains the reasons why there may, or may not be, increased performance arising from the privatization of public services. Much of this theory is borrowed from or overlaps with economic theory. For instance, the theory of X-efficiency (Leibenstein, 1966) makes an argument that firms (including public agencies) will only minimize costs if circumstances force them to do so. This is in contrast to public-choice theorists (Buchanan, 1978; Downs, 1967; Niskanen, 1971) who argue public bureaucracies do a poor, inefficient job of translating public demand into services. These theorists also argue that the public employee is more likely to pursue goals that are risk aversive and that promote the expansion of government programs beyond required needs in order to insure their jobs. Property-rights theorists (Langford, 1982) argue that government ownership is too diffuse, that managers have no equity interests in government programs, and that there are no incentives to manage resources efficiently.

The principal-agent theorists (Eisenhardt, 1989) argue that the line staff (agents) may have goals that conflict with their managers (principal) and that it is too expensive for the principal to verify what the agent is actually doing. Volumes have been written about these and other organizational theories. We have provided only a glimpse of what these organizational theories represent. Clearly, many of these theories overlap with economic arguments, for and against privatization, that we cover in chapters 6 and 7.

The Link between Performance and Privatization

Public administration researchers and writers have also linked the interest in performance measurement to privatization of public services. Bavon (1995) discusses this link as a by-product of the development of an international interest in the privatization of public services. From this point of view, performance measurement is a technique that measures public work effectiveness in an effort to compare it to, and to make it as efficient as, the private sector. Bavon notes that although the facts do not necessarily support the contention that the public sector is less efficient than the private sector, "the perception persists . . . spawning the resurgence of performance measurement concepts as a solution to the public sector inefficiency problem" (Bavon, 1995: 502). While Bavon discusses some of the public administration theories that purport to explain the inefficiency of the public sector, these can all be characterized as interest-maximizing theories similar to the arguments proposed by some economists that we covered in earlier chapters.

Bavon reasons that public sector managers can make the goals of the organization explicit, and then use the performance measures to insure those goals are met. Incentives and disincentives can be used to support the system. Bavon also cites public administration literature that indicates that the process of explicitly setting goals can itself have positive consequences because it infuses the organization with a kind of private corporate culture. Bavon also points out that while some developing countries and a few more economically advanced countries such as Britain, Australia, and New Zealand have subscribed to government performance measurement for some time, the U.S. federal government has only adopted the idea since the development of the Government Performance and Results Act (GPRA) of 1993. Even many of the states and localities were ahead of the federal government in developing performance measurement systems.

Government Accountability

Holzer and Halachmi (1996) emphasize the use of performance measurement systems to insure government accountability. The idea is that legislators, the public, and other external monitors who have an interest in government performance have the same information as managers of the public agencies when they use it to make policy decisions and to evaluate the agency's performance. Measurement, these authors argue, makes government decision making more transparent. These authors go on to cite a wealth of available resources on performance available in the public domain. These include reports, books, a quarterly journal—*Public Productivity and Management Review*—and handbooks. These resources address issues of data collection, development of performance measures, critical analysis, management issues, tools, formulae, and recommendations on setting up the performance measurement system. These resources have been written for all levels of government—local, state, and federal. These authors also cite examples of model programs in which performance measurement systems helped solve problems, improve services, and increase efficiency.

Empirical Analysis of Performance Measurement Systems

In recent years, the public administration literature contains articles that use survey and other techniques to evaluate the effectiveness of performance measurement systems. For example, Streib and Poister's (1999) research uses a survey of municipal districts with a population above twenty-five thousand that have developed centralized, citywide performance measurement systems. The responses to their questionnaire show some parallels to what we have suggested for prison performance measurement. For example, Streib and Poister found 65 percent of their respondents indicated that performance measures were derived from the mission, goals, and standards of the city programs and departments. For the most part, the city managers used the system to track performance over time. Although survey respondents were more equivocal about whether the measures were developed because of data availability or because of the importance of the process being monitored, there did seem to be logistical problems in keeping the system up to date and in distributing the information. While the great majority of municipalities used managers to develop their system, jurisdictions did not typically use lower-level employees during development. The respondents did indicate that there was some trouble in maintaining support for the system from lower-level employees, managers, and sometimes citizens.

Streib and Poister also asked questions about the functionality of the performance measurement systems—the extent to which the system resulted in improvements in their jurisdictions. The respondents indicated that the measurement system did improve manager accountability, helped improve the focus of employees on organizational goals, and somewhat improved service quality. However, on the other side of the ledger, it had less of an effect on the cost of city operations and employee motivation. Although these data are interesting, they are based on responses of a senior official in each surveyed municipality. It would have been informative to survey employees at all levels of city government. We suspect that senior officials have more of a stake in the system than junior employees.

Kelley and Swindell (2002) offer another perspective on the evaluation of performance measurement. They compared administrative measures with citizen satisfaction surveys in different municipalities. Earlier in this book, we consider different perspectives on who is the true consumer of prison services. While there is disagreement about the consumer of prison services, there is much less ambiguity in defining the consumer of most municipal services, namely, the citizens for whom these services are intended.

Kelly and Swindell analyzed administrative performance measures and customer satisfaction surveys in thirty jurisdictions for services provided by police, fire and medical emergency personnel, road maintenance employees, and parks and recreation staff. In prior research, when there were discrepancies between administrative measures and citizen surveys, researchers concluded that there was either no link between the two, or that citizens were not good judges of these services (Brown and Coulter, 1983; Percy, 1986; Stipak, 1979). Kelly and Swindell, on the other hand, emphasize the idea that changes in administrative data may not influence citizen perception because an individual's interaction with a government service may have little or nothing to do with the dimensions captured by the administrative data. They provide the example of perceptions of police performance. While the police managers may monitor crime and have an indication that crime is decreasing, citizens may evaluate police performance based on their everyday non-crime-related interactions. Thus, rather than focus on the level of crime in their neighborhood, especially if there is a low crime rate, citizens may judge performance on how traffic is handled, or how they are treated during a routine police contact. Thus, Kelly and Swindell propose that there should only be congruence between some administrative outcomes and citizen satisfaction.

While Kelly and Swindell found the relationship between administrative outputs and citizen satisfaction to be relatively low, they chose not to dismiss the citizen surveys. They noted that the low relationships could have been due to survey methods and also that labor intensive services (fire and police) may be evaluated differently by citizens than capital intensive services (roads and parks). Furthermore, it may be the citizen's personal experiences with a service that determine his or her attitudes. If someone never experiences a fire, or rarely is involved in a crime, what experiential basis do they use? Thus, rather than dismiss citizen surveys, it is important to investigate further where and why they may diverge from administrative measures. Prison administrators might heed this advice and monitor prison performance by measuring the opinions of inmates, staff, and citizen constituencies as part of their performance measurement system.

Wang (2002) distinguishes outputs from outcomes in the same way that we have differentiated processes and outcomes. Another way of making this point is to distinguish intermediate outcomes or outputs from the outcomes representing program or policy goals. Thus, an output is a measure of the amount of a service or intervention, while outcome is a measure of the achievement of a service or policy goal. Wang argues that U.S. governments have historically collected output measures; however, a more recent emphasis has refocused attention on outcomes. Wang was also interested in the services provided by municipal governments, and the extent to which elected officials, as opposed to city managers, police chiefs, and finance directors, were more interested in outcomes than outputs. The service he focused on was policing, which is apparently the local agency that is most likely to develop performance measures. The output measures Wang used were number of calls for services, officer patrol miles, number of investigations, the arrest rate per policeman, and the number of patrol dispatches per policeman. The outcome measures included resident's ratings, clearance rate (the rate at which police solve crimes), crime rate, victimization rate, perceptions of citizen safety, citizen's ratings of police courteousness, and police response time. All of the officials, elected or appointed, preferred outcomes over outputs as performance measures. Police chiefs strongly favored citizen-evaluation measures. So even though Kelly and Swindell found little congruence between administrative and citizen evaluations, it appears that at least in Wang's sample of jurisdictions, police chiefs prefer feedback from citizens.

Boyne, Gould-Williams, Law, and Walker (2002) examined the impact of what are called Best Value performance plans in the United Kingdom on the development of performance measures, and ultimately on the accountability of jurisdictions to consumers and elected officials. These plans were the result of law requiring jurisdictions to provide a plan specifying how managers responsible for a service and the consumers of the service could judge or rate the jurisdiction's performance. The researchers examined the implementation of performance plans in Wales. These plans were supposed to include measures of the quantity, quality, speed, and efficiency of services, as well as customer satisfaction and direct measures of progress and improvements in the equity of service. Boyne et al. found that the Best Value performance plans did not generate information that was particularly useful for holding the jurisdictions accountable. However, their assessment occurred at an early point in the development of these plans and data improvement did occur over the course of the pilot period.

Heinrich (2002) addresses a fundamental question in her analysis of performance measures. She poses the question as to whether outcome measures in the absence of a control or comparison group can provide meaningful information. To address this question, she analyzed data that were collected in conjunction with the Job Training Partnership Act (JTPA). This program is a $5 billion, federally sponsored, employment and training program; however, the responsibility for operating the program rests primarily with state and local jurisdictions. The primary goals of the JTPA are to increase long-term wages for participants and to reduce welfare roles. Data have been collected to monitor the value of this program. Heinrich capitalized on individual-level, experimentally derived data along with information about sixteen different jurisdictions providing the training. The data were collected for three years, 1987 through 1989. This provides forty-eight level-2 measurements of the sixteen different training jurisdictions, allowing her to perform multilevel modeling. Her primary substantive interest was whether measuring performance outcomes is a meaningful way to evaluate a program.

In her analysis, the dependent variable was the wages earned by program participants in the first year after the training ends. Heinrich's distinction between outcome and impact is much different than the distinction we have been drawing between outputs and impact. To measure *outcome*, she analyzed the wage data for only the *program participants*. To assess *impact*, she used the data for both *program participants* and *experimental controls*, and included in her model a factor (parameter) that tests for the difference in wages as a result of whether or not the person participated in a JTPA program. In both analyses, she used characteristics of the training jurisdiction, such as its location; whether a private industry council administered the program; the percentage of services provided by the contract administrators; the percentage of performance-based contracts in the jurisdiction; the minimum number of standards the contractor providing the job training service must meet to get a performance bonus; and whether the contract administrators used performance bonuses to service "hard-to-serve" groups. She then compared the results of the two analyses, examining whether these jurisdictional-level factors were significant determinants of post-program wages in both models. If the models yield the same understanding, then this demonstrates that one can look only at program outcomes over time without having to construct an impact assessment—whether an experiment or quasi-experiment. She found that the jurisdictional factors we listed above were important determinants of post-program wages, regardless of whether she used only the data from those receiving training or whether she used the experimental and control clients, and tested the training effect. This supports the conclusion that at least for JTPA performance measurement, you only need to look at outcomes for *program participants*.

One of the factors she examined was the weight a jurisdiction assigned to the employment rate that was achieved. In other words, managers in those districts closely monitored how many trainees were actually getting jobs. She writes that this is one of the most important performance standards in the JTPA program. The greater the weight a jurisdiction gave to the employment rate, the higher the average earnings of participants in that jurisdiction. A one-percent increase in this weight resulted in a $94 increase in the one-year wage for the program participants compared to the control group. Thus, jurisdictions that emphasize the employment rate they are achieving for their clients produce higher average wages for those clients. This is strong evidence that if there is local accountability for a program and there is a commitment to monitoring programs outcomes, this can have a dramatic effect on program success. This should be true of prisons as well as other government services.

Heinrich's analysis is extremely important, because it is based on an experimental assessment of the JTPA. This allows us to rule out possible artifactual results, and instead, concentrate on whether we can measure jurisdictional indicators that predict program impacts. In the context of prison performance, there have been many quasi-experimental evaluations of programs and policies that have established the impact of a particular intervention. With this knowledge in hand, we can experiment with different performance measures to see how they are related to program goals without having to reconfirm the program impacts with an experimental or quasi-experimental design.

Heinrich's work does raise the question, however, of whether we need to do an impact analysis of an intervention or procedure prior to using process data in a prison performance model. We think that this depends on the complexity and "face validity" of the intervention or procedure, and perhaps the cost as well. For example, if we were to spend a great deal of money to pilot equipment to interdict drugs in the prison visiting room, and we had no evidence beforehand that the procedure indeed works, we may want to do a formal evaluation first. Once the effectiveness of the interdiction technique is established, then we may only need to measure process indicators such as the percentage or number of visitors screened as an intermediate output and use the random urinalysis drug hit rate as the impact measure to monitor institution performance over time. However, if prison health officials wanted to reduce the rate of transmission of tuberculosis and introduced screening procedures as the intervention, there is already evidence from the public health literature on the effectiveness of screening. Rather than do a formal evaluation of the efficacy of screening, one could measure the proportion of the population screened (output or process measure) and the incidence of tuberculosis over time (outcome measure) to monitor the performance of prison health services.

Government Contracts and Performance Measurement

There has also been an attempt in the public administration literature to examine the nature of government contracts with private firms that provide public services, and link this to performance standards. Blasi (2002) examined government contracts for human services provided by for-profit and nonprofit organizations. Blasi reviewed forty-six contracts held by either a city or county agency. He determined whether there were performance criteria set forth in the contract and whether the contract had any accountability clauses. Most of the time the contracts called for the reporting of some level of services delivered. In a few cases, customer satisfaction surveys were required. It was rare that the contracts specified the measurement of long-term goals of the program. Unfortunately, Blasi's study was restricted to only two jurisdictions.

The recent report by McDonald et al. (2003) describes how the federal and state governments monitor their prison contracts. In their report, McDonald et al. cite the performance-based contract developed by the Federal Bureau of Prisons. The bureau wrote into its contract with Wackenhut Corrections Corporation a set of vital functions the contractor had to meet to fulfill its obligations in operating the prison in Taft, California. It provided financial incentives for Taft to reach certain performance goals and gave Wackenhut responsibility for establishing its own quality control system to insure that the vital functions were being met.

As McDonald et al. further note, most jurisdictions do not monitor institution performance measures for their contract facilities. Instead, they focus almost exclusively on contract compliance and occasionally on cost comparisons. As these authors point out, comparing the performance of public and private facilities within the same jurisdiction will require a well-developed automated data system, a contractual obligation for the private company to participate in the performance measurement system (and be compensated for participation), a system's ability to account for institutional differences in the composition of the prison populations, and the capability of analyzing performance differences, recognizing that it requires trained social scientists to accomplish these tasks. McDonald et al. advocate neither for nor against progress toward such a system, but point out the barriers that must be overcome.

Multilevel Models in the Public Administration Literature

While we have already emphasized the importance of multilevel models in the analysis of performance measurement, we found another example in the public administration literature demonstrating why multilevel models are the preferred technique.

We have already reviewed Heinrich's (2002) paper in the section on empirical analysis of performance measurement systems. She used a multilevel model to conduct that work. However, Heinrich and Lynn (2000) have also published a paper to demonstrate why multilevel models are the preferred approach to analyzing the performance of government jurisdictions. Since their results offer yet another insight into the advantages of multilevel modeling, we review their work in this section.

Heinrich and Lynn (2000) discuss the state of the art in analyzing the relationship of governance to institutional and individual performance. *Governance* is a term used in the public administration literature to refer to the organization and structure of public administration. They try to show how operational definitions of governance can be directly translated and measured in a multilevel design.

To demonstrate how to use multilevel models, Heinrich and Lynn used two separate data sets to analyze the Job Training Partnership Act programs. They investigated the administrative structures and management incentive policies that various sites used to enhance job training. They characterized administrative structures depending on whether the organization responsible for training was public nonprofit, private nonprofit, or for profit. They also examined the influence of performance incentives in service provider contracts on client outcomes. To contrast analytical strategies, Heinrich and Lynn used Hierarchical Linear Models (HLM) and ordinary least squares regression (OLS) procedures to analyze their data. To conduct an OLS analysis of individual outcomes, Heinrich and Lynn linked the site level data to the appropriate individual records. For the OLS analysis of the site-level outcomes, they aggregated (typically averaged) the individual level data for a given site and then linked these data to the site level data. Thus, there were three analyses: an HLM approach which organized the individual (level-1) and organizational (level-2) echelons hierarchically, each level having its own set of variables predicting the outcomes; the OLS analysis of individual level data that merged the level-2 organizational data onto the level-1 individual level records; and the OLS analysis of level-2 data, which aggregated the individual level information, and then assigned that data to the appropriate level-2 organizational unit.

In one data set, there were only sixteen level-2 organizational units, while in the second data set there were four hundred level-2 units. HLM procedures allow the analyst to test the extent to which there is site variation in the individual level outcomes. This is done by calculating the intra-class correlation, which measures the level of inter-site variation relative to both the inter-site and within-site variation. Heinrich and Lynn found that in the first data set about 3 percent of the variation in outcomes was due to differences in sites. In the second data set, they found that up to 39 percent of the variation in outcomes was due to site differences.

The dependent variable in these studies was the post-program earnings of the participants. In comparing the HLM and the OLS estimates for the first study, where the between site variation was small (3 percent), there were no substantive differences in interpretation of the effects of the individual and organizational level variables. Either model gave the same insights. Despite the fact that both analytical approaches yielded similar interpretation, Heinrich and Lynn note that the HLM procedure allows the analyst to describe how much of the variation in individual outcomes is attributable to individual-level characteristics or organizational influences. This clearly allows the policy maker to understand how important the organizational variables are relative to the attributes and characteristics of the individuals.

In the second data set, where the inter-site variation was much higher, there were substantial differences in interpretation of both the individual and organizational variables when comparing the HLM to the OLS analysis of the individual level effects, although, as Heinrich and Lynn noted, there was also a great deal of similarity in the results. In the final comparison, however, the OLS analysis of the aggregated data produced much different results than the HLM model.

The HLM models indicated that relative to the public nonprofit contractors, the for-profit contractor and the private nonprofit contractors achieved higher post-program wages. Furthermore, sites that were given performance incentives also achieved higher post-program outcomes than their counterparts. The HLM model showed that these site effects were stronger than site effects represented in the OLS analysis of *individual data*. The OLS analysis of *aggregated data* indicated that only the for-profit contractors achieved better results. This model gave no indication of the importance of performance incentives. Furthermore, an analyst would have mistakenly concluded that private, nonprofit contractors did no better than their public nonprofit counterparts.

As Heinrich and Lynn's analysis demonstrates, using HLM models allows the analyst to advise policy makers on the importance of organizational influences. In both cases, individual characteristics have more of an influence than organizational characteristics, although this was much less true of the second data set. Furthermore, they were able to show that individual factors do not account for a great deal of the variation encompassed in individual variation in wages. Factors such as age, race, sex, whether a welfare recipient, whether single head of household, extent of education, work record, training services received, and prior earnings only accounted for 9 percent of this individual (within) level of wage variation. The contract characteristics accounted for 68 percent of wage variation that was attributable to the organizational characteristics. Just to be clear about this, it is typical in these HLM models that variations in the characteristics of individuals typically account for (explain, predict) more variation in the dependent variable than differences in sites or organizations. However, when you try to model individual characteristics and organizational characteristics, you are more likely to find factors that account for a higher percentage of the organizational variation than you are for the individual variation. This is true of prisons, schools, and hospitals as well.

The public policy consequences implied by the results of many HLM models is that characteristics of individuals are more likely to account for program outcomes such as wages, finding a job, school success, and desisting from crime than organizational features. However, when interventions or programs can have an impact on the individual and there are important jurisdictional or organizational factors that determine success, these latter factors are typically very important in "driving" those success rates.

The Unintended Consequences of Performance Measurement Systems

One of the most compelling publications we have found, to date, in the public administration literature is an article by Peter Smith (1995) on the unintended consequences of using performance data. We found this piece compelling because it was the most thorough and insightful examination of issues we have only tangentially or superficially considered. We devote the rest of this chapter to Smith's paper, using his section headings to represent his dissection of the problem. Where we could, we provide examples on the unintended consequences of monitoring prison performance.

The paper by Smith (1995) drew upon his experience with the United Kingdom's public sector. At the heart of his analysis is the idea that the performance measurement of humans can be corrupted by the very fact that the "controller," who is monitoring such performance, can be frustrated by the "self-controlling human beings." While performance measurement of physical systems allows for feedback and correction, the measurement process does not typically affect the performance of the system itself (absent the Heisenberg principle of uncertainty in quantum mechanics). However, human agency can contravene the measurement process of human performance.

Smith discusses eight sources of unintended consequences. His examples anticipate possible problems with the process of prison performance measurement. Understanding how these problems arose in the United Kingdom may help managers avoid these problems when they implement these systems in their respective jurisdictions. He argues that the primary purpose of performance measurement is to monitor the activities of the organization relative to an implicit or explicit set of goals. This allows the managers to set targets and then try to influence the behavior of line staff to move in the direction of those targets. Since line staff will know there are consequences to meeting those goals, both rewards and punishments, the line staff may act to subvert those goals if they are not aligned with their own immediate circumstances. As Smith also notes, "any divergence of objectives between the two parties compromises the ability of the principal [manager] to secure an appropriate level of effort from the agent [staff member]" (Smith, 1995: 283). As a result of this tension between principal and agent, Smith argues that there are eight distinct types of unintended consequences of performance measurement: tunnel vision, suboptimization, myopia, measure fixation, misrepresentation, misinterpretation, gaming, and ossification. He claims that all eight of these unintended consequences result from the divergence between the goals of the staff and their managers. We use both his examples and those from our own experience to amplify the eight principles.

Tunnel Vision

Tunnel vision is the unintended consequence that follows from management's selection and emphasis of a performance indicator "at the expense of unquantified aspects of performance" (Smith, 1995: 284). Smith discusses the performance indicator adopted by the UK National Health Service to monitor the perinatal mortality rate. This is certainly a key indicator of the effectiveness of maternity services. But as Smith points out, by focusing almost exclusively on this measure, the UK National Health Service was inadvertently causing a distortion in the nature of maternity services with regard to the overall quality and "experience of pregnancy and childbirth for healthy mothers" (Smith, 1995: 284). Smith mentions here that one of the attendant dangers of trying to measure too much is that it becomes very difficult to change behavior along too many dimensions. He also notes that unlike the private sector, which can usually focus on a single unifying measure of revenues and profits, the public sector may lose focus by concentrating on one measure to the exclusion of others. Unfortunately, public sector organizations usually have broad mandates, and many service impacts fall outside of the set of outcomes that are measured.

There are several lessons to be learned for the measurement of prison performance. The first is that the performance measurement process must be carefully considered and rethought over time. Were we only to concentrate on measures of control, we would lose sight of other important correctional goals involving inmates once they are released from prison. Second, it may be easy to overwhelm administrators with too many performance measures. We have presented some rather complicated models involving a great many performance measures and other factors that must be accounted for in order to draw meaningful conclusions. The good news is that senior managers need not have the responsibility to monitor every facet of the system we are proposing. In fact, it is more practical to allow midlevel managers to specialize in their particular prison domains. The security experts track the security indicators. Health administrators monitor health indicators. Then these components all report to senior managers what they have observed and their particular insights into the process. We have observed that certain managers in the Bureau of Prisons closely monitor performance indicators and use that information to correct problems. For example, we observed an expert in security issues closely monitor drug hit rates and drug misconduct across institutions. As he observed anomalies, he would call institutions to find out why they had not met their quota of drug tests, and more importantly, what they were doing about high hit rates. This kind of proactive use of performance measurement analysis is what statisticians call continuous process monitoring. To a prison administrator, it is continuous observation and accountability.

Suboptimization

Suboptimization, as it is defined by Smith, "is the pursuit of narrow local objectives by managers at the expense of the objectives of the organization as a whole" (Smith, 1995: 286). This is particularly problematic when the local goals and targets conflict with the "central office" goals and targets. This problem becomes more acute the more management is devolved. Thus, if a penal system provides a tremendous amount of discretion to the warden, it is more difficult to make the local and the central office goals and targets compatible. We argue that without performance measurement, there would be little or no proof of the narrow pursuits of the local administration.

Myopia

Myopia occurs when it takes a long time for an organizational policy change to impact the behavior of the line staff. Since most performance indicators are snapshots of a point in time, it is sometimes difficult to capture the long-term targets. Thus, some performance indicators that are being measured now are the result of management interventions that occurred in the past. Furthermore, interventions occurring now may only have an effect sometime into the future. This is particularly true of recidivism as a prison performance measurement. When an analyst measures a one-year recidivism rate of a release cohort he or she is evaluating interventions, procedures, and policy several years back in time. Complicating the interpretation is the fact that a release cohort is a mixture of individuals who have vastly different exposures to prison. The release population is a distribution of offenders who have spent a few months to many years in prison. How do we hold people accountable, and how do we sort out the consequences of different policy interventions? This is a case where an evaluation study would yield a great deal more than the simple monitoring of the performance indicator. The performance measure may indicate that further attention must be given to a phenomenon; however, it is more likely that further research will have to be conducted to draw conclusions about cause and effect. A General Accounting Office report (1997) recommends evaluation studies as a way of supplementing information garnered from performance measurement systems, and as a way of accounting for external influences that may affect the program's intended outcomes. As we argue above, however, this may only be necessary for complex or costly interventions.

One of the by-products of myopia, according to Smith, is that if managers move around constantly, it is difficult to hold them accountable for long-term strategies. If a warden moves every two years, it is difficult either to praise or blame him or her for the success or failure of long-term goals. As Smith points out, in those public sector organizations that only have short-term targets, this is not a problem. He mentions refuse pickup and welfare payments. But he points to education and policing as being particularly susceptible to myopia. Clearly some corrections outcomes would also fall into this latter group of measures.

Smith provides several strategies to circumvent and overcome myopia. One may measure outputs instead of outcomes. If the long-term goal is to reduce a particular infectious disease, one can hold an agency accountable by measuring contemporaneous processes such as vaccination rates. Smith argues, however, that performance indicators are almost always intrinsically myopic. He also claims that "long term issues can usually never be satisfactorily captured by performance indicators. It may be necessary to encourage managers to pursue long term objectives by means other than formal performance measurement schemes" (Smith, 1995: 290).

As we mentioned, formal evaluations can address questions about policy interventions. In fact, we have provided many such evaluations ourselves to prison management. Our experience with these evaluations is that management is often impatient about waiting for the results and they think evaluation outcomes have a short shelf life. According to this point of view, any finding that is more than a year or two old may no longer be true. This latter criticism may, in fact, be relevant. Perhaps a performance system should integrate findings from an evaluation that can be used to generate process and outcomes measures that will give managers some assurance that contemporaneous performance indicators are consistent (or not) with the results of prior evaluation research. For example, using a quasi-experimental design, Saylor and Gaes (1997) found that vocational training (VT) and prison industrial work experience decreased the likelihood that inmates would be rearrested after they had been released from prison. This study was conducted during the period 1983 to 1987. But, have there been changes in the effectiveness of training over time? Or, have there been changes in the economy that make it more or less likely that inmates will be able to find a job after their release? A performance measurement system that tracks institutional rates of prison VT training and work experience, and also tracks post-release outcomes, may at least suggest whether such impacts hold up over time.

Measure Fixation

Measure fixation means that managers attend to the performance indicator rather than the objective itself. This is especially true if the performance indicator does not fully capture the intent and meaning of the goal that it is designed to represent. Smith describes the UK government objective of reducing waiting time for elective surgery. The performance measure that was developed portrayed the number of patients who had to wait more than two years for elective surgery. In fact, the UK "Patient's Charter" stated that no one should wait more than two years for elective surgery. The performance measure indicated no patient in the United Kingdom had to wait more than two years; however, this resulted in the average wait time increasing for patients and in an undesired effect that patients with minor surgery were benefiting from the waiting time initiative, while those with more serious elective surgery were suffering.

As strategies to reduce measure fixation, Smith recommends the development of multiple indicators and the judicious choice of those indicators. In the case of health consequences, he also discusses seeking the opinions of clients. As he further notes, sometimes it is not easy to identify all clients. He provides the example of welfare benefits. If one were only concerned about the client satisfaction of the welfare recipient, the agency might ignore the taxpayer as client. The latter may be more concerned about welfare fraud.

It is easy to think of a parallel fixation with measurement in corrections. Indicators similar to the ones noted by Smith on reduced waiting time for elective surgery can be developed for many health performance measures inside of a prison. For example, in an effort to increase the use of diabetes clinics, where inmates learn to cope with their illness, a health professional may monitor the proportion of known diabetics who actually attend the clinic. But this may miss entirely the purpose of such measurement. Diabetics who learn to monitor their blood sugar levels, who keep their weight down, and who are taught to look for signs of debilitation can guard against advances in the disease. Simply knowing whether they attend a clinic does not insure they actually come away better prepared. Thinking through these performance measures is a way of guarding against measure fixation. In the diabetes example, in addition to tracking the proportion of ill inmates who attend the clinic, it is also important to monitor outcomes such as acute episodes associated with diabetes.

Misrepresentation

Misrepresentation is the "deliberate manipulation of data so that reported behavior differs from actual behavior" (Smith, 1995: 292). Smith claims that as the importance of a performance indicator rises, there is more pressure to deliberately manipulate the performance measurement system. This may be especially true if the information is input by those who have a high stake in the outcomes. Readers may recall an event reported in the newspapers several years ago in which a post office supervisor was directly manipulating the major performance goal of fast delivery by personally delivering the specially marked mail to other post offices. Auditing and sanctions for misrepresentation can limit the fraudulent manipulation of data. Smith also notes that there are creative ways that are not fraudulent to "shape" the data. He provides an example of a medical provider who may have the choice of a diagnostic code for a patient and chooses the one that implies the greatest workload. In corrections, staff may make similar choices.

We have found that one way to reduce the process of creative or fraudulent manipulation of data is to design a performance measurement system that is not so transparent or obvious to the people entering the data. Because most of the data that has been collected by the Bureau of Prisons comes from the database used by staff to record their interactions with inmates, each transaction is viewed as part of the daily routine of entering data. Thus, instead of viewing these data ultimately as measures of performance, they are seen by the staff member as important administrative data to conduct their business.

While this safeguards against manipulation, it does not guarantee it. Staff members may be given instructions by their supervisors on how to enter certain kinds of data. In fact, in some circumstances supervisors may give subtle or implicit signals that the recording of certain kinds of data may jeopardize their jobs. In the competitive environment of prison privatization, both public and private sector employees may feel pressured to creatively enter the data. When the data come directly from summarized pieces of paper, performance indicators are even easier to manipulate. We have seen quite a few systems of performance measurement in the correctional setting that are based upon some summary sheet of information that is used to record monthly data on significant incidents such as the number of assaults, drug "hits," and walkaways. Rather than keeping a running tally, or culling the data from an administrative database, the person charged with the responsibility calls the captain's office for the month's totals. This invites deception and exaggeration. Line staff may be less likely to have a vested interest in the institution outcomes. Vesting them with the responsibility for entering data in an administrative record based on their daily interactions with inmates may minimize manipulation.

Misinterpretation

Misinterpretation results from the complicated circumstances arising from publicly run organizations. Smith's explanation of this phenomenon bears repeating.

> In practice, many of the production processes in the public sector are immensely complex, and building a realistic model of them is severely taxing. This problem is intensified by the fact that most public sector organizations must continue to operate however difficult the local environment, in contrast to firms, which can continue to cease trading in adverse conditions. Full account must therefore be taken of the external environment in which public sector organizations are operating when inferring the nature of the production function and assessing performance. Thus, even if the available data were a perfect representation of reality, the problem of interpreting the signals emerging from the data is often complex. In other words, although in possession of all of the facts,

bounded rationality might cause the controller [manager] systematically to *misinterpret* them, and to send the wrong policy signals to the agent [line staff]. (Smith, 1995: 294)

Smith goes on to discuss the external environment in which organizational decision making takes place. We see this kind of exposition as yet another reason for the methodology we have advocated throughout this book—modeling the performance measures to account for differences in inmates, staff, and organizational variables. This provides insights into both individual and organizational context. Smith's example of misinterpretation helps to make our point.

The United Kingdom central government has called for the publication of the results of examinations for all public schools. There were, as to be expected, dramatic differences among the school districts. Rather than seeking to understand these differences, Smith argues that local governments with low-performing schools were, by implication, pressured to devote resources to improve the test scores. Without understanding the differences in jurisdictions, Smith notes that this may have resulted in an inefficient use of resources. Implicit in this argument is that compositional differences among the students may have been a more important factor in the student outcomes than the management of the schools (a multilevel problem).

Recently, the problem of school achievement in the United States has also been elevated by the public policy debate surrounding the "No Child Left Behind" act of 2002.[1] This act allows states to set their own achievement standards for math, reading, and eventually science. Once those standards are established, the states must test students to monitor their performance achievement up through twelfth grade. Schools will be held accountable if they do not make adequate progress toward the state-established standards. One of the prevailing themes of No Child Left Behind (NCLB) is that disadvantaged groups, such as economically depressed students, will have access to funds to improve their performance once a school has been identified as needing improvement. Recent press releases found at the NCLB website (see chapter note 1 for the address) emphasize the role states have had in establishing their own standards. While there has been a controversy about the funding available to achieve the goals of this legislation, there seems to be less dispute about the importance of establishing performance standards for the schools.

Some of the key elements of the NCLB legislation are (1) first standards are developed; (2) standards will be state specific; (3) students will be compared based on characteristics that measure their background, especially those characteristics that may create a disadvantage to their achievement; and (4) students will be able to get additional resources if their school is identified as substandard. Those resources will include the ability to transfer to a better performing public school. In contrast to Smith's portrayal of the United Kingdom's mandate to publish public school examination results without the assessment of student composition, the NCLB legislation requires context to interpret the data. Yet, without properly specified models, such as the ones we have recommended, possible differences in schools may lead to inappropriate policy decisions based on a misunderstanding of the causes of school achievement differences. The multilevel models may not be a complete solution to understanding jurisdictional context, but at least they explicitly represent and reveal jurisdictional differences at the same time the analyst is studying individual differences among the clients, whether they are students, patients, welfare recipients, or prisoners (to name a few).

Smith also discusses "creative misinterpretation." He argues that in the corporate (private) sector, investors are willing to pay for accurate and timely advice. Therefore, misinterpretation is less likely. In the public sector, he notes, there is no equivalent market. This, of course, was written prior to the debacle of Enron, Global Crossings, WorldCom, and the realization that some financial analysts had a stake in the economic health of corporations they were auditing. It is true that, once this was uncovered, the marketplace determined the true value of both the corporations and their auditors. Governments use both private and public auditing agencies to monitor other government functions. Separation of the interests of the auditor and audited should insure accurate representation, reducing "creative" misinterpretation.

Gaming

Because performance appraisal is so complex for many government functions, it is difficult to set a benchmark without referring to past performance. This leads to a kind of "ratchet" effect. One year's performance level sets the standard for the next. If there is an expectation of improving performance over time, this is clearly not possible and could result in gaming by the manager or the line staff to set much lower performance expectations. Cost reductions are a good example of performance indicators that may lead to gaming. If you squeeze costs one year, does this set you up for a similar reduction next year? At some point, the marginal savings are extremely hard to achieve. Smith notes that if managers only anticipate being in a position for a short period of time, they may be more willing to adopt a short horizon goal of meeting some performance measure expectation. However, if managers anticipate being in a position for a long period of time, they may resort to gaming to lower year-to-year performance improvement expectations.

Ossification

Any performance system should not be set in stone. Managers should be encouraged to constantly re-evaluate their performance goals. Perhaps changing key performance indicators over time is a way to avoid ossification. Ossification is the opposite of innovation. It is an environment of rigid policies where performance indicators, once cast, can never be redesigned. There may be key concepts and performance measures in corrections that do not change over time; however, even managers will have to be cognizant of the potential gaming that may result. One way of circumventing the problem is to develop absolute benchmarks of performance achievement. If a urinalysis hit rate of 1 percent is an achievable and sustainable goal that does not negatively affect other areas of institutional operations, then as long as an institution achieves that level or below, it should get high marks. On the contrary, by setting a benchmark that is not achievable, say zero percent urinalysis hit rates for penitentiaries, not only will the system produce unintended consequences, the additional money and procedures to reach such a goal may interfere with other important goals of corrections. To eliminate drug importation into an institution, you may have to stop contact visiting, minimize inmate-staff contact, and constantly keep staff under surveillance. Such procedures might reduce the hit rate to under 1 percent, but how will they affect the program participation among inmates who, in fact, do not use illicit drugs in prison? The additional resources devoted to trying to lower the urinalysis hit rate unreasonably then become opportunity costs that take money, and other resources, away from other important correctional goals.

Summary

Social scientists publishing in the public administration literature have examined how performance measurement can influence many different public services such as law enforcement, road maintenance, trash collection, parks and recreation, emergency responsiveness, and job training. However, despite the emphasis by the professional groups representing public administration, many localities, states, and federal agencies have been slow to develop performance measurement systems. As we argue elsewhere in this book, these systems only make sense if they are, for the most part, a by-product of the automated data collection one uses in providing the service for individual clients. When police file a crime report, when welfare agents conduct the case management of their clients, when public hospitals collect information on someone being treated for an infectious disease, these data become the grist for the performance measurement mill. Likewise, in a prison, case managers, correctional officers, nurses, teachers, vocational trainers, and industry foremen all record their individual interactions with inmates and these data translate into performance measurement indicators. Client satisfaction, audits, and other survey instruments are actually samples of performance measures that complement what is referred to as administrative data in the public administration domain.

Whether performance measurement in corrections gained ascendancy as a result of the challenge provided by prison privatization, it has achieved momentum in many jurisdictions where progressive administrators see it as a means of insuring government accountability. This is also true in jurisdictions where there has been very little external pressure to privatize prison beds. This is clearly the emphasis in the public administration literature in which theorists and analysts try to understand how governments meet their service mandates while holding public officials accountable. The paradigm we have developed in preceding chapters to measure prison performance clearly could be applied to almost any government service.

LOOKING BACKWARD AND LOOKING FORWARD

I n this book, we range far and wide in our investigation of prison performance. We start with an examination of the stated purposes of
prisons, step through different approaches to measurement, discuss
the relevance of recent advancements in criminal life course theory and
methods, and conclude with a chapter showing how the paradigm we develop throughout the book can be applied to almost any government service. We discuss the advantages and disadvantages of prison audits, surveys
of staff and inmates, behavioral or operational data, and narratives of the
context in which prisons have been evaluated. We hope administrators and
policy analysts will have a greater appreciation for the utility of inmate and
employee surveys as a tool for monitoring prison performance. With recent
advances in computer applications, the administration, scoring, and sum-
marization of these data are becoming faster and cheaper. We also want administrators and policy makers to consider expanding the use of prison
audits beyond their primary use as a local tool. A small investment in the
development of an audit tool will transform it into a measurement device
that will give prison administrators a greater understanding of prison operations and their impact on important outcomes.

At almost every turn, we provide examples from the prison privatization literature that demonstrate how these alternative performance devices
can be used. These examples also show that much of the prison privatization research literature is fraught with problems in analysis and interpretation. Despite the claims of both proponents and opponents of prison
privatization, we argue that it is premature to draw conclusions about the
relative quality or cost of privately versus publicly operated prisons.

A recent paper by Perrone and Pratt (2003) concluded that the "empirical evidence regarding whether private prisons are more cost-effective

and whether they provide a higher quality of confinement to inmates, however, is inconclusive" (Perrone and Pratt, 2003: 301). These researchers evaluated nine studies comparing the quality of privately and publicly operated prisons and concluded that the results were mixed. Furthermore, many studies failed to equate prisons on their age, capacity, and security level composition. Perrone and Pratt selected a few indicators that were represented in all, or most, of the studies such as escapes, assaults, audits of medical services, program services, and sick leave, to try to assess differences in quality of confinement across as many of Logan's domains as they could. Perrone and Pratt noted that the inconsistency in results could be due to differences in managerial style and different data collection methods. They also noted that the studies involved very few prisons and rarely employed statistical tests to assess whether there were actual differences.

We do not disagree with Perrone and Pratt's conclusions regarding the research literature comparing private versus public quality of confinement. However, the limitations they describe do not go far enough. Such conclusions await the development and application of the methods we describe in this book.

Perrone and Pratt were also critical of the cost-effectiveness studies. These authors reviewed many of the dimensions we have covered to insure a "level playing field." They mention: type and location of prisons; number of inmates; hidden costs of financial liability, contract writing, and monitoring; the cost of construction; prison security level and geographic area; and different accounting techniques. Perrone and Pratt found that there was a median difference of $3.40 per diem favoring the private sector. However, due to methodological limitations, such as poor matching techniques, the authors emphasize caution in concluding that private prisons are cheaper.

Again, we do not disagree with the Perrone and Pratt conclusion, but once again, it did not go far enough. We devote a great deal of time and space in this book to the consideration of prison costs. That discussion, in particular, may seem arcane. It may evoke images of the accountant with green eyeshades. We thought it was necessary, however, to inform the reader about the care that must be given to analyses of alternative cost scenarios, and ultimately, about the methods one uses to choose between the private or public operation of the prison. The methodology we sketch for comparing prison costs relies on the concept of avoidable costs. If a cost is avoidable, it is based on a task that can be assumed by the contractor. If it is unavoidable, then despite the work of the contractor, the government must still pay for the task or function. No matter how many prisons may be privatized in a jurisdiction, the government will still bear the unavoidable cost associated with strategic planning and oversight. The smaller the scope of privatization, the larger the unavoidable share of costs that will be borne by the government. While there are many potential pitfalls in calculating avoidable and unavoidable costs, one of the most difficult cost dimensions is the calculation of the avoided proportion of the overhead rate for a system. Using the template and data provided by the state of Oklahoma, we showed how this calculation should be computed. The calculation of the avoided overhead rate alone can push the private-public comparison in favor of one sector or the other.

We also argue that, for the most part, when an analyst is making a comparison between public and private costs, it is not necessary to know how the funds are being spent by the contractor. This will trouble some people, who want to argue that the private sector spends too little on staff or too little on medical care. By considering only the total price, we cannot uncover the company's profit margin. Strictly speaking, how the company uses its payments to cover expenses is not important in comparing the public and private costs. However, the expenses do become important when we want to analyze a particular institution function to understand how costs relate to performance. Thus, if we were to compare the public and private delivery of prison health care, and we were to find that by measuring morbidity and mortality one sector was better than the other, we might begin to ask questions about training, staffing patterns, and the money spent in delivering the health care.

Chapter 6 also covers economic theory that rationalizes why the public or the private sector may be less costly in the production of goods or services. We mentioned theories by Starr, Niskanen, Moore, Volokh, Hart et al., and Schleifer, among others. McDonald et al. (2003) have summarized many of these arguments into a set of discrete propositions without attributing the theories on which they are based. On the side of private markets are the following arguments: private firms are not subject to rule-ridden procurement procedures; without organized labor, private firms manage labor better; private firms bear risk unlike public management, thus increasing cost efficiency; competition among private firms lowers

179

costs; incentives for government management are structured so as to increase rather than conserve money; government managers neither benefit nor suffer from their financial decisions reducing the incentives to save money; and civil service regulations limit managers' control of government labor. The arguments in support of government provision include the following: government contracts actually increase expenditures because of hidden contract costs; private firms cut corners to make a profit resulting in inexperienced staff or poor quality goods and services; corruption can increase costs and lower quality; private firms abandon their contracts if they cannot make a profit, leaving the government at risk; private firms are subject to strikes; the initial bids of private firms are "lowball" offers, and private firms either raise prices later, once they have a foothold in the market, or they fail to deliver quality services because the original negotiated price was too low.

The Hart et al. argument of residual rights of control suggests that because it is difficult to completely specify the expectations of prison performance in a contract, the private firm can exercise discretion in delivering services that may lead to relatively poorer quality. One possible outcome of the Hart et al. thesis is that increases in privatization will lead to degradation in services to the inmate population in both public and private prisons in a jurisdiction. One outcome of the paradigm presented in this book is that it could lead to performance-based contracts that could be closely monitored. This would increase private accountability. However, as we argue above, publicly managed prisons can be held to the same standards. Contrary to the point of view of some scholars, we do not see how a contract offers an advantage over public provision. Our goal in presenting these arguments is to be theoretically comprehensive, and to show how the merits of any of these propositions depend on the ability to measure prison performance.

The ability to compare public and private prisons in a meaningful way can inform penal policy. The comparison process itself can also be an impetus in promoting better prison performance. By comparing prisons and making the data available to outsiders, we nurture an environment of accountability. There is no doubt that the competition between the public and private sectors for prison beds motivated our interest in prison performance. While the impetus to study prison performance may have originated with the introduction of privately operated prisons into the criminal justice system in the 1980s, the benefits of that study extend far beyond the narrow focus upon private prisons. The ongoing work of the American Correctional Association and the Association of State Correctional Administrators to develop objective performance measures is indicative of the recognition that better prison operations can be obtained when we have the ability to compare prison operations both within as well as across jurisdictions.

To move beyond the current confusion in methods and approaches in evaluating prison privatization, Perrone and Pratt (2003) recommended that researchers move beyond the case study to larger-scale analyses. In the event that case studies continue to be conducted, Perrone and Pratt recommend that management practices should be scrutinized to directly examine the claims made by privatization advocates of more cost-effective strategies for prison administration. Finally, they advocate for a centralized database of information on private and public facilities. These are all good recommendations but depend on the extent to which we have common jurisdictional definitions and on the techniques we use to evaluate prison performance.

To address these kinds of concerns, we also introduce the technique of multilevel modeling, a proven methodology that has been used to evaluate and rank schools and hospitals. We demonstrate how the method can be used to rate prison performance. We believe it is important for the reader to appreciate the value of multilevel models to study prison performance. Although it is certainly not the breakthrough the microscope was to the study of microbes, or the telescope to the study of astronomy, multilevel models do allow the analyst to simultaneously measure the individual and the institution. We can use the results of the model to infer the extent to which prisoner or institutional characteristics are more important for a given dimension of performance. We can rank the institutions relative to what we would expect based on the characteristics of the inmates, staff, and the prisons themselves. This ranking, as we demonstrate with both hospitals and prisons, is a more accurate portrayal of the relative performance of prisons than one based on simply calculating an aggregate value. We call this latter measure an unadjusted measure, and the former an expected or adjusted measure. The unadjusted measure may "misrepresent" the prison because it does not take into account the nature of the inmate population or the composition of the prison employees. By leveling the playing field, the multilevel model gives a truer picture of prison performance.

Since multilevel modeling forces us to think about prison performance on two levels, the template we presented for evaluating prison security introduced features of the prison and characteristics of the prisoners. When we conceive of performance measurement this way, then it becomes more apparent that some dimensions of prison performance can be aggregations of inmate characteristics. For example, while the security score of an inmate is a crucial prisoner dimension, the average security score of the inmates in an institution is an important prison dimension. When we introduced multilevel modeling we also cautioned against confusing the meaning and interpretation of the individual and aggregate characteristic. When we examine relationships between variables, a relationship at the institution level should not be confused with a relationship at the individual level. As we pointed out, both levels require careful consideration. For example, if we find a positive relationship between the percentage of inmates who are Caucasian and the rate of drug misconduct (the more whites, the greater the drug misconduct) at the level of the institution, this does not necessarily imply that Caucasians are more likely to use drugs. Instead, it may mean that prisons that have more Caucasians have lower drug surveillance to detect and deter drug use, have fewer drug programs to treat addiction, or have lower security constraints so that there are more opportunities for drug introduction. If we also measure race at the individual level and find no relationship between being a Caucasian and drug misconduct, that would begin to clarify our understanding of the institutional-level relationship. However, the most systematic approach is to use a multilevel model.

The methods for comparing prisons that we present here primarily apply to comparing prisons within a single jurisdiction, whether those prisons are publicly or privately operated. In part, this focus is a product of the incompatibility in the data systems and measures collected across prison jurisdictions. Conceptually, however, there is nothing to prevent the application of these methods to comparisons of entire prison systems. From a methodological standpoint, the comparison of prison systems involves adding another level to the measurement models we have proposed. As noted above, the models would then incorporate levels for the individual inmates, the prisons in which the inmates are housed, and the prison administration (typically the state) responsible for operating the individual prisons. Comparisons would be possible at all three levels. Practically speaking, however, such models are only possible if appropriate data are easily available. Hopefully, this is where the work of ACA and ASCA will provide tangible benefits in the future.

We have devoted a lot of discussion to the problems inherent in using recidivism as a measure of prison performance. The problems are formidable. As we note, some criminal justice theorists have argued that we ought not to hold prison systems responsible for such outcomes. The linchpin of this argument is that prisons should not be held accountable for outcomes over which they have no control. We reject this argument. We recognize that there are many influences that impact on the ability of inmates to desist from crime. But just as we should hold individuals accountable for their failures, we should hold administrators of prisons accountable for the efforts they make in insuring successful reintegration. We are cautiously optimistic that by recognizing the measurement problems, by incorporating safeguards to insure that recidivism is not dependent on release context, and by evaluating prison performance in relation to the life course of the offender's criminal career, we may be on the verge of a better understanding of recidivism as both an individual and organizational measure.

The key life course concept applicable to prison performance is that offenders come into prison having different criminal trajectories. Inmates commit crime at different rates prior to imprisonment and this has an important influence on what their rates of misconduct will be inside of prison and what their rates of crime will be when they are released. Without understanding this phenomenon, or taking it into account when we measure the continuation of that trajectory when a prisoner is released, we lose sight of an important dimension of criminal behavior. Life course scholars have conducted limited studies on the impact of incarceration on post-release trajectories, but we are unaware of systematic research that examines the trajectories prior to, during, and after incarceration. If recidivism is an important dimension of prison performance, and we argue that it is, future work will have to clarify the significance of life course theory and methods to the analysis of prison performance.

The paradigm we have developed in this book can also serve as a model for the analysis of any government service. While there have been many texts and papers in the public administration literature that advocate some of the same techniques we have proposed, we think there is an advantage in starting with a specific domain, an analysis of prison services, and then generalizing it to other government services. Since we collectively have almost seventy years of experience in analyzing all aspects of prison operations, we think that by bringing that expertise to bear on prison performance and accountability, we can inform the public policy debate on these issues. This is the coherent way to resolve both the ambiguities and misunderstandings found in the prison privatization literature as well.

While we make no claims to having solved all problems involved in measuring prison performance, we sincerely believe that we have outlined the type of framework necessary to take the assessment of prison performance to another level. As such, we have benefited greatly from the pioneering work of thoughtful researchers such as Chuck Logan. To paraphrase our opening comments, the framework we have provided will, we hope, move us beyond rhetoric and speculation about the relative merits of private and public prisons. We also envision a new era of development in prison standards, a vision we share with the American Correctional Association, based on the paradigm we have developed throughout this book.

We end where we began. *Measuring Prison Performance* is one of those intellectual skirmishes in the global movement toward replacing government with the marketplace. We have tried to be intellectually honest by not advocating one sector over the other. Instead, we have tried to advance the global marketplace of ideas by developing a systematic methodology to reach an honest conclusion. The current weight of the evidence on prison privatization in the United States is so light that it defies interpretation. There have been some privatization successes, some failures. However, mostly there have been poorly conceived and poorly executed analyses. This book is about thinking intelligently about privatization and accountability. In the end, whether you favor one sector over the other, the import of this book is to develop the tools that allow researchers and managers to make the comparison. In the past, these tools have been inaccurate, crude, or nonexistent. These new measurement tools let one measure, compare, and decide. They also give us some assurance that we have the knowledge to hold the executor of the services accountable—public or private.

APPENDIX

The approach taken in an Archambeault and Deis type of study can be expressed as follows.

$$\beta^*_{0j} = \gamma_0 + \sum_{j=1}^{J}\gamma_j$$

The parameter β^* is used to facilitate later discussion of multilevel models, but it can refer to either a mean of a continuous variable, a count, or even a rate, without the form of the model losing relevance. For this example, we are measuring inmate misconduct. Simply put, the model states that the average value of misconduct for any of the J institutions is equal to an overall grand "mean," γ_0, plus or minus the deviation noted for that institution, the respective γ_j. The statistical test then is whether the deviations from the grand mean are significant.

As suggested above, one of the problems with this model is that the β^* do not come from prisons holding randomly assigned inmates. In other words, there are systematic differences between the prisons in terms of the inmate populations that generate the β^* values. Plus, we know from previous research (Harer, 1994), that inmates with different characteristics are differentially predisposed to commit misconduct. As such, it is necessary to control for these individual differences when generating the estimates of β^*. If the data are available, this task is easily accomplished with the following formula:

$$y_{ij} = \beta_{0j} + \sum_{k=1}^{K}\beta_k x_k + r_{ij}$$

In other words, the predicted value of the outcome of interest is a function of the mean value of the institution in which the inmate is housed, as captured by β_{0j}, and the K covariates entered at the individual level. As we see shortly, the β_{0j} are also affected by covariates at the organizational level. The variables at the organizational level can either be aggregates of individual-level characteristics of inmates or staff (such as average sentence length of inmates or average tenure for staff) or truly global measures such as the budget for programs. It should be noted that the functional form specified in this equation is for an outcome measured on a continuous scale. However, the general form of the model holds for nonlinear specifications of counts or rates with the appropriate transformations of the outcome variable and with different specifications of the error term.

As noted, there is the possibility that there are contextual effects associated with the types of inmates held at the respective prisons or other organizational-level effects. Contextual effects arise when the propensity to observe an outcome is not only affected by the individual-level characteristic of an inmate, but also the proportion of inmates with a given characteristic at a prison. Take the hypothetical characteristic of inmates with a gambling addiction. Misconduct, especially gaming types of misconduct, would be influenced not only by whether individuals at the prison have this characteristic, but also by whether or not other individuals at the prison have this same characteristic. It is easy to imagine gambling misconduct becoming a problem in a way that is not a simple function of the individual characteristics, but of the group characteristics at the prison. An analogy can be drawn to school performance. Learning is affected not only by the innate ability of an individual child, but also the abilities of the other children in the class. The progress of a gifted child may be held back if the child is placed in a class that moves too slowly for the child's abilities.

It is possible to model these contextual/organizational effects, simultaneously with the individual-level effects, with multilevel models as described by Bryk and Raudenbush (1992). For simplicity's sake, we do not combine the two levels into one equation, but both the individual-level model and the contextual/organizational level model are combined during estimation (simply substitute the re-expression of β_{0j} into the individual-level equation above). The organizational-level model looks like the following:

$$\beta_{0j} = \gamma_{00} + \sum_{m=1}^{M} \gamma_m W_m + \mu_j$$

Generally speaking, any individual-level effect can be tested to see whether it has a contextual effect by entering the aggregated values for each institution and including these effects among the M covariates predicting β_{0j}. In addition, other organizational-level covariates without corresponding individual-level effects can be incorporated into the model, what we called global measures above. One of the more interesting features of multilevel models is that any of the β coefficients can be treated as random variables, although only β_{0j} is treated this way in this discussion. It is the ability to independently estimate the error term (and variance) associated with the organizational level deviations, the μ_j, that distinguishes multilevel models from other forms of regression analysis.

NOTES

Introduction

1. We unabashedly borrow this phraseology from the subtitle of *Privatizing Prisons: Rhetoric and Reality* by Adrian L. James, A. Keith Bottomley, Alison Liebling, and Emma Clare.

Chapter 1

1. The discussion is restricted to these jurisdictions because they are the ones with which we are most familiar; however, all of our approaches and arguments could apply to any government in any country concerned with these issues.

2. We recognize that adherence to standards established by the federal courts and professional bodies such as the American Correctional Association impose some conformity across jurisdictions. Nonetheless, we argue that these are minimal standards, and each jurisdiction has considerable latitude in establishing policy, such as the extent to which rehabilitation is emphasized.

3. Remand prisoners are those awaiting trial. Thus, the comparable U.S. term would be pre-trial prisoners.

4. For those unfamiliar with the structure of government in England, the Home Office is a government department that has responsibility for criminal justice functions similar to the U.S. Department of Justice. The Home Office website, http://homeoffice.gov.uk, lists the following functions: community policy, crime reduction, criminal justice, drug prevention, immigration and nationality passports, the category of race, equality, and diversity, and research and statistics.

5. *Regime* is a very broad term in the vernacular of English prisons. It implies the level of programming, custody, and the nature of the interaction between inmates and staff.

6. A reader of this book suggested that we strengthen this subsection by noting that jurisdictions tend to overemphasize public safety. He argued that this

perverts the goal of post-release supervision by inverting the goal of reintegration from reform to revocation. Since offenders will eventually be released through some mandatory release mechanism, the goal of public safety may be undermined in the long term. While we are in agreement with that principle, we still need a way of measuring the difference between a jurisdiction that emphasizes supervision and revocation from one that emphasizes reintegration.

Chapter 3

1. The description of James et al. of direct supervision sounds like the concept of unit management in American corrections. In contrast, American correctional professionals use direct supervision to refer to line of sight contact with inmates, or to housing units in which staff can easily observe inmates. Unit management is the idea that case managers are dedicated to a specific housing unit and have their offices on that unit rather than a central location somewhere in the administration building. Unit management encourages more one-on-one staff-inmate interaction.

Chapter 4

1. Level 2 of a multilevel model can also represent an individual when the level 1 unit of analysis is individual behavior measured over different periods of time.

2. Statistically, these dependencies cause the standard errors to be misestimated, as a result of the intraclass correlation that occurs due to cluster sampling.

3. Technically, if you make multiple comparisons, the confidence intervals need to be adjusted with a Bonferroni or similar procedure. But for informal examination, and when the differences are as large as those noted between YAZ and TAF, this type of visual examination is sufficient.

Chapter 5

1. For those interested in this issue, one place to start is a recent workshop summary of these problems prepared by the National Research Council, J. V. Pepper and C. V. Petrie, Eds. (2003), *Measurement Problems in Criminal Justice Research: Workshop Summary* (Washington, D.C., The National Academies Press).

2. For the technically inclined, it was a Z-score Likert scale.

3. One of the reasons staff at the privately operated institution may have had a higher commitment to the institution is that the BOP emphasizes commitment

to the organization, rather than the institution. Staff are encouraged to move around the country and assume different leadership and administrative roles at different institutions. This emphasis is an organizational goal to reduce the possibility of "homesteading" at a particular prison and to increase the transfer of knowledge across institutions with the aim of supporting a consistent and uniform interpretation of policy and procedures. It is not clear whether private correctional organizations share these same goals. For many of the smaller companies, there is typically less opportunity to move about the country among different prison settings, although the larger companies, CCA and WCC, have the opportunity and capacity.

Chapter 6

1. This section updates the analysis of these issues reported by Nelson (1999).

2. Although the OPPAGA is a unit of the Office of the Auditor General, it reports directly to the state legislature.

3. Commissioners are appointed by the governor and with the approval of the state senate. The commission's mission statement appears on its website, located at www.fcc.state.fl.us.

4. These estimates are reproduced and analyzed in Florida Department of Corrections (1998).

5. This trust fund is an account containing the revenue (in excess of expenses) from the prison commissary, vending concessions, and inmate telephone service.

6. A fourth small adjustment by CCA remains unexplained: the "unadjusted" per diem reported by CCA for Lawtey exceeds that found in the OPPAGA report by $.36.

7. According to OPPAGA, CCA sought to claim credit for taxes paid on income from other facilities.

8. According to OPPAGA, this trust account is established in the name of the private contractor operating the prison. However, current law requires the contractor to obtain the approval of the CPC commissioner before using these funds for anything other than the purchase of items for resale. In contrast, state profits from the prison commissary and inmate phone usage are used to offset prison operating costs.

9. See, for example, comments made by the Chair of the Privatization Ad Hoc Group of the U.S. Chamber of Commerce, James A. Dobkin, quoted in Sorett (1998).

10. See chapter 1, Section E.3, for a discussion of cost waivers in the case of service quality improvements.

11. See Tennessee Select Oversight Committee on Corrections (1995), Executive Summary (Wright et al., 1997) for a listing of public and private expenditures categorized both by function (security, administration, health, etc.) and by line item (salaries, supplies, utilities, etc.).

12. Martin (1993); the Colorado Commission on Privatization (1997); and Treasury Board of Canada (1997).

13. See Nelson (1998) for a more complete discussion of this bias.

14. Department of Defense (1995). The more recent DOD A-76 Costing Manual Department of Defense (Department of Defense, 2001) modifies this guidance to some extent. Defense Department analysts are instructed to use the 12 percent overhead rate specified in the A-76 guidelines, but only apply it to civilian personnel costs. The (avoidable) overhead cost of military personnel is included in the "military composite rate" used to calculate the cost of military staff. The DOD Financial Management Regulation (Department of Defense, 2000) defines this military support adjustment to be a 6 percent markup on the compensation of officers and an 18 percent markup on the compensation of enlisted personnel. This revised cost comparison approach appears to imply an overhead cost rate that exceeds ones used by DOD in the past: in 1998 the GAO reported that less than 2 percent of the air force cost estimates they examined included overhead allowances above 3 percent (General Accounting Office, 1998).

15. This table is available on the Oklahoma DOC website at www.doc. state.ok.us/DOCS/rates.htm.

Chapter 7

1. Actually, the claim put forward by Wackenhut Corrections Corporation (WCC) is that federal government procurement rules, specifically the Service Contract Act, force WCC to pay wages above the market rate at the Taft, California, prison they operate for the Federal Bureau of Prisons. As a point of evidence, they note that WCC pays wages about half those at Taft at the nearby facility, McFarland CC, which is operated by WCC for the state and which is not subject to the Service Contract Act.

2. Private prison operators also point out that they can purchase materials associated with building and operating prisons more cheaply than the public sector as they are not bound by public-sector procurement rules. Even granting the claims of efficiencies in procuring goods, savings in this area do not account for a significant portion of potential cost savings. The greatest potential for cost savings comes from reductions in employee salaries and benefits, which often account for 70 percent of a prison's operating expenses.

Chapter 9

1. Bushway et al. demonstrate what they mean by the random component of crime by showing how a Poisson process can represent a rate of criminality. If we assume that the true underlying rate of criminality is, say, three crimes per year, then a Poisson distribution would yield such a rate 22.4 percent of the time in one year. Under these same assumptions, two crimes would occur 22.4 percent of the time, one crime 14.9 percent of the time, and five crimes 5 percent of the time. In other words, if there is a random component to crime separate from propensity and opportunity, we should expect this kind of variation when we measure crime.

2. We are currently in the process of trying to assemble such a database using official arrest records for over 600,000 federal offenders, some of who have been released from prison for twenty-two years.

3. We owe a thanks to Shawn Bushway for his comments on this chapter and particularly in pointing out how the prior criminal rate is more important than the prior amount of crime.

Chapter 11

1. For an explanation of the No Child Left Behind Act of 2002, see www.nclb.gov/next/overview/index.html.

REFERENCES

AFSCME. American Federation of State, County and Municipal Employees.
2001. The evidence is clear: Crime shouldn't pay. Retrieved from the World Wide Web: www.afscme.org/private/evidtc.htm.

Allison. G.
1969. Conceptual models and the Cuban missile crisis. *The American Political Science Review* 63: 689–718.

American Correctional Association.
1999. *American Correctional Association Directory: Juvenile and Adult Correctional Departments, Institutions, Agencies, and Paroling Authorities.* Lanham, MD: American Correctional Association.

——.
2000. *Performance-Based Standards for Adult Community Residential Services.* Lanham, MD: American Correctional Association.

——.
2002. *Performance-Based Standards for Correctional Health Care in Adult Correctional Institutions.* Lanham, MD: American Correctional Association.

Ammons, D.
1996. *Municipal Benchmarks: Assessing Local Performance and Establishing Community Needs.* Thousand Oaks, CA: Sage.

Andrews, D. A., and Bonta, J.
1998. *The Psychology of Criminal Conduct.* Cincinnati, OH: Anderson Publishing.

Archambeault, W. G., and Deis, D. R.
1996. Cost Effectiveness Comparisons of Private Versus Public Prisons in

Louisiana: A Comprehensive Analysis of Allen, Avoyelles, and Winn Correctional Centers. Unpublished paper, Baton Rouge, Louisiana State University.

Atherton, P., Czerniak, L., Franklin, M., and Palmateer, J.
1999. *Security Audit Program: A "How To" Guide and Model Instrument for Adaptation to Local Standards, Policies, and Procedures.* Washington, DC: National Institute of Corrections.s

Austin, J., and Coventry, G.
2003. A second look at the private prison debate. *The Criminologist* 28(5): 1–9.

Bavon, A.
1995. Innovations in performance measurement systems: A comparative perspective. *International Journal of Public Administration* 18(2–3): 491–519.

Berk, R. A., and de Leeuw, J.
1999. Evaluation of California's inmate classification system using a generalized regression discontinuity design. *Journal of the American Statistical Association* 94(448): 1045–52.

Berk, R. A., Ladd, H., Graziano, H., and Baek, J. H.
2003. A randomized experiment testing inmate classification systems. *Criminology & Public Policy* 2: 215–42.

Biles, D., and Dalton, V.
1999. *Deaths in Private Prisons 1990–99: A Comparative Study.* Canberra: Australian Institute of Criminology.

Blasi, G. J.
2002. Government contracting and performance measurement in human services. *International Journal of Public Administration* 25(4): 519–38.

Blumstein, A., Cohen, J., Roth, J. A., and Visher, C. A.
1986. *Criminal Careers and "Career Criminals."* Washington, DC: National Academy Press.

Boyne, G., Gould-Williams, J., Law, J., and Walker, R.
2002. Plans, performance information and accountability: The case of best value. *Public Administration Review* 80(4): 691–710.

Britton, D. M.
1997. Perceptions of the work environment among correctional officers: Do race and sex matter? *Criminology* 35(1): 85–105.

Brown, K., and Coulter, P. B.
1983. Subjective and objective measures of police service delivery. *Public Administration Review* 43(1): 50–58.

Bruckner, E., and Mayer, K. U.
1998. Collecting life history data: Experiences from the German Life History study. In J. Z. Giele and J. Glen H. Elder (Eds.), *Methods of Life Course Research: Qualitative and Quantitative Approaches* (152–81). Thousand Oaks, CA: Sage.

Bryk, A. S., and Raudenbush, S. W.
1992. *Hierarchical Linear Models: Applications and Data Analysis Methods.* Newbury Park, CA: Sage.

Buchanan, J.
1978. *The Economics of Politics.* London: Institute of Economic Affairs.

Bureau of Justice Statistics.
1993. *Performance Measures for the Criminal Justice System.* Washington, DC: Bureau of Justice Statistics.

Bureau of Research and Data Analysis.
1998. *Preliminary Assessment of a Study Entitled "A Comparative Recidivism Analysis of Releasees from Private and Public Prisons in Florida."* Tallahassee: Florida Department of Corrections.

Bushway, S., Brame, R., and Paternoster, R.
2003. Connecting desistance and recidivism: Measuring changes in criminality over the lifespan. In S. Maruna and R. Immarigeon (Eds.), *Desistance from Crime and Ex-Convict Reentry.* Albany, NY: SUNY Press.

Bushway, S. D., Piquero, A. R., Broidy, L. M., Cauffman, E., and Mazerolle, P.
2001. An empirical framework for studying desistance. *Criminology* 39(2): 491–515.

Cadora, E., and Swartz, C.
1999. *Analysis for the Community Justice Project at the Center for Alternative Sentencing and Employment Services (CASES).* Retrieved from the World Wide Web: www.communityjusticeproject.org.

Camp, C. G., and Camp, G. M.
1999. *The Corrections Yearbook 1999: Adult Corrections.* Middletown, CT: Criminal Justice Institute, Inc.

REFERENCES

Camp, S. D.
    1999. Do inmate survey data reflect prison conditions? Using surveys to assess prison conditions of confinement. *The Prison Journal* 79(2): 250–68.

Camp, S. D., and Gaes, G. G.
    2000. *Private Prisons in the United States, 1999: An Assessment of Growth, Performance, Custody Standards, and Training Requirements.* Washington, DC: Federal Bureau of Prisons.

———.
    2001. Private adult prisons: What do we really know and why don't we know more? In D. Shichor and M. Gilbert (Eds.), *Privatization of Criminal Justice: Past, Present and Future* (283–98). Cincinnati, OH: Anderson.

———.
    2002. Growth and quality of U.S. private prisons: Evidence from a national survey. *Criminology & Public Policy* 1(3): 427–49.

———.
    2004. *Are Prisons Criminogenic? Some Experimental Evidence.* Washington, DC: Federal Bureau of Prisons.

Camp, S. D., Gaes, G. G., Klein-Saffran, J., Daggett, D. M., and Saylor, W. G.
    2002. Using inmate survey data in assessing prison performance: A case study comparing private and public prisons. *Criminal Justice Review* 27(1): 26–51.

Camp, S. D., Gaes, G. G., Langan, N. P., and Saylor, W. G.
    2003. The influence of prisons on inmate misconduct: A multilevel investigation. *Justice Quarterly* 20(3): 501–33.

Camp, S. D., Gaes, G. G., and Saylor, W. G.
    2002. Quality of prison operations in the federal sector: A comparison with a private prison. *Punishment & Society* 4(1): 27–53.

Camp, S. D., Saylor, W. G., and Harer, M. D.
    1997. Aggregating individual-level evaluations of the organizational social climate: A multilevel investigation of the work environment at the Federal Bureau of Prisons. *Justice Quarterly* 14(4): 739–61.

Camp, S. D., Saylor, W. G., and Wright, K. N.
    1999. Creating performance measures from survey data: A practical discussion. *Corrections Management Quarterly* 3(1): 71–80.

Camp, S. D., and Steiger, T. L.
    1995. Gender and racial differences in perceptions of career opportunities and

the work environment in a traditionally male occupation: Correctional workers in the Federal Bureau of Prisons. In N. A. Jackson (Ed.), *Contemporary Issues in Criminal Justice: Shaping Tomorrow's System* (258–77). New York: McGraw-Hill.

Colorado Commission on Privatization.
1997. *More Competitive Government: A Report to the General Assembly.* Denver: Colorado Department of Public Health and Environment.

Crane, R.
2001. *Monitoring Correctional Services Provided by Private Firms.* Washington, DC: Correctional Programs Office, U.S. Department of Justice.

Crants, D. R.
1991. Private prison management: A study in economic efficiency. *Journal of Contemporary Criminal Justice* 7(1): 49–59.

Cummins, C. E.
2001. *Private Prisons in Texas, 1987–2000.* Unpublished doctoral dissertation, American University, Washington, D.C.

Department of Defense.
1995. *Commercial Activities Program Procedures* (DODI 4100.33). Washington, DC: Department of Defense.

———.
2000. *Financial Management Regulation* (Volume 11a). Washington, DC: Department of Defense.

———.
2001. *A-76 Costing Manual.* Washington, DC: Department of Defense.

Department of Energy.
1995. *How to Measure Performance: A Handbook of Techniques and Tools.* Washington, DC: Department of Energy.

DiIulio, J. J., Jr.
1990. *Governing Prisons: A Comparative Study of Correctional Management.* New York: Free Press.

———.
1993. Rethinking the criminal justice system: Toward a new paradigm. In L. Greenfield (Ed.), *Performance Measures for the Criminal Justice System* (1–18). Washington, DC: Bureau of Justice Statistics.

REFERENCES

Downs, A.
1967. *Inside Bureaucracy*. Boston: Little, Brown.

Edwards, G. C.
1980. *Implementing Public Policy*. Washington, DC: Congressional Quarterly Inc.

Eisenhardt, K.
1989. Agency theory: An assessment and review. *Academy of Management Review* 14: 57–74.

Farabee, D., and Knight, K.
2002. *A Comparison of Public and Private Prisons in Florida: During and Post-Prison Performance Indicators*. Los Angeles: Query Research.

Fleisher, M. S., and Decker, S. H.
2001. An overview of the challenge of prison gangs. *Corrections Management Quarterly* 5(1): 1–9.

Florida Department of Corrections.
1998. *Privatization in the Florida Department of Corrections*. Tallahassee: Florida Department of Corrections.

Gaes, G. G., Camp, S. D., and Saylor, W. G.
1998. Appendix 2: Comparing the quality of publicly and privately operated prisons: A review. In D. McDonald, E. Fournier, M. Russell-Einhorn, and S. Crawford (Eds.), *Private Prisons in the United States: An Assessment of Current Practice* (1–38). Boston: Abt Associates Inc.

Gaes, G. G., and Kendig, N.
2002, January 30–31, 2002. *The skill sets and health care needs of releasing offenders*. Paper presented at the National Policy Conference, From Prison to Home: The Effect of Incarceration and Reentry on Children, Families, and Communities, Natcher Conference Center, National Institutes of Health, Bethesda, MD.

Gendreau, P., Little, T., and Goggin, C.
1996. A meta-analysis of the predictors of adult offender recidivism. *Criminology* 34(4): 575–607.

General Accounting Office.
1997. *The Government Performance and Results Act: 1997 Governmentwide Implementation Will Be Uneven* (GAO/GGD-97-109). Washington, DC: General Accounting Office.

———.

1998. *Defense Outsourcing: Better Data Needed to Support Overhead Rates for A-76 Studies* (GAO/NSIAD-98-62). Washington, DC: General Accounting Office.

Gilbert, M. J.

2001. How much is too much privatization in criminal justice? In D. Schicor and M. J. Gilbert (Eds.), *Privatization in Criminal Justice: Past Present, and Future* (41–80). Cincinnati, OH: Anderson Publishing Company.

Gillespie, W.

2003. *Prisonization: Individual and Institutional Factors Affecting Inmate Conduct.* New York: LFB Scholarly Publishing LLC.

Glaser, D.

1969. *The Effectiveness of a Prison and Parole System.* New York: The Bobbs-Merrill Company, Inc.

Glueck, S., and Glueck, E. T.

1966. *Criminal Careers in Retrospect.* New York: Kraus Reprint Corporation.

Goffman, E.

1961. *Asylums: Essays on the Social Situation of Mental Patients and Other Inmates.* Garden City, NY: Anchor Books.

Goggin, M. L., Bowman, A. O. M., Lester, J. P., and O'Toole, L. J.

1990. *Implementation Theory and Practice: Toward a Third Generation.* Glenview, IL: Scott Foresman/Little, Brown Higher Education.

Goldstein, H.

1995. *Multilevel Statistical Models.* New York: Wiley.

Gottfredson, M. R., and Hirschi, T.

1990. *General Theory of Crime.* Palo Alto: Stanford University Press.

Greene, J.

1999. Comparing private and public prison services and programs in Minnesota: Findings from prisoner interviews. *Current Issues in Criminal Justice* 2(2): 202–232.

———.

2002. Lack of correctional services. In A. Coyle, A. Campbell, and R. Neufield (Eds.), *Capitalist Punishment: Prison Privatization and Human Rights.* Gardena, CA: Clarity Press.

REFERENCES

Grogger, J.
1995. The effect of arrest on the employment and earnings of young men. *Quarterly Journal of Economics* 110(1): 51–71.

Hagan, J.
1991. Density and drift: Subcultural preferences, status attainments, and the risks and rewards of youth. *American Sociological Review* 56(5): 567–82.

———.
1993. Social embeddednesss of crime and unemployment. *Criminology* 31(4): 465–91.

Harding, R.
2001. Private prisons. In M. Tonry (Ed.), *Crime and Justice: A Review of Research* (vol. 28, 265–346). Chicago: University of Chicago Press.

Harer, M. D.
1994. *Recidivism among Federal Prisoners Released in 1987.* Washington, DC: Federal Bureau of Prisons.

Hart, O., Shleifer, A., and Vishny, R. W.
1997. The proper scope of government: Theory and an application to prisons. *The Quarterly Journal of Economics* 112(4): 1127–61.

Hatry, H. P.
1999. *Performance Measurement: Getting Results.* Washington, DC: The Urban Institute Press.

Hatry, H. P., Blair, L. H., Fisk, D. M., Greiner, J. M., Hall, J. R., and Schaenman, P. S.
1992. *How Effective Are Your Community Services?* Washington, DC: The Urban Institute.

Heinrich, C. J.
2002. Outcomes-based performance management in the public sector: Implications for government accountability and effectiveness. *Public Administration Review* 62(6): 712–25.

Heinrich, C. J., and Lynn, L. E.
2000. Means and ends: A comparative study of empirical methods for investigating governance and performance. *Journal of Public Administration and Theory* 11(1): 109–38.

Hill, P. W., and Goldstein, H.
1998. Multilevel modeling of educational data with cross-classification and

missing identification for units. *Journal of Educational and Behavioral Statistics* 23(2): 117–28.

Holzer, M., and Halachmi, A.
1996. Measurement as a means of accountability. *International Journal of Public Administration* 19(11–12): 1921–43.

Howell, S.
1997. *Performance Measurement Models Displayed Via Interactive Bar Charts* (version 1.0). Washington, DC: Federal Bureau of Prisons.

———.
2001. *Parallel Coordinates Display* (version 2.0). Washington, DC: Federal Bureau of Prisons.

Inselburg, A., and Dimsdale, B.
1990. *Parallel Coordinates: A Tool for Visualizing Multi-Dimensional Geometry.* Paper presented at the First IEEE Conference on Visualization, San Francisco, California.

James, A. L., Bottomley, A. K., Liebling, A., and Clare, E.
1997. *Privatizing Prisons: Rhetoric and Reality.* Thousand Oaks, CA: Sage.

Jones, B. L., Nagin, D. S., and Roeder, K.
2001. A SAS procedure based on mixture models for estimating developmental trajectories. *Sociological Methods and Research* 29: 374–93.

Kahn, A. E.
1988. *The Economics of Regulation: Principles and Institutions.* Cambridge, MA: MIT Press.

Kearney, R. C., and Bergman, E. M.
1999. *Public Sector Performance: Management, Motivation, and Measurement.* Boulder, CO: Westview Press.

Kelley, J.
1984. *Costing Government Services: A Guide for Decision Making.* Chicago: Government Finance Officers Association.

Kelly, J. M., and Swindell, D.
2002. A multiple indicator approach to municipal service evaluation: Correlating performance measurement and citizen satisfaction across jurisdictions. *Public Administration Review* 62(5): 610–21.

Kling, J.
1999. *The Effect of Prison Sentence Length on the Subsequent Employment and*

REFERENCES

Earnings of a Criminal Defendant (Economics Discussion Paper 208). Princeton, NJ:Woodrow Wilson School.

Land, K. C., McCall, P. L., and Nagin, D. S.
1996. A comparison of Poisson, negative binomial, and semiparametric mixed Poisson regression models with application to criminal careers data. *Sociological Methods and Research* 24: 387–441.

Langford, J.
1982. Public corporations in the 1980's: Moving from rhetoric to analysis. *Canadian Public Administration* 25: 619–37.

Lanza-Kaduce, L., and Maggard, S.
2001. *The long-term recidivism of public and private prisoners.* Paper presented at the National Conference of the Bureau of Justice Statistics and Justice Research and Statistics Association, New Orleans.

Lanza-Kaduce, L., and Parker, K. F.
1998. *A Comparative Recidivism Analysis of Releasees from Public and Private Prisons in Florida.* Unpublished manuscript, Gainesville.

Lanza-Kaduce, L., Parker, K. F., and Thomas, C. W.
1999. A comparative recidivism analysis of releasees from private and public prisons. *Crime & Delinquency* 45(1): 28–47.

Laub, J. H., and Sampson, R. J.
1998. Integrating quantitative and qualitative data. In J. Z. Giele and J. Glen H. Elder (Eds.), *Methods of Life Course Research: Qualitative and Quantitative Approaches* (213–30). Thousand Oaks, CA: Sage.

———.
2001. Understanding desistance from crime. In M. Tonry (Ed.), *Crime and Justice: A Review of Research* (1–69). Chicago: University of Chicago Press.

Lazarsfeld, P. F., and Menzel, H.
1972. On the relation between individual and collective properties. In P. F. Lazarsfeld, A. K. Pasanella, and M. Rosenbert (Eds.), *Continuities in the Language of Social Research* (225–37). New York: Free Press.

Leibenstein, H.
1966. Allocative efficiency and X-efficiency. *American Economic Review* 56: 392–415.

Lin, A. C.
2000. *Reform in the Making: The Implementation of Social Policy in Prisons.* Princeton, NJ: Princeton University Press.

Lincoln, J. R., and Zeitz, G.

1980. Organizational properties from aggregate data: Separating individual and structural effects. *American Sociological Review* 45(3): 391–408.

Logan, C. H.

1991. *Well Kept: Comparing Quality of Confinement in a Public and a Private Prison.* Washington, DC: National Institute of Justice.

———.

1992. Well kept: Comparing quality of confinement in private and public prisons. *The Journal of Criminal Law and Criminology* 83(3): 577–613.

———.

1993. Criminal justice performance measures for prisons. In L. Greenfield (Ed.), *Performance Measures for the Criminal Justice System* (1–18). Washington, DC: Bureau of Justice Statistics.

Lynch, J. P., and Sabol, W. J.

2001. *Prisoner reentry in perspective* (3). Washington, DC: Urban Institute.

Maguire, K., and Pastore, A. L.

1999. *Sourcebook of Criminal Justice Statistics 1998.* Washington, DC: U.S. Department of Justice, Bureau of Justice Statistics.

Maltz, M.

1984. *Recidivism.* Orlando, FL: Academic Press.

Martin, L.

1993. *How to Compare Costs between In-House and Contracted Services.* Los Angeles: Reason Foundation.

Matsueda, R. L., and Heimer, K.

1997. Symbolic interactionist theory of role-transitions, role-commitment, and delinquency. In T. P. Thornberry (Ed.), *Developmental Theories of Crime and Delinquency* (163–213). Piscataway, NJ: Transaction Publishers.

McDonald, D., Fournier, E., Russell-Einhourn, M., and Crawford, S.

1998. *Private Prisons in the United States: An Assessment of Current Practices.* Cambridge, MA: Abt Associates, Inc.

McDonald, D., Patten, C., Fournier, E., and Crawford, S.

2003. *Governments' Management of Private Prisons.* Cambridge, MA: Abt Associates, Inc.

REFERENCES

Moffitt, T. E.
1993. "Life course persistent" and "adolescent limited" antisocial behavior: A developmental taxonomy. *Psychological Review* 100: 674–701.

Moore, A. T.
1998. *Private Prisons: Quality Corrections at a Lower Cost.* Los Angeles: Reason Public Policy Institute.

Morris, N., and Tonry, M.
1990. *Between Prison and Probation: Intermediate Punishments in a Rational Sentencing System.* Oxford: Oxford University Press.

Nagin, D. S., and Land, K. C.
1993. Age, criminal careers, and population heterogeneity: Specification and estimation of a nonparametric, mixed Poisson model. *Criminology* 31: 327–62.

Nelson, J.
1998. Comparing public and private prison costs. In D. McDonald, E. Fournier, M. Russell-Einhorn, and S. Crawford (Eds.), *Private Prisons in the United States: An Assessment of Current Practice.* Boston: Abt Associates, Inc.

———.
1999. *Taft Prison Facility: Cost Scenarios.* Washington, DC: National Institute of Corrections.

———.
2002. *Measuring the Cost of Public and Private Prison Facilities.* Bethesda, MD: J. W. Partners.

Niskanen, W.
1971. *Bureaucracy and Representative Government.* Chicago: Aldine-Atherton.

Normand, S. L., Glickman, M. E., and Gatsonis, C. A.
1997. Statistical models for profiling providers of medical care: Issues and application. *Journal of the American Statistical Association* 92(439): 803–14.

Office of Management and Budget.
1996. *Circular A-76. Revised Supplemental Handbook: Performance of Commercial Activities.* Washington, DC: Office of Management and Budget.

Office of Program Policy Analysis and Government Accountability.
1998. *(97–68) Review of Bay Correctional Facility and Moore Haven Correctional Facility.* Tallahassee, FL: Office of Program Policy and Government Accountability.

———.
2000. *(99–46) Progress Report: Bay and Moore Haven Private Prison Contracts Renewed; Bay Costs Increase.* Tallahassee, FL: Office of Program Policy and Government Accountability.

Osborne, D., and Gaebler, T.
1992. *Reinventing Government.* New York: Addison-Wesley.

Pepper, J. V., and Petrie, C. V. (Eds.).
2003. *Measurement Problems in Criminal Justice Research: Workshop Summary.* Washington, DC: The National Academies Press.

Percy, S. L.
1986. In defense of citizen evaluations as performance measures. *Urban Affairs Quarterly* 22(1): 66–83.

Perrone, D., and Pratt, T. C.
2003. Comparing the quality of confinement and cost-effectiveness of public versus private prisons: What we know, why we do not know more, and where to go from here. *The Prison Journal* 83(3): 301–22.

Petersilia, J.
1993. Measuring the performance of community corrections. In L. Greenfield (Ed.), *Performance Measures for the Criminal Justice System* (1–18). Washington, DC: Bureau of Justice Statistics.

Piquero, A. R., Blumstein, A., Brame, R., Haapanen, R., Mulvey, E. P., and Nagin, D. S.
2001. Assessing the impact of exposure time and incapacitation on longitudinal trajectories of criminal offending. *Journal of Adolescent Research* 16(1): 54–74.

Pratt, T. C., and Maahs, J.
1999. Are private prisons more cost-effective than public prisons? A meta-analysis of evaluation research studies. *Crime & Delinquency* 45(3): 358–71.

President's Commission on Privatization.
1988. *Privatization: Toward More Effective Government.* Washington, DC: President's Commission on Privatization.

Pressman, J. L., and Wildavsky, A.
1984. *Implementation.* Berkeley: University of California Press.

Rasbash, J., Browne, W., Goldstein, H., Yang, M., Plewis, I., Healey, M., Woodhouse, G., Draper, D., Langford, I., and Lewis, T.
2000. *A User's Guide to MLwiN: Version 2.1.* London: Institute of Education, University of London.

REFERENCES

Raudenbush, S. W., and Bryk, A. S.
2002. *Hierarchical Linear Models: Applications and Data Analysis Methods.* Thousand Oaks, CA: Sage Publications.

Raudenbush, S. W., and Sampson, R.
1999a. Assessing direct and indirect effects in multilevel designs with latent variables. *Sociological Methods & Research* 28(2): 123–53.

———.
1999b. Ecometrics: Toward a science of assessing ecological settings, with application to the systematic social observation of neighborhoods. In M. Sobel (Ed.), *Sociological Methodology* (1–41). Oxford: Blackwell Publishers.

Rensberger, B.
1997, March 12. How honest data can mislead. *The Washington Post,* H05.

Ritzer, G.
1993. *The McDonaldization of Society: An Investigation into the Changing Character of Contemporary Social Life.* Newbury Park, CA: Pine Forge Press.

———.
1998. *The McDonaldization Thesis: Explorations and Extensions.* Thousand Oaks, CA: Sage.

Robinson, W. S.
1950. Ecological correlation and the behavior of individuals. *American Sociological Review* 15: 351–57.

Rosenbaum, P. R., and Rubin, D. B.
1984. Reducing bias in observational studies using subclassification on the propensity score. *Journal of the American Statistical Association* 79(387): 516–24.

Sampson, R. J., and Laub, J. H.
1993. *Crime in the Making: Pathways and Turning Points through Life.* Cambridge, MA: Harvard University Press.

Saylor, W. G.
1984. *Surveying Prison Environments.* Washington, DC: Federal Bureau of Prisons.

———.
1997. *Modeling and Graphing Organizational Processes in Pursuit of Performance Benchmarks: Methods for Establishing and Evaluating Performance Measures.* Washington, DC: Federal Bureau of Prisons.

Saylor, W. G., and Gaes, G. G.
  1997. PREP: Training inmates through industrial work participation and vocational and apprenticeship instruction. *Corrections Management Quarterly* 1(20): 32–43.

Schmidt, P., and Witte, A. D.
  1988. *Predicting Recidivism Using Survival Models.* New York: Springer-Verlag.

Sechrest, D. K., and Shichor, D.
  1994. *Final Report: Exploratory Study of California's Community Correctional Facilities.* Parole and Community Services Division, California Department of Corrections.

———.
  1996. Comparing Public and Private Correctional Facilities in California: An Exploratory Study. In G. L. Mays and T. Gray (Eds.), *Privatization and the Provision of Correctional Services* (133–51). Cincinnati, OH: Anderson Publishing.

Segal, J., and Moore, A. T.
  2002. *Weighing the Watchmen: Evaluating the Costs and Benefits of Outsourcing Correctional Services* (290). Los Angeles: Reason Public Policy Institute.

Shleifer, A.
  2001. *State versus Private Ownership.* Cambridge, MA: Department of Economics, Harvard University.

Smith, P.
  1995. On the unintended consequences of publishing performance data in the public sector. *International Journal of Public Administration* 18(2–3): 277–310.

Sorett, S. M.
  1998. *OMB Circular A-76 in 1998: Its Context and Structure.* Retrieved from the World Wide Web: www.amc.army.mil/amc/command_counsel/resources/documents/a76/PAPER.PDF.

Starr, P.
  1987. *The Limits of Privatization.* Washington, DC: Economic Policy Institute.

Stewart, T. L.
  2000. *Arizona Department of Corrections: Public-Private Prison Comparison.* Phoenix: Arizona Department of Corrections.

REFERENCES

Stipak, B.
1979. Citizen satisfaction with urban services: Potential misuse as a performance measure. *Public Administration Review* 39(1): 46–52.

Streib, G. D., and Poister, T. H.
1999. Assessing the validity, legitimacy, and functionality of performance measurement systems in municipal governments. *American Review of Public Administration* 29(2): 107–23.

Taylor, F. W.
1911. *Scientific Management*. Westport, CT: Greenwood.

Tennessee Select Oversight Committee on Corrections.
1995. *Comparative Evaluation of Privately-Managed Corrections Corporation of America Prison (South Central Correctional Center) and State-Managed Prototypical Prisons (Northeast Correctional Center, Northwest Correctional Center)—Executive Summary*. Nashville: Tennessee Select Oversight Committee on Corrections.

Thomas, C. W.
1997. *Comparing the Cost and Performance of Public and Private Prisons in Arizona*. Gainesville: Center for Studies in Criminology and Law, University of Florida.

Treasury Board of Canada.
1997. *Stretching the Tax Dollar: Make or Buy*. Ottawa, Ontario: Treasury Board of Canada Secretariat.

Uggen, C., and Massoglia, M.
2001. Desistance from crime and deviance as a turning point in the life course (draft). In J. T. Mortimer and M. Shanahan (Eds.), *Handbook of the Life Course*. New York: Plenum Publishing.

Urban Institute.
1989. *Comparison of Privately and Publicly Operated Correctional Facilities in Kentucky and Massachusetts*. Washington, DC: U.S. Department of Justice, National Institute of Justice.

Volokh, A.
2002. A tale of two systems: Cost, quality, and accountability in private prisons. *Harvard Law Review* 115: 1868–90.

Wang, X.
2002. Perception and reality in developing an outcome performance measurement system. *International Journal of Public Administration* 25(6): 805–29.

Wholey, J. S., and Hatry, H. P.
1992. The case for performance monitoring. *Public Administration Review* 52(6): 604–10.

Wilson, J. Q.
1993. The problem of defining agency success. In L. Greenfield (Ed.), *Performance Measures for the Criminal Justice System* (1–18). Washington, DC: Bureau of Justice Statistics.

Woolf, H. K., and Tumim, S.
1991. *Prison Disturbances, April 1990: Report of an Inquiry by the Rt. Hon. Lord Justice Woolf (Parts 1 and 2) and His Honour Judge Stephen Tumim* (Cm. 1456). London: Stationery Office.

Woolredge, J., Griffin, T., and Pratt, T.
2001. Considering hierarchical models for research on inmate behavior: Predicting misconduct with multi-level data. *Justice Quarterly* 18(1): 203–31.

Wright, K.
2002. *Key Indicators of ASCA Performance Standards (with Counting Rules)*. Middletown, CT: Association of State Correctional Administrators.

Wright, K. N., Saylor, W. G., Gilman, E. B., and Camp, S. D.
1997. Job control and occupational outcomes among prison workers. *Justice Quarterly* 14(3): 525–46.

Yergin, D., and Stanislaw, J.
1998. *The Commanding Heights: The Battle Between Government and the Marketplace That Is Remaking the World*. New York: Simon and Schuster.

INDEX

213

expenditures: borne by taxpayers, 95; unchanging, 95–97

familial reintegration, 132–33; programs for, 136
Federal Bureau of Prisons. *See* Bureau of Prisons
federal prisons, privatization of, 91–94
female prisoners, recidivism rates of, 27
Florida: prison privatization in, cost issues and, 89–91, 101–2; recidivism rates of public versus private prisons in, 24–29
Florida Corrections Commission, 89

Gaebler, Ted, 154
gaming, 174–75
gang activity, 81–82, 82*f*; management of, 136–38
GED completion rates, as performance measure, 29
General Accounting Office, 169
German Life History Study, 124
goals, xii, 1; of adult correctional agencies in U.S. and Canada, 8–18, 10*t*–16*t*
governance, term, 163
government(s): interests of, 48; relationship to economies, ix, 105
government accountability, x; public administration literature on, 156
Government Performance and Results Act (GPRA), 155
Group 4, 19–20, 41–42

halfway house placement, 118
Harding, Richard, x
Hatry, Harry, 1, 154
Health Care Financing

Administration (HCFA), 66–67
hierarchical linear models (HLM), 163–65. *See also* multilevel models
homicides, as performance measure, 119
hospital performance, multilevel model of, 66–67

implementation theory, 45
incapacitation, recidivism and, 20
individual-level model, 54, 54*f*; results of analysis in, 55, 55*f*
in-house operations, avoidable cost of, 95
inmates: and inexperienced staff, 41; misconduct of, multilevel model of, 66, 68–72, 68*f*; movement of, and use of recidivism as performance measure, 22, 28; prisonization of, 71; risk classification systems for, 52, 68, 129–30; surveys of, 73–84
interjurisdictional comparisons, 117–22
inventory, perpetual, and audits, 36

Job Training Partnership Act (JTPA), 159–61, 163
justice: in confinement model, 7–8; definition of, 5
Justice, William Wayne, 46

knifing off, 134

labeling phenomenon, 136
labor: meaningful, in prison missions, 9; shortages, at Wolds, 40. *See also* staff
Laub, John, 124
Lawtey prison, 90, 102

215

ABOUT THE AUTHORS

Gerald G. Gaes is currently a visiting scientist at the National Institute of Justice and a criminal justice consultant. He received his Ph.D. in social psychology from the State University of New York at Albany in 1980. He joined the Bureau of Prisons (BOP) in 1980 and worked in the Office of Research from 1980 to 2002, with the exception of a two-year period (1982, 1983) when he served as a research analyst at the Federal Correctional Institution in Otisville, New York. He also spent over two years on detail at the United States Sentencing Commission from 1985 to 1987 to develop a population projection microsimulation and an expert system to apply U.S. sentencing guidelines. In 1988, he was appointed director of the Office of Research at the BOP and held that position until his retirement in August 2002. He has published in professional journals and has written chapters in edited books. His most recent publications have appeared in *Criminal Justice Review, Criminology and Public Policy, Punishment & Society,* and *Justice Quarterly.* In July 2000, Gerry received the U.S. Department of Justice Attorney General's Distinguished Service Award for the correctional research he has conducted throughout his career. This is the second highest award given by the Department of Justice. Gerry's current research interests include statistical techniques for minimizing selection bias, cost-benefit analysis of criminal justice interventions, prison privatization, evaluation methodology, inmate gangs, inmate classification, simulating criminal justice processes, prison crowding, prison violence, prison rape, and the effectiveness of prison program interventions on post-release outcomes.

Scott D. Camp, Ph.D., is a senior social science analyst with the Office of Research at the Federal Bureau of Prisons. He completed his Ph.D.

in sociology at the Pennsylvania State University with a minor in statistics in 1991. Prior to joining the BOP in 1992, he spent five years working for the Pennsylvania State University as a computer instructional specialist and a sociology instructor. Much of his current research focuses on performance measurement, especially using survey and operational data to compare prisons. He also publishes on diversity issues and prison privatization. His most recent publications have appeared in the *Journal of Criminal Justice Education*, *Criminal Justice Review*, *Criminology and Public Policy*, *Punishment & Society*, *The Prison Journal*, and *Justice Quarterly*. He has ongoing research projects on the topics of sick leave use by correctional workers, criminogenic effects of prisons on inmates, faith-based prison programs, education programs in prisons, mental health prevalence among inmates, and longitudinal effects of prisons upon inmate misconduct.

Julianne B. Nelson has more than twenty years of experience working on a wide range of topics as an economic and financial analyst. As a consultant in the corrections field, she has compared public and privately managed prison facilities in terms of their cost of operations, their methods of doing business, and the quality of services provided. Her work analyzes the financial impact—on government budgets and ultimately on taxpayers—of competition and partnerships between the public employees and their private sector counterparts. Her clients include the Federal Bureau of Prisons, as well as the state departments of corrections in Minnesota, Oklahoma, and Washington. She has also served as full-time member of the faculty at the Stern School of Business at New York University and the School of Public Affairs at American University, where the courses she taught emphasized the economic analysis of law and public policy, as well as decisions made in everyday life. Her previously published works include *Women Working It Out: Career Plans and Business Decisions*, as well as articles on topics ranging from the quality of prison health care to the economics of tort law and public policy. She received an M.P.A. from the Woodrow Wilson School and a Ph.D. from the economics department of Princeton University.

William G. (Bo) Saylor received his B.A. and master's degrees in criminology from the University of Maryland. He joined the Office of Research and Evaluation of the Federal Bureau of Prisons in 1977. In 1988, he was named deputy director of the office. In 2002, he was selected as director of research and currently holds that position. He is the lead statistical research methodologist for the office in addition to directing research projects. Among the projects he has conceptualized and directed are: the Post Release Employment Project (PREP)—a multiyear, longitudinal evaluation of the bureau's job training programs; the Prison Social Climate Survey (PSCS)—questionnaires administered to Bureau of Prisons staff and inmates to measure impressions of working and living conditions; the Key Indicators Strategic Support System (KI/SSS)—a CD and intranet-based information system designed to provide the bureau's managers with on-demand access to information required to monitor and evaluate institutional and organizational performance, and to provide support for policy formulation and policy impact assessment; and an Inmate Medical Classification System—designed to augment the bureau's current security designation/custody classification system. In July 2000, Saylor received the Bureau of Prisons' Myrl E. Alexander Award for Personal Initiative and Leadership for conceptualizing and directing the development of the Bureau's Key Indicators Strategic Support System and the Prison Social Climate Survey.